Expository Thoughts on
The Gospel of Matthew

Register This New Book

Benefits of Registering*

✓ FREE **replacements** of lost or damaged books

✓ FREE **audiobook** – *Pilgrim's Progress,*
   audiobook edition

✓ FREE information about new titles
   and other **freebies**

www.anekopress.com/new-book-registration

*See our website for requirements and limitations.

Expository Thoughts on
The Gospel of Matthew

J. C. Ryle

We love hearing from our readers. Please contact us
at www.anekopress.com/questions-comments with
any questions, comments, or suggestions.

Expository Thoughts on the Gospel of Matthew – J. C. Ryle
Revised Edition Copyright © 2019
First edition published 1856

Cover Design: J. Martin
Cover Background: ilolab/Shutterstock
Editors: Ruth Clark; Jeremiah Zeiset

Printed in the United States of America
Aneko Press
www.anekopress.com
Aneko Press, Life Sentence Publishing, and our logos are trademarks of
Life Sentence Publishing, Inc.
203 E. Birch Street
P.O. Box 652
Abbotsford, WI 54405

RELIGION / Biblical Commentary / New Testament / Jesus, the Gospels & Acts
Paperback ISBN: 978-1-62245-669-7
eBook ISBN: 978-1-62245-670-3
10 9 8 7 6 5 4 3 2 1
Available where books are sold

Contents

Preface

IN SENDING FORTH THE FIRST VOLUME of a new expository work upon the Gospels, I feel it necessary, in order to prevent misunderstanding, to offer some explanation of the character and design of the work.

The *Expository Thoughts*, which are now before the reader, are not a learned, critical commentary. I do not profess to expound every verse of the Gospels, grapple with every difficulty, attempt the solution of every hard text, and examine every disputed reading or translation.

The *Expository Thoughts* are not a continuous and homiletic exposition containing practical remarks on every verse like the commentaries of Brentius and Gualter.

The plan I have adopted in drawing up the *Expository Thoughts* is as follows: I have divided the sacred text into sections or passages averaging about twelve verses in each. I have then supplied a continuous series of short, plain expositions of each of these passages. In each exposition, I have generally begun by stating as briefly as possible the main scope and purpose of the passage under consideration. I have then selected two, three, or four prominent points in the passage, singled them out from the rest, dwelt exclusively on them, and endeavored to enforce them plainly and vigorously on the reader's attention. The points selected will be found to be sometimes doctrinal and sometimes practical. The only rule in selection has been to seize on the really leading points of the passage.

In style and composition, I frankly avow that I have endeavored, as far as possible, to be plain and pointed and to choose what an old preacher calls "picked and packed" words. I have striven to place myself in the position of one who is reading aloud to others and must arrest their attention if he can. I have said to myself in writing each exposition, "I am addressing a mixed company and I have but a short time." Keeping this in view, I have constantly left unsaid many things that might have been said, and have endeavored to dwell chiefly on the things needful to salvation. I have deliberately passed over many subjects of secondary importance in order to say something that might strike and stick in consciences. I have felt that a few points, well remembered and fastened down, are better than a quantity of truths lying loosely and thinly scattered over the mind.

I cannot, of course, expect that the opinions expressed in these expositions, whether about doctrine, practice, or prophecy, will be satisfactory and acceptable to everyone. I can only say I have spoken out freely and kept back nothing that seemed true to me. I have set down nothing but what I conscientiously believe to be the real meaning of the inspired writer and the mind of the Spirit. I have always held that truth is most likely to be reached when men on all sides conceal nothing, but tell out all their minds. Right or wrong, I have endeavored to tell out my own mind. It is my firm conviction that I have said nothing in these expositions which is not in perfect harmony with the thirty-nine articles of my own church and which does not agree in the main with all the Protestant confessions of faith. The words of an old preacher will explain the kind of theology to which I ever desire to conform:

I know no true religion but Christianity; no true Christianity but the doctrine of Christ; of His divine person (Colossians 1:15), of His divine office (1 Timothy 2:5), of His divine righteousness (Jeremiah 23:6), and of His divine Spirit which all that are His receive (Romans 8:9). I know no true ministers of Christ but such as make it their business in their calling to commend Jesus Christ, in His saving fullness of grace and glory, to the faith and love of men. I know no true Christian but one united to Christ by faith and abiding in Him by faith and love to the glorifying of the name of Jesus Christ in the beauties of gospel holiness. Ministers and Christians of this spirit have for many years been my brethren and companions, and I hope ever shall be, whithersoever the hand of the Lord may lead me. – Traill's Preface to *13 Sermons on the Throne of Grace*

I am deeply aware of the many imperfections and defects of the volume which is now sent forth. No one perhaps will see them more clearly than I do myself. At the same time, I think it only fair to say that no exposition in this volume has been composed without deliberate reflection and laborious examination of other men's opinions. There are very few passages handled in these expositions concerning which I have not at least *looked* at the views of the following writers: Chrysostom, Augustine, Theophylact, Euthymius, Calvin, Brentius, Bucer, Musculus, Gualter, Beza, Bullinger, Pellican, Calovius, Cocceius, Baxter, Poole, Hammond, Lightfoot, Hall, Duveil, Whitby, Piscator, Paraeuse, Ferus, Jansenius, Leigh, Ness, Mayer, Trapp, Henry, Gill, Doddridge, Burkitt, Quesnel, Bengel, Scott, A. Clarke, Pearce, Adams, Watson, Olshausen, Alford, Barnes, and Stier. I can say that I have spent hours, days, and weeks in examining the opinions of these writers and that when I differ from them, it is not because I do not know their views.

Commentaries and expositions of Scripture are so numerous in the present day that I feel it necessary to say something as to the class of readers whom I have specially had in view in putting forth these *Expository Thoughts*.

In the first place, I indulge the hope that the work may be found *suitable for use at family prayers.* The supply of works adapted for this purpose has never yet been equal to the demand.

In the next place, I cannot help hoping that the work may prove *an aid to those who visit the sick and the poor.* The number of people who visit hospitals and sickrooms with an earnest desire to do spiritual good is now very great. There is reason to believe that proper books for reading on such occasions are much wanted.

Last, but not least, I trust that the work may not be found unprofitable *for private reading, as a companion to the Gospels.* There are not a few whose callings and engagements make it impossible for them to read large commentaries and expositions of God's Word. I have thought that such may find it helpful to their memories to have a few leading points set before their minds in connection with what they read.

I now send forth the volume with an earnest prayer that it may tend to the promotion of pure and undefiled religion, help to extend the knowledge of Christ, and be a humble instrument in aid of the glorious work of converting and edifying immortal souls.

Matthew Chapter 1

Matthew 1:1-17

The record of the genealogy of Jesus the Messiah, the Son of David, the Son of Abraham: Abraham was the father of Isaac, Isaac the father of Jacob, and Jacob the father of Judah and his brothers. Judah was the father of Perez and Zerah by Tamar, Perez was the father of Hezron and Hezron the father of Ram. Ram was the father of Amminadab, Amminadab the father of Nahshon, and Nahshon the father of Salmon. Salmon was the father of Boaz by Rahab, Boaz was the father of Obed by Ruth, and Obed the father of Jesse. Jesse was the father of David the king. David was the father of Solomon by Bathsheba who had been the wife of Uriah. Solomon was the father of Rehoboam, Rehoboam the father of Abijah, and Abijah the father of Asa. Asa was the father of Jehoshaphat, Jehoshaphat the father of Joram, and Joram the father of Uzziah. Uzziah was the father of Jotham, Jotham the father of Ahaz, and Ahaz the father of Hezekiah. Hezekiah was the father of Manasseh, Manasseh the father of Amon, and Amon the father of Josiah. Josiah became the father of Jeconiah and his brothers, at the time of the deportation to Babylon. After the deportation to Babylon: Jeconiah became the father of Shealtiel, and Shealtiel the father of Zerubbabel. Zerubbabel was the father of Abihud, Abihud the father of Eliakim, and Eliakim the father of Azor. Azor was the father of Zadok, Zadok the father of Achim, and Achim the father of Eliud. Eliud was the father of Eleazar, Eleazar the father of Matthan, and Matthan the father of Jacob. Jacob was the father of Joseph the husband of Mary, by whom Jesus was born, who is called the Messiah. So all the generations from Abraham to David are fourteen generations; from David to the deportation to Babylon, fourteen generations; and from the deportation to Babylon to the Messiah, fourteen generations. (Matthew 1:1-17)

THESE VERSES BEGIN THE NEW TESTAMENT. Let us always read them with serious and solemn feelings. The book before us contains not the word of men but of God. Every verse in it was written by inspiration of the Holy Spirit.

Let us thank God daily for giving us the Scriptures. The poorest Englishman who understands his Bible knows more about religion than the wisest philosophers of Greece and Rome.

Let us remember our deep responsibility. We shall all be judged at the last day according to our light. To whomsoever much is given, of them much will be required.

Let us read our Bibles reverently and diligently, with an honest determination to believe and practice all we find in them. It is no light matter how we use this book. Eternal life or death depends on the spirit in which it is used.

Above all, let us humbly pray for the teaching of the Holy Spirit. He alone can apply truth to our hearts and make us profit by what we read.

The New Testament begins with the life, death, and resurrection of our Lord Jesus Christ. No part of the Bible is so important as this, and no part is so full and complete. Four distinct Gospels tell us the story of Christ's doing and dying. Four times over we read the precious account of His works and words. How thankful we ought to be for this! To know Christ is life eternal. To believe in Christ is to have peace with God. To follow Christ is to be a true Christian. To be with Christ will be heaven itself. We can never hear too much about Jesus Christ.

The Gospel of Matthew begins with a long list of names. Sixteen verses are taken up with tracing a pedigree from Abraham to David, and from David to the family in which Jesus was born. Let no one think that these verses are useless. Nothing is useless in creation. The least mosses and the smallest insects serve some good end. Nothing is useless in the Bible. Every word of it is inspired. The chapters and verses which seem at first sight unprofitable are all given for some good purpose. Look again at these sixteen verses and you will see in them useful and instructive lessons.

Learn from this list of names that *God always keeps His word*. He had promised that in Abraham's seed all the nations of the earth should be blessed. He had promised to raise up a Savior of the family of David (Genesis 12:2-3; Isaiah 11:1). These sixteen verses prove that Jesus was the son of David and the son of Abraham, and that God's promise was fulfilled. Thoughtless and ungodly people should remember this lesson and be afraid. Whatever they may think, God will keep His word. If they repent not, they will surely perish. True Christians should remember this lesson and take comfort. Their Father in heaven will be true to all His engagements. He has said that He will save all believers in Christ. If He has said it, He will certainly do it. *God is not a man, that He should lie. He remains faithful, for He cannot deny Himself* (Numbers 23:19; 2 Timothy 2:13).

Learn next from this list of names *the sinfulness and corruption of human nature.* Observe how many godly parents in this catalogue had wicked and ungodly sons. The names of Rehoboam, Joram, Amon, and Jeconiah should teach us humbling lessons. They all had pious fathers, but they were all wicked men. Grace does not run in families. It needs something more than good examples and good advice to make us children of God. Those who are born again are not born of blood, nor of the will of the flesh, nor of the will of man, but of God (John 1:13). Praying parents should pray night and day that their children may be born of the Spirit.

Learn lastly from this list of names *how great is the mercy and compassion of our Lord Jesus Christ*. Think how defiled and unclean our nature is, and then think what a condescension it was in Him to be born of a woman and *made in the likeness of men*. Some of the names we read in this catalogue remind us of shameful and sad histories. Some of the names are those of people never mentioned elsewhere in the Bible. But at the end of it all comes the name of the Lord Jesus Christ. Though He is the eternal God, He humbled Himself to become man

3

in order to provide salvation for sinners. *Though He was rich, yet for your sake He became poor.*

We should always read this catalogue with thankful feelings. We see here that no one who partakes of human nature can be beyond the reach of Christ's sympathy and compassion. Our sins may have been as black and great as those of any whom Matthew names. But they cannot shut us out of heaven if we repent and believe the gospel. If Jesus was not ashamed to be born of a woman whose pedigree contained such names as those we have read today, we need not think that He will be ashamed to call us brethren and to give us eternal life.

Matthew 1:18-25

Now the birth of Jesus Christ was as follows: when His mother Mary had been betrothed to Joseph, before they came together she was found to be with child by the Holy Spirit. And Joseph her husband, being a righteous man and not wanting to disgrace her, planned to send her away secretly. But when he had considered this, behold, an angel of the Lord appeared to him in a dream, saying, "Joseph, son of David, do not be afraid to take Mary as your wife; for the Child who has been conceived in her is of the Holy Spirit. She will bear a Son; and you shall call His name Jesus, for He will save His people from their sins." Now all this took place to fulfill what was spoken by the Lord through the prophet: "Behold, the virgin shall be with child and shall bear a Son, and they shall call His name Immanuel," which translated means, "God with us." And Joseph awoke from his sleep and did as the angel of the Lord commanded him, and took Mary as his wife, but kept her a virgin until she gave birth to a Son; and he called His name Jesus. (Matthew 1:18-25)

These verses begin by telling us two great truths. They tell us how the Lord Jesus Christ took our nature upon Himself and became man. They tell us also that His birth was miraculous. His mother Mary was a virgin.

These are *very mysterious subjects.* They are depths which we have no line to fathom. They are truths which we have not mind enough to comprehend. *Let us not attempt to explain things which are above our feeble reason. Let us be content to believe with reverence and not speculate about matters which we cannot understand. It is enough for us to know that with Him who made the world nothing is impossible.* Let us rest in the words of the Apostles' Creed: "Jesus Christ was conceived by the Holy Spirit, and born of the Virgin Mary."

Let us observe *the conduct of Joseph* described in these verses. It is a beautiful example of godly wisdom and tender consideration for others. He saw the appearance of evil in her who was his espoused wife, but he did nothing rashly. He waited patiently to have the line of duty made clear. In all probability he laid the matter before God in prayer. *He who believes . . . will not be disturbed* (Isaiah 28:16).

The patience of Joseph was graciously rewarded. He received a direct message from God upon the subject of his anxiety and was at once relieved from all his fears. How good it is to wait upon God! Who has ever cast his cares upon God in hearty prayer and found him failing? *In all your ways acknowledge Him, and He will make your paths straight* (Proverbs 3:6).

Let us observe *the two names* given to our Lord in these verses. One is *Jesus,* the other is *Immanuel.* One describes His office, the other His nature. Both are deeply interesting.

The name *Jesus* means "Savior." It is the same name as *Joshua* in the Old Testament. It is given to our Lord because *He will save His people from their sins.* This is His special office. He saves them from the guilt of sin by washing them in His own atoning blood. He saves them from the dominion of sin by putting in their hearts the sanctifying Spirit. He saves them from the presence of sin when He takes them out of this world to rest with Him forever. He will save them from all the consequences of sin when He shall give them a glorious body at the last day. Blessed and holy are Christ's people! From sorrow, cross, and conflict they are not saved, but they are saved from sin forevermore. They are cleansed from guilt by Christ's blood. They are made fit for heaven by Christ's Spirit. This is salvation. *He who cleaves to sin is not yet saved.*

Jesus is a *very encouraging name to heavy-laden sinners*. He who is King of Kings and Lord of Lords might lawfully have taken some more high-sounding title. But He does not do so. The rulers of this world have often called themselves "great," "conquerors," "bold," "magnificent," and the like. The Son of God is content to call Himself *Savior*. The souls which desire salvation may draw near to the Father with boldness, and they have access with confidence through Christ. It is His office and His delight to show mercy. *For God did not send the Son into the world to judge the world, but that the world might be saved through Him* (John 3:17).

Jesus is a name *which is peculiarly sweet and precious to believers*. It has often done them good when the favor of kings and princes would have been heard of with unconcern. It has given them what money cannot buy, even inward peace. It has eased their wearied consciences and given rest to their heavy hearts. The Song of Solomon speaks to the experience of many when it says, *"Your name is like purified oil"* (Song of Solomon 1:3). Happy is that person who trusts not merely in vague notions of God's mercy and goodness, but also in Jesus.

The other name in these verses is scarcely less interesting than that just referred to. It is the name which is given to our Lord from His nature, as "God manifest in the flesh." He is called *Immanuel*, "God with us."

Let us take care that we have clear views of our Lord Jesus Christ's *nature and person*. It is a point of the deepest importance. We should settle it firmly in our minds that our Savior is perfect man as well as perfect God, and perfect God as well as perfect man. If we once lose sight of this great foundational truth, we may run into fearful heresies. The name *Immanuel* takes in the whole mystery. Jesus is "God with us." He had a nature like our own in all things, sin only excepted. But though Jesus was "with us" in human flesh and blood, He was at the same time very God.

We shall often find, as we read the Gospels, that our Savior could be weary and hungry and thirsty, and could weep and groan and feel pain like ourselves. In all this we see *the man* Christ Jesus. We see the nature He took on Himself when He was born of the Virgin Mary.

But we shall also find in the same Gospels that our Savior knew men's hearts and thoughts, that He had power over devils, that He could work the mightiest of miracles with a word, that He was ministered to by angels, that He allowed a disciple to call Him *my God*, and that He said, *"Before Abraham was born, I am,"* and *"I and the Father are one."* In all this we see *the eternal God.* We see Him *who is over all, God blessed forever. Amen* (Romans 9:5).

Would you desire to have a strong foundation for your faith and hope? Then keep in constant view your Savior's *divinity.* He in whose blood you are taught to trust is the almighty God. All power is His in heaven and earth. None can pluck you out of His hand. If you are a true believer in Jesus, let not your heart be troubled or afraid.

Would you desire to have sweet comfort in suffering and trial? Then keep in constant view your Savior's *humanity.* He is the man Christ Jesus, who lay on the bosom of the Virgin Mary as a little infant, and who knows the heart of a man. He can be touched with the feeling of your infirmities. He has Himself experienced Satan's temptations. He has endured hunger. He has shed tears. He has felt pain. Trust Him at all times with all your sorrows. He will not despise you. Pour out all your heart before Him in prayer, and keep nothing back. He can sympathize with His people.

Let these thoughts sink down into our minds. Let us bless God for the encouraging truths which the first chapter of the New Testament contains. It tells us of One who *will save His people from their sins.* But this is not all. It tells us that this Savior is Immanuel, God Himself, and yet God *with us*, God manifest in human flesh like our own. This is glad tidings. This is indeed good news. Let us feed on these truths in our hearts by faith with thanksgiving.

Matthew Chapter 2

Matthew 2:1-12

Now after Jesus was born in Bethlehem of Judea in the days of Herod the king, magi from the east arrived in Jerusalem, saying, "Where is He who has been born King of the Jews? For we saw His star in the east and have come to worship Him." When Herod the king heard this, he was troubled, and all Jerusalem with him. Gathering together all the chief priests and scribes of the people, he inquired of them where the Messiah was to be born. They said to him, "In Bethlehem of Judea, for this is what has been written by the prophet: 'And you, Bethlehem, land of Judah, are by no means least among the leaders of Judah; for out of you shall come forth a Ruler Who will shepherd My people Israel.'" Then Herod secretly called the magi and determined from them the exact time the star appeared. And he sent them to Bethlehem and said, "Go and search carefully for the Child; and when you have found Him, report to me, so that I too may come and worship Him." After hearing the king, they went their way; and the star, which they had seen in the east went on before them until it came and stood over the place where the Child was. When they saw the star, they rejoiced exceedingly with great joy. After coming into the house they saw the Child with Mary His mother; and they fell to the ground and worshiped Him. Then, opening their treasures, they presented to Him gifts of gold, frankincense, and myrrh. And having been warned by God in a dream not to return to Herod, the magi left for their own country by another way. (Matthew 2:1-12)

IT IS NOT KNOWN WHO THESE MAGI WERE. Their names and dwelling place are alike kept back from us. We are only told that they came *from the east*. Whether they were Chaldeans or Arabians we cannot say. Whether they learned to expect Christ from the ten tribes who went into captivity or from the prophecies of Daniel, we do not know. It matters little who they were. The point which concerns us most is the rich instruction which their history conveys.

These verses show us that *there may be true servants of God in places where we would not expect to find them*. The Lord Jesus has many "hidden ones" like these magi. Their history on earth may be as little known as that of Melchizedek and Jethro and Job. But their names are in the Book of Life, and they will be found with Christ in the day of His appearing. It is well to remember this. We must not look around the earth and say hastily, "All is barren." The grace of God is not tied to places and families. The Holy Spirit can lead souls to Christ without the help of many outward means. Men may be born in dark places of the earth, like these magi, and yet like them be given *the wisdom that leads to salvation*. There are some traveling to heaven at this moment of whom the church and the world know nothing. They flourish in secret places like the lily among thorns and "waste their sweetness on the desert air." But Christ loves them, and they love Christ.

These verses teach us that *it is not always those who have the most religious privileges who give Christ most honor*. We might have thought that the scribes and Pharisees would have been the first to hasten to Bethlehem on the lightest rumor that the Savior was born. But it was not so. A few unknown strangers from a distant land were the first, except the shepherds mentioned by Luke, to rejoice at His birth. *He came to His own, and those who were His own did not receive Him*. What a mournful picture this is of human nature! How often the same kind of thing may be seen among ourselves! How often the very people who live nearest to a church are those who neglect it most! There is only too much truth in the old proverb, "The nearer the church, the further from God." Familiarity with sacred things has a dreadful tendency to make men despise them. There are many who from residence and convenience ought to be first and foremost in the worship of God and yet are always last. There are many who might well be expected to be last who are always first.

These verses teach us *that there may be knowledge of Scripture in the head, while there is no grace in the heart.* Notice how King Herod sends to inquire of the priests and elders *where the Messiah was to be born.* Notice what a ready answer they return to him and what an acquaintance with the words of Scripture they show. But they never went to Bethlehem to seek for the coming Savior. They would not believe in Him when He ministered among them. Their heads were better than their hearts. Let us all beware of resting satisfied with head-knowledge. It is an excellent thing when rightly used. But a man may have much of it and yet perish everlastingly. What is the state of our hearts? This is the great question. A little grace is better than many gifts. Gifts alone save no one. But grace leads on to glory.

The conduct of the wise men described in this chapter is *a splendid example of spiritual diligence.* What trouble it must have cost them to travel from their homes to the place where Jesus was born! How many weary miles they must have journeyed! The fatigues of an Eastern traveler are far greater than we today can at all understand. The time that such a journey would occupy must necessarily have been very great. The dangers to be encountered were neither few nor small. But none of these things moved them. They had set their hearts on seeing Him *who has been born King of the Jews*, and they never rested until they saw Him. They prove to us the truth of the old saying, "Where there's a will, there's a way."

It would be well for all professing Christians if they were more ready to follow the magi's example. Where is our self-denial? What pains do we take for our souls? What diligence do we show about following Christ? What does our religion cost us? These are serious questions. They deserve serious consideration.

Last but not least, the conduct of the magi is *a striking example of faith.* They believed in Christ when they had never seen Him – but that was not all. They believed in Him when the scribes and Pharisees were unbelieving – but that again was not all. They believed in Him when they saw Him as a little infant on Mary's knee and worshiped

Him as a king. This was the crowning point of their faith. They saw no miracles to convince them. They heard no teaching to persuade them. They beheld no signs of divinity and greatness to overawe them. They saw nothing but a newborn infant, helpless and weak, and needing a mother's care like any one of us. And yet when they saw that infant, they believed that they saw the divine Savior of the world. *They fell to the ground and worshiped Him.*

We can hardly read of greater faith than this in the whole volume of the Bible. It is a faith that deserves to be placed side by side with that of the penitent thief. The thief saw one dying the death of a malefactor and yet implored Him and called Him *Lord.* The magi saw a newborn babe on the lap of a poor woman and yet worshiped Him and confessed that He was the Christ. Blessed indeed are those who can believe in this fashion!

This is the kind of faith, let us remember, that *God delights to honor.* We see the proof of that at this very day. Wherever the Bible is read, the conduct of these magi is known and told as a memorial of them. Let us walk in the steps of their faith. Let us not be ashamed to believe in Jesus and confess Him, even though those all around us remain careless and unbelieving. Have we not a thousandfold more evidence than the magi had to make us believe that Jesus is the Christ? Beyond doubt we have. Yet where is our faith?

Matthew 2:13-23

Now when they had gone, behold, an angel of the Lord appeared to Joseph in a dream and said, "Get up! Take the Child and His mother and flee to Egypt, and remain there until I tell you; for Herod is going to search for the Child to destroy Him." So Joseph got up and took the Child and His mother while it was still night, and left for Egypt. He remained there until the death of Herod. This was to fulfill what had been spoken by the Lord through the prophet: "Out of Egypt I called My Son." Then when Herod saw that he had been tricked by the magi, he became very enraged, and sent and slew all the male children who were in Bethlehem and all its vicinity, from two years old and under, according to the time which he had determined from the magi. Then what had been spoken through Jeremiah the prophet was fulfilled: "A voice was heard in Ramah, weeping and great mourning, Rachel weeping for her children; and she refused to be comforted, because they were no more." But when Herod died, behold, an angel of the Lord appeared in a dream to Joseph in Egypt, and said, "Get up, take the Child and His mother, and go into the land of Israel; for those who sought the Child's life are dead." So Joseph got up, took the Child and His mother, and came into the land of Israel. But when he heard that Archelaus was reigning over Judea in place of his father Herod, he was afraid to go there. Then after being warned by God in a dream, he left for the regions of Galilee, and came and lived in a city called Nazareth. This was to fulfill what was spoken through the prophets: "He shall be called a Nazarene." (Matthew 2:13-23)

Observe in this passage how true it is that *the rulers of this world are seldom friendly to the cause of God.* The Lord Jesus comes down from heaven to save sinners, and at once we are told that Herod the king sought to destroy Him.

Greatness and riches are perilous possessions for the soul. They know not what they seek who seek to have them. They lead men into many temptations. They are likely to fill the heart with pride and to chain the affections down to things below. *Not many mighty, not many noble are called. "It is hard for a rich man to enter the kingdom of heaven."*

Do you envy the rich and great? Does your heart say, "Oh, that I had their place and rank and substance?" Beware of giving way to the feeling. The very wealth which you admire may be gradually sinking its possessor down into hell. A little more money might be your ruin. Like Herod, you might run into every excess of wickedness and cruelty. *"Beware, and be on your guard against every form of greed."* Be content with what you have.

Do you think that Christ's cause depends on the power and patronage

13

of princes? You are mistaken. They have seldom done much for the advancement of true religion. They have far more frequently been the enemies of the truth. *Do not trust in princes.* Those who are like Herod are many. Those who are like Josiah and Edward VI of England are few.

Observe how *the Lord Jesus was "a man of sorrows" even from His infancy.* Trouble awaits Him as soon as He enters the world. His life is in danger from Herod's hatred. His mother and Joseph are obliged to take Him away by night and *flee to Egypt.* It was only a type and figure of all His experience upon earth. The waves of humiliation began to beat over Him even when He was a nursing child.

The Lord Jesus is just the Savior that the suffering and sorrowful need. He knows well what we mean when we tell Him in prayer of our troubles. He can sympathize with us when we cry to Him under cruel persecution. Let us keep nothing back from Him. Let us make Him our bosom friend. Let us pour out our hearts before Him. He has had great experience of affliction.

Observe how *death can remove the kings of this world like other men.* The rulers of millions have no power to retain life when the hour of their departure comes. The murderer of helpless infants must himself die. Joseph and Mary hear the tidings that *Herod died,* and at once they return in safety to their own land.

True Christians should never be greatly moved by the persecution of man. Their enemies may be strong and they may be weak, but still they ought not to be afraid. They should remember that *the triumphing of the wicked is short.* What has become of the Pharaohs and Neros and Diocletians who at one time fiercely persecuted the people of God? Where is the enmity of Charles IX of France and Bloody Mary of England? They did their utmost to cast the truth down to the ground. But the truth rose again from the earth and still lives; and they are dead and moldering in the grave. Let not the heart of any believer fail. *Death is a mighty leveler* and can take any mountain out of the way of Christ's church. *The Lord lives* forever. His enemies are only men. The truth shall always prevail.

Observe, in the last place, *what a lesson of humility is taught us by the dwelling place of the Son of God* when He was on earth. He dwelt with His mother and Joseph *in a city called Nazareth*. Nazareth was a small town in Galilee. It was an obscure, retired place, not so much as once mentioned in the Old Testament. Hebron, Shiloh, Gibeon, and Bethel were far more important places. But the Lord Jesus passed by them all and chose Nazareth. This was humility.

In Nazareth the Lord Jesus lived thirty years. It was there He grew up from infancy to childhood, and from childhood to boyhood, and from boyhood to youth, and from youth to man's estate. We know little of the manner in which those thirty years were spent. That He was *in subjection to* Mary and Joseph we are expressly told. That He worked in the carpenter's shop with Joseph is highly probable. We only know that almost five-sixths of the time that the Savior of the world was on earth was passed among the poor of this world and passed in complete privacy. Truly this was humility.

Let us learn wisdom from our Savior's example. We are far too ready to be *seeking great things* in this world. Let us seek them not. To have a place and a title and a position in society is not nearly so important as people think. It is a great sin to be covetous, worldly, proud, and carnal-minded, but it is no sin to be poor. It matters not so much where we live as what we are in the sight of God. Where are we going when we die? Shall we live forever in heaven? These are the main things to which we should attend.

Above all, let us daily strive to copy our Savior's humility. Pride is the oldest and most common of sins. Humility is the rarest and most beautiful of graces. For humility let us labor. For humility let us pray. Our knowledge may be scanty. Our faith may be weak. Our strength may be small. But if we are disciples of Him who lived in Nazareth, let us at any rate be humble.

Matthew Chapter 3

Matthew 3:1-12

Now in those days John the Baptist came, preaching in the wilderness of Judea, saying, "Repent, for the kingdom of heaven is at hand." For this is the one referred to by Isaiah the prophet when he said, "The voice of one crying in the wilderness, 'Make ready the way of the LORD, make His paths straight!'" Now John himself had a garment of camel's hair and a leather belt around his waist; and his food was locusts and wild honey. Then Jerusalem was going out to him, and all Judea and all the district around the Jordan; and they were being baptized by him in the Jordan River, as they confessed their sins. But when he saw many of the Pharisees and Sadducees coming for baptism, he said to them, "You brood of vipers, who warned you to flee from the wrath to come? Therefore bear fruit in keeping with repentance; and do not suppose that you can say to yourselves, 'We have Abraham for our father'; for I say to you that from these stones God is able to raise up children to Abraham. The ax is already laid at the root of the trees; therefore every tree that does not bear good fruit is cut down and thrown into the fire. As for me, I baptize you with water for repentance, but He who is coming after me is mightier than I, and I am not fit to remove His sandals; He will baptize you with the Holy Spirit and fire. His winnowing fork is in His hand, and He will thoroughly clear His threshing floor; and He will gather His wheat into the barn, but He will burn up the chaff with unquenchable fire." (Matthew 3:1-12)

THESE VERSES DESCRIBE THE MINISTRY OF JOHN THE BAPTIST, the forerunner of our Lord Jesus Christ. It is a ministry that deserves close attention. Few preachers ever produced such effects. *Jerusalem was going out to Him, and all Judea and all the district around the Jordan.* None ever received such praise from the Lord. Jesus calls him *the lamp that was burning and was shining.* The great bishop of souls Himself declares that *"among those born of women there has not arisen anyone greater than John the Baptist!"* Let us then study the leading features of his ministry.

John the Baptist *spoke plainly about sin.* He taught the absolute necessity of repentance before anyone can be saved. He preached that repentance must be proved by its fruits. He warned men not to rest on outward privileges or outward union with the church.

This is just the teaching that we all need. We are naturally dead, blind, and asleep in spiritual things. We are ready to content ourselves with a mere formal religion, and to flatter ourselves that if we go to church we shall be saved. We need to be told that except we repent and are converted, we shall all perish.

John the Baptist *spoke plainly about our Lord Jesus Christ.* He taught people that one far mightier than himself was coming among them. He was nothing more than a servant – the coming One was the King. He himself could only *baptize them with water*; the coming One could *baptize them with the Holy Spirit*, take away sins, and would one day judge the world.

This again is the very teaching that human nature requires. We need to be sent directly to Christ. We are all ready to stop short of this. We want to rest in our union with the church, regular use of the sacraments, and diligent attendance at an established ministry. We ought to be told the absolute necessity of union with Christ Himself by faith. He is the appointed fountain of mercy, grace, life, and peace. We must each have personal dealings with Him about our souls. What do we know of the Lord Jesus? What have we got from Him? These are the questions on which our salvation hinges.

John the Baptist *spoke plainly about the Holy Spirit.* He preached that there was such a thing as the baptism of the Holy Spirit. He taught that it was the special office of the Lord Jesus to give it to men.

This again is a teaching which we greatly need. We need to be told that forgiveness of sin is not the only thing necessary for salvation. There is another thing yet, and that is the baptizing of our hearts by the Holy Spirit. There must not only be the work of Christ *for* us, but also the work of the Holy Spirit *in* us. There must not only be a title to heaven by the blood of Christ, but also a preparedness for heaven wrought in us by the Spirit of Christ. Let us never rest until we know something by experience of the baptism of the Spirit. The baptism of water is a great privilege, but let us see to it that we also have the baptism of the Holy Spirit.

John the Baptist *spoke plainly about the dreadful danger of the impenitent and unbelieving.* He told his hearers that there was a *wrath to come.* He preached of an *unquenchable fire* in which the chaff would one day be burned.

This again is a teaching which is deeply important. We need to be warned that it is no light matter whether we repent or not. We need to be reminded that there is a hell as well as a heaven, and an everlasting punishment for the wicked as well as everlasting life for the godly. We are fearfully apt to forget this. We talk of the love and mercy of God, and we do not remember sufficiently His justness and holiness. Let us be very careful on this point. It is no real kindness to keep back the terrors of the Lord. It is good for us all to be taught that it is possible to be lost forever, and that all unconverted people are hanging over the brink of the pit.

In the last place, John the Baptist spoke plainly *about the safety of true believers.* He taught that there was a *barn* for all who are Christ's wheat, and that they would be gathered together there in the day of His appearing.

This again is a teaching which human nature greatly needs. The best of believers need much encouragement. They are yet in the body. They live in a wicked world. They are often tempted by the devil. They ought to be often reminded that Jesus will never leave them nor forsake them. He will guide them safely through this life and at last give them eternal glory. They shall be hidden in the day of wrath. They shall be as safe as Noah in the ark.

Let these things sink down deeply into our hearts. We live in a day of much false teaching. Let us never forget the leading features of a faithful ministry. Happy would it have been for the church of Christ if all its ministers had been more like John the Baptist!

Matthew 3:13-17

Then Jesus arrived from Galilee at the Jordan coming to John, to be baptized by him. But John tried to prevent Him, saying, "I have need to be baptized by You, and do You come to me?" But Jesus answering said to him, "Permit it at this time; for in this way it is fitting for us to fulfill all righteousness." Then he permitted Him. After being baptized, Jesus came up immediately from the water; and behold, the heavens were opened, and he saw the Spirit of God descending as a dove and lighting on Him, and behold, a voice out of the heavens said, "This is My beloved Son, in whom I am well-pleased." (Matthew 3:13-17)

You have here the account of our Lord Jesus Christ's baptism. This was His first step when He entered His ministry. When the Jewish priests took up their office at the age of thirty, they were washed with water. When our Great High Priest begins the great work He came into the world to accomplish, He is publicly baptized.

Let us learn from these verses *to regard the sacrament of baptism with reverence.* An ordinance of which the Lord Jesus Himself partook is not to be lightly esteemed. An ordinance to which the Lord submitted ought to be ever honorable in the eyes of professing Christians.

There are few subjects in religion on which greater mistakes have arisen than baptism. There are few which require so much fencing and guarding. Let us arm our minds with two general cautions.

Let us beware on the one hand *that we do not attach a superstitious importance to the water of baptism.* We must not expect that water to act as a charm. We must not suppose that all baptized people as a matter of course receive the grace of God in the moment that they are baptized. To say that all who come to baptism obtain like and equal benefit, and that it matters not a jot whether they come with faith and prayer or in utter carelessness, appears to contradict the plainest lessons of Scripture.

Let us beware on the other hand *that we do not dishonor the sacrament of baptism.* It is dishonored when it is thrust out of sight and never publicly noticed in the congregation. A sacrament ordained by Christ Himself ought not to be treated in this way. The admission of every new member into the ranks of the visible church, whether young or grown-up, is an event which ought to excite a lively interest in a Christian assembly. It is an event that ought to call forth the fervent prayers of all praying people. The more deeply we are convinced that baptism and grace are not inseparably tied together, the more we ought to feel bound to join in prayer for a blessing whenever anyone is baptized.

The baptism of our Lord Jesus Christ was attended by circumstances of peculiar solemnity. Such a baptism never will be again, as long as the world stands.

We are told of *the presence of all three persons of the blessed Trinity.* God the Son, manifest in the flesh, is baptized. God the Spirit descends like a dove and lights upon Him. God the Father speaks from heaven with a voice. In a word we have the manifested presence of Father, Son, and Holy Spirit. Surely we may regard this as a public announcement that the work of Christ was the result of the eternal counsels of all three. It was the whole Trinity, which at the beginning of creation said, *"Let Us make man."* It was the whole Trinity again, which at the beginning of the gospel seemed to say, "Let Us *save* man."

We are told of *a voice out of the heavens* at our Lord's baptism. This was a circumstance of singular solemnity. We read of no voice from heaven before this except at the giving of the law on Sinai. Both occasions were of peculiar importance. It therefore seemed good to our Father in heaven to mark both with peculiar honor. At the introduction both of the law and the gospel, He Himself speaks.

How striking and deeply instructive are the Father's words! *"This is My beloved Son, in whom I am well-pleased."* He declares in these words that Jesus is the divine Savior sealed and appointed from all eternity to carry out the work of redemption. He proclaims that He accepts Him as the Mediator between God and man. He seems to publish to the world that He is satisfied with Him as the propitiation, the substitute, the ransom-payer for the lost family of Adam, and the Head of a redeemed people. In Him He sees His holy law magnified and made honorable. Through Him He can *be just and the justifier of the one who has faith in Jesus* (Romans 3:26).

May we ponder these words well! They are full of rich food for thought. They are full of peace, joy, comfort, and consolation for all who have fled for refuge to the Lord Jesus Christ and committed their souls to Him for salvation. Such may rejoice in the thought that though in themselves they are sinful, yet in God's sight they are counted righteous. The Father regards them as members of His beloved Son. He sees in them no spot, and for His Son's sake is *well-pleased* (Ephesians 1:6).

Matthew Chapter 4

Matthew 4:1-11

*Then Jesus was led up by the Spirit into the wilderness to be
tempted by the devil. And after He had fasted forty days and
forty nights, He then became hungry. And the tempter came and
said to Him, "If You are the Son of God, command that these
stones become bread." But He answered and said, "It is written,
'Man shall not live on bread alone, but on every word that proceeds out of the mouth of God.'" Then the devil took Him into the
holy city and had Him stand on the pinnacle of the temple, and
said to Him, "If You are the Son of God, throw Yourself down; for
it is written, 'He will command His angels concerning You'; and
'On their hands they will bear You up, so that You will not strike
Your foot against a stone.'" Jesus said to him, "On the other hand,
it is written, 'You shall not put the LORD your God to the test.'"
Again, the devil took Him to a very high mountain and showed
Him all the kingdoms of the world and their glory; and he said
to Him, "All these things I will give You, if You fall down and
worship me." Then Jesus said to him, "Go, Satan! For it is written, 'You shall worship the LORD your God, and serve Him only.'"
Then the devil left Him; and behold, angels came and began to
minister to Him.* (Matthew 4:1-11)

THE FIRST EVENT in our Lord's ministry which Matthew records
after His baptism is His temptation. This is a deep and mysterious subject. There is much in the history of it which we cannot explain. But

there lie on the face of the history plain, practical lessons to which we shall do well to take heed.

Let us learn, in the first place, *what a real and mighty enemy we have in the devil.* He is not afraid to assault even the Lord Jesus Himself. Three times over he attacks God's own Son. Our Savior was *tempted by the devil.* It was the devil who brought sin into the world at the beginning. This is he who vexed Job, deceived David, and gave Peter a heavy fall. This is he whom the Bible calls a *murderer,* a *liar,* and a *roaring lion.* This is he whose enmity toward our souls never slumbers and never sleeps. This is he who for nearly six thousand years has been working at one work: to ruin men and women and draw them to hell. This is he whose cunning and subtlety pass man's understanding and who often appears as *an angel of light.*

Let us all watch and pray daily against his devices. There is no enemy worse than an enemy who is never seen and never dies, who is near to us wherever we live, and who goes with us wherever we go. Not least let us beware of levity and jesting about the devil which is so unfortunately common. Let us remember every day that if we are saved, we must not only crucify the flesh and overcome the world but also *resist the devil.*

Let us learn in the next place *that we must not count temptation a strange thing.* "*A disciple is not above his teacher, nor a slave above his master.*" If Satan came to Christ, he will also come to Christians.

It would be well for all believers if they would remember this. They are too apt to forget it. They often find evil thoughts arising within their minds which they can truly say they hate. Doubts, questions, and sinful imaginings are suggested to them, against which their whole inward man revolts. But let not these things destroy their peace and rob them of their comforts. Let them remember there is a devil, and not be surprised to find him near them. To be tempted is in itself no sin. It is the yielding to the temptation and giving it a place in our hearts which we must fear.

Let us learn in the next place *that the chief weapon we ought to use in resisting Satan is the Bible.* Three times the great Enemy offered temptations to our Lord. Three times his offer was refused, with a text of Scripture as the reason: "*It is written.*"

Here is one among many reasons we ought to be diligent readers of our Bibles. The Word is the sword of the Spirit. We shall never fight a good fight if we do not use it as our principal weapon. The Word is the lamp for our feet. We shall never keep the King's highway to heaven if we do not journey by its light. It may well be feared that there is not enough Bible-reading among us. It is not sufficient to have the Book. We must actually read it and pray over it ourselves. It will do us no good if it only lies still in our houses. We must actually be familiar with its contents and have its texts stored in our memories and minds. Knowledge of the Bible never comes by intuition. It can only be obtained by diligent, regular, daily, attentive, and wakeful reading. Do we grudge the time and trouble this will cost us? If we do, we are not yet fit for the kingdom of God.

Let us learn in the last place *what a sympathizing Savior the Lord Jesus Christ is. For since He Himself was tempted in that which He has suffered, He is able to come to the aid of those who are tempted* (Hebrews 2:18).

The sympathy of Jesus is a truth which ought to be peculiarly dear to all believers. They will find in it a mine of strong consolation. They should never forget that they have a mighty Friend in heaven who feels for them in all their temptations and can enter into all their spiritual anxieties. Are they ever tempted by Satan to distrust God's care and goodness? So was Jesus. Are they ever tempted to presume on God's mercy and run into danger without warrant? So also was Jesus. Are they ever tempted to commit some one great private sin for the sake of some great seeming advantage? So also was Jesus. Are they ever tempted to listen to some misapplication of Scripture as an excuse for doing wrong? So also was Jesus. He is just the Savior that a tempted people need. Let them flee to Him for help and spread before Him all their troubles. They will find His ear ever ready to hear and His heart ever ready to feel. He can understand their sorrows.

May we all know the value of a sympathizing Savior by experience! There is nothing to be compared to it in this cold and deceitful world. Those who seek their happiness in this life only, and despise the religion of the Bible, have no idea what true comfort they are missing.

Matthew 4:12-25

Now when Jesus heard that John had been taken into custody, He withdrew into Galilee; and leaving Nazareth, He came and settled in Capernaum, which is by the sea, in the region of Zebulun and Naphtali. This was to fulfill what was spoken through Isaiah the prophet: "The land of Zebulun and the land of Naphtali, by the way of the sea, beyond the Jordan, Galilee of the Gentiles – The people who were sitting in darkness saw a great light, and those who were sitting in the land and shadow of death, upon them a Light dawned." From that time Jesus began to preach and say, "Repent, for the kingdom of heaven is at hand." Now as Jesus was walking by the Sea of Galilee, He saw two brothers, Simon who was called Peter, and Andrew his brother, casting a net into the sea; for they were fishermen. And He said to them, "Follow Me, and I will make you fishers of men." Immediately they left their nets and followed Him. Going on from there He saw two other brothers, James the son of Zebedee, and John his brother, in the boat with Zebedee their father, mending their nets; and He called them. Immediately they left the boat and their father, and followed Him. Jesus was going throughout all Galilee, teaching in their synagogues and proclaiming the gospel of the kingdom, and healing every kind of disease and every kind of sickness among the people. The news about Him spread throughout all Syria; and they brought to Him all who were ill, those suffering with various diseases and pains, demoniacs, epileptics, paralytics; and He healed them. Large crowds followed Him from Galilee and the Decapolis and Jerusalem and Judea and from beyond the Jordan.
(Matthew 4:12-25)

We have in these verses the beginning of our Lord's ministry among men. He enters on His labors among a dark and ignorant people. He chooses men to be His companions and disciples. He confirms His ministry by miracles which rouse the attention of *all Syria* and draw multitudes to hear Him.

Let us notice *the way in which our Lord commenced His mighty work. He began to preach.* There is no office so honorable as that of the preacher. There is no work so important to the souls of men. It is an office which the Son of God was not ashamed to take up. It is an office to which He appointed His twelve apostles. It is an office to which Paul in his old age specially directs Timothy's attention. He charges him with almost his last breath to *preach the Word.* It is the means which God has always been pleased to use above any other for the conversion and edification of souls. The brightest days of the church have been those when preaching has been honored. The darkest days of the church have been those when it has been lightly esteemed. Let us honor the sacraments and public prayers of the church and reverently use them. But let us beware that we do not place them above the preaching of the Word.

Let us notice *the first doctrine which the Lord Jesus proclaimed to the world.* He began by saying, "*Repent.*" The necessity of repentance is one of the great foundations which lie at the very bottom of Christianity. It needs to be pressed on all mankind without exception. High or low, rich or poor, all have sinned and are guilty before God, and all must repent and be converted if they would be saved. And true repentance is no light matter. It is a thorough change of heart about sin, a change showing itself in godly sorrow and humiliation, in heartfelt confession before the throne of grace, in a complete breaking off from sinful habits, and in an abiding hatred of all sin. Such repentance is the inseparable companion of saving faith in Christ. Let us prize the doctrine highly. It is of the highest importance. No Christian teaching can be called sound which does not constantly bring forward *repentance toward God and faith in our Lord Jesus Christ* (Acts 20:21).

Let us notice *the class of men whom the Lord Jesus chose to be His disciples.* They were of the poorest and humblest rank in life. Peter, Andrew, James, and John were all fishermen.

The religion of our Lord Jesus Christ was not intended for the rich and learned alone. It was intended for all the world – and the majority of all the world will always be the poor. Poverty and ignorance of books excluded thousands from the notice of the boastful philosophers of the heathen world. They exclude no one from the highest place in the service of Christ. Is a man humble? Does he feel his sins? Is he willing to hear Christ's voice and follow Him? If this be so, he may be the poorest of the poor, but he shall be found as high as any in the kingdom of heaven. Intellect and money are worth nothing without grace.

The religion of Christ must have been from heaven or it never could have prospered and overspread the earth as it has done. It is vain for infidels to attempt to answer this argument. It cannot be answered. A religion which did not flatter the rich, the great, and the learned – a religion which offered no license to the carnal inclinations of man's heart – a religion whose first teachers were poor fishermen without wealth, rank, or power – such a religion could never have turned the world upside down if it had not been of God. Look at the Roman emperors and the heathen priests with their splendid temples on the one side! Look at a few unlearned working men with the gospel on the other! Were there ever two parties so unequally matched? Yet the weak proved strong and the strong proved weak. Heathenism fell and Christianity took its place. Christianity must be of God.

Let us notice, in the last place, *the general character of the miracles by which our Lord confirmed His mission.* Here we are told of them in the mass. Hereafter we shall read many of them described particularly. And what is their character? They were miracles of mercy and kindness. Our Lord *went about doing good.*

These miracles are meant to teach us our Lord's power. He who could heal sick people with a touch, and cast out devils with a word, is *able also to save forever those who draw near to God through Him.* He is almighty.

These miracles are meant to be *types and emblems* of our Lord's skill as a spiritual physician. He before whom no bodily disease proved incurable is mighty to cure every ailment of our souls. There is no broken heart that He cannot heal. There is no wound of conscience that He cannot cure. Fallen, crushed, bruised, and plague-stricken as we all are by sin, Jesus by His blood and Spirit can make us whole. Only let us go to Him.

These miracles not least of all are intended *to show us Christ's heart.* He is a most compassionate Savior. He rejected no one who came to

Him. He refused no one, however loathsome and diseased. He had an ear to hear all, and a hand to help all, and a heart to feel for all. There is no kindness like His. His compassions fail not.

May we all remember that Jesus is *the same yesterday and today and forever.* High in heaven at God's right hand, He is not in the least altered. He is just as able to save, just as willing to receive, and just as ready to help as He was eighteen hundred years ago. Would we have spread out our needs before Him then? Let us do the same now. He can *heal every kind of disease and every kind of sickness.*

Matthew Chapter 5

Matthew 5:1-12

When Jesus saw the crowds, He went up on the mountain; and after He saw down, His disciples came to Him. He opened His mouth and began to teach them, saying, "Blessed are the poor in spirit, for theirs is the kingdom of heaven. Blessed are those who mourn, for they shall be comforted. Blessed are the gentle, for they shall inherit the earth. Blessed are those who hunger and thirst for righteousness, for they shall be satisfied. Blessed are the merciful, for they shall receive mercy. Blessed are the pure in heart, for they shall see God. Blessed are the peacemakers, for they shall be called sons of God. Blessed are those who have been persecuted for the sake of righteousness, for theirs is the kingdom of heaven. Blessed are you when people insult you and persecute you, and falsely say all kinds of evil against you because of Me. Rejoice and be glad, for your reward in heaven is great; for in the same way they persecuted the prophets who were before you." (Matthew 5:1-12)

EVERY WORD OF THE LORD JESUS ought to be most precious to professing Christians. It is the voice of the chief Shepherd. It is the charge of the great bishop and head of the Church. It is the Master speaking. It is the word of Him who spoke as never man spoke, and by whom we shall all be judged at the last day.

Would we know what kind of people Christians ought to be? Would we know the character at which Christians ought to aim? Would we know the outward walk and inward habit of mind which are suitable to a follower of Jesus? Then let us often study the Sermon on the Mount. Let us often ponder each sentence and prove ourselves by it. Not least of all let us often consider who they are who are called *blessed* at the beginning of the sermon. Those whom the Great High Priest blesses are blessed indeed.

The Lord Jesus calls those blessed who are *poor in spirit.* He means the humble, the lowly-minded, and the self-abased. He means those who are deeply convinced of their own sinfulness in God's sight. These are they who are not *wise in their own eyes and clever in their own sight.* They are not *rich and wealthy.* They do not imagine that they need nothing. They regard themselves as *wretched and miserable and poor and blind and naked.* Blessed are all such! Humility is the very first letter in the alphabet of Christianity. We must begin low if we would build high.

The Lord Jesus calls those blessed who *mourn.* He means those who sorrow over sin and grieve daily over their own shortcomings. These are they who trouble themselves more about sin than about anything on earth. The remembrance of it is grievous to them. The burden of it is intolerable. Blessed are all such! *The sacrifices of God are a broken spirit; a broken and a contrite heart.* One day they shall weep no more. *They shall be comforted.*

The Lord Jesus calls those blessed who are *gentle.* He means those who are of a patient and contented spirit. They are willing to put up with little honor here below. They can bear injuries without resentment. They are not ready to take offense. Like Lazarus in the parable, they are content to wait for their good things. Blessed are all such! They are never losers in the long run. One day they shall *reign upon the earth* (Revelation 5:10).

The Lord Jesus calls those blessed who *hunger and thirst for righteousness.* He means those who desire above all things to be entirely conformed to the mind of God. They long not so much to be rich or wealthy or learned as to be holy. Blessed are all such! They shall have

Blessed

enough one day. They shall *be satisfied with [God's] likeness when [they] awake* (Psalm 17:15).

The Lord Jesus calls those blessed who are *merciful*. He means those who are full of compassion towards others. They pity all who are suffering either from sin or sorrow, and are tenderly desirous to make their sufferings less. They are full of good works and endeavors to do good. Blessed are all such! Both in this life and that to come they shall reap a rich reward.

The Lord Jesus calls those blessed who are *pure in heart*. He means those who do not aim merely at outward correctness but at inward holiness. They are not satisfied with a mere external show of religion. They strive to keep a heart and conscience void of offense and to serve God with the spirit and the inner man. Blessed are all such! The heart is the man. *"Man looks at the outward appearance, but the LORD looks at the heart"* (1 Samuel 16:7). He who is most spiritually-minded will have most communion with God.

The Lord Jesus calls those blessed who are *peacemakers*. He means those who use all their influence to promote peace and charity on earth, in private and in public, at home and abroad. He means those who strive to make all men love one another by teaching that gospel which says, *Love is the fulfillment of the law*. Blessed are all such! They are doing the very work which the Son of God began when He came to earth the first time and which He will finish when He returns the second time.

Lastly, the Lord Jesus calls those blessed who *have been persecuted for the sake of righteousness*. He means those who are laughed at, mocked, despised, and ill-used because they endeavor to live as true Christians. Blessed are all such! They drink of the same cup of which their Master drank. They are now confessing Him before men, and He will confess them before His Father and the angels at the last day. *"Their reward in heaven is great."*

Such are the eight foundation stones which the Lord lays down at the beginning of the Sermon on the Mount. Eight great testing truths are placed before us. May we well notice each one of them and learn wisdom!

Let us learn how entirely contrary are the principles of Christ to the principles of the world. It is vain to deny it. They are almost diametrically opposed. The very characters which the Lord Jesus praises, the world despises. The very pride, thoughtlessness, high tempers, worldliness, selfishness, formality, and unlovingness which abound everywhere, the Lord Jesus condemns.

Let us learn how unhappily different is the teaching of Christ from the practice of many professing Christians. Where shall we find men and women among those who go to churches and chapels who are striving to live up to the pattern we have read of today? Alas! there is much reason to fear that many baptized people are utterly ignorant of what the New Testament contains.

Above all, let us learn how holy and spiritually-minded all believers should be. They should never aim at any standard lower than that of the Sermon on the Mount. Christianity is eminently a practical religion. Sound doctrine is its root and foundation, but holy living should always be its fruit. And if we would know what holy living is, let us often recall who they are whom Jesus calls *blessed*.

Matthew 5:13-20

"You are the salt of the earth; but if the salt has become tasteless, how can it be made salty again? It is no longer good for anything, except to be thrown out and trampled under foot by men. You are the light of the world. A city set on a hill cannot be hidden; nor does anyone light a lamp and put it under a basket, but on the lampstand, and it gives light to all who are in the house. Let your light shine before men in such a way that they may see your good works, and glorify your Father who is in heaven. Do not think that I came to abolish the Law or the Prophets; I did not come to abolish but to fulfill. For truly I say to you, until heaven and earth pass away, not the smallest letter or stroke shall pass from the Law until all is accomplished. Whoever then annuls one of the least of these commandments, and teaches others to do the same, shall be called least in the kingdom of heaven; but whoever

keeps and teaches them, he shall be called great in the kingdom of heaven. For I say to you that unless your righteousness surpasses that of the scribes and Pharisees, you will not enter the kingdom of heaven." (Matthew 5:13-20)

In these verses the Lord Jesus speaks of two subjects. One is the character which true Christians must support and maintain in the world. The other is the relation between His doctrines and those of the Old Testament. It is of great importance to have clear views on both of these subjects.

True Christians are to be in the world like salt. Now salt has a peculiar taste of its own, utterly unlike anything else. When mingled with other substances, it preserves them from corruption. It imparts a portion of its taste to everything it is mixed with. It is useful so long as it preserves its savor, but no longer than that. Are we true Christians? Then behold here our place and its duties!

True Christians are to be in the world like light. Now it is the property of light to be utterly *distinct* from darkness. The least spark in a dark room can be seen at once. Of all things created, light is the most *useful*. It fertilizes. It guides. It cheers. It was the first thing called into being. Without it the world would be a gloomy blank. Are we true Christians? Then behold again our position and its responsibilities!

Surely, if words mean anything, we are meant to learn from these two figures that there must be something marked, distinct, and peculiar about our character if we are true Christians. It will never do to idle through life, thinking and living like others, if we mean to be owned by Christ as His people. Have we grace? Then it must be *seen*. Have we the Spirit? Then there must be *fruit*. Have we any saving religion? Then there must be a difference of habits, tastes, and turn of mind between us and those who think only of the world. It is perfectly clear that true Christianity is something more than being baptized and going to church. *Salt* and *light* evidently imply *peculiarity* both of heart and life, of faith and practice. We must dare to be singular and unlike the world if we mean to be saved.

The relation between our Lord's teaching and that of the Old Testament is cleared up by our Lord in one striking sentence. He says,

"Do not think that I came to abolish the Law or the Prophets; I did not come to abolish but to fulfill." These are remarkable words. They were deeply important when spoken, as satisfying the natural anxiety of the Jews on the point. They will be deeply important as long as the world stands as a testimony that the religion of the Old and New Testaments is one harmonious whole.

The Lord Jesus came to fulfill *the predictions of the prophets* who had long foretold that a Savior would one day appear. He came to fulfill *the ceremonial law* by becoming the great sacrifice for sin to which all the Mosaic offerings had ever pointed. He came to fulfill *the moral law* by yielding to it a perfect obedience which we could never have yielded, and by paying the penalty for our breach of it with His atoning blood which we could never have paid. In all these ways He exalted the Law of God and made its importance more evident even than it had been before. In a word, He made *the law great and glorious* (Isaiah 42:21).

There are deep lessons of wisdom to be learned from these words of our Lord. Let us consider them well and lay them up in our hearts.

Let us *beware of despising the Old Testament* under any pretense whatsoever. Let us never listen to those who bid us throw it aside as an obsolete, antiquated, and useless book. The religion of the Old Testament is the embryo of Christianity. The Old Testament is the gospel in the bud. The New Testament is the gospel in full flower. The Old Testament is the gospel in the blade. The New Testament is the gospel in full ear. The saints in the Old Testament saw many things through a glass darkly. But they all looked by faith to the same Savior and were led by the same Spirit as ourselves. These are no light matters. Much infidelity begins with an ignorant contempt for the Old Testament.

Let us, for another thing, *beware of despising the law of the Ten Commandments.* Let us not suppose for a moment that it is set aside by the gospel or that Christians have nothing to do with it. The coming of Christ did not alter the position of the Ten Commandments one hair's breadth. If anything, it established and raised their authority (Romans 3:31). The law of the Ten Commandments is God's eternal measure of right and wrong. By it is the knowledge of sin. By it the Spirit shows men their need of Christ and drives them to Him. To it Christ refers

His people as their rule and guide for holy living. In its right place it is just as important as *the glorious gospel*. It cannot save us. We cannot be justified by it. But never, never let us despise it. It is a symptom of an ignorant and unhealthy state of religion when the law is lightly esteemed. The true Christian *joyfully concur[s] with the law of God* (Romans 7:22).

In the last place, let us *beware of supposing that the gospel has lowered the standard of personal holiness,* and that the Christian is not intended to be as strict and particular about his daily life as the Jew. This is an immense mistake, but one that is unfortunately very common. So far from this being the case, the sanctification of the New Testament saint ought to exceed that of him who has nothing but the Old Testament for his guide. The more light we have, the more we ought to love God. The more clearly we see our own complete and full forgiveness in Christ, the more heartily ought we to work for His glory. We know what it cost to redeem us far better than the Old Testament saints did. We have read what happened in Gethsemane and on Calvary, and they only saw it dimly and indistinctly as a thing yet to come. May we never forget our obligations! The Christian who is content with a low standard of personal holiness has much to learn.

Matthew 5:21-37

"You have heard that the ancients were told, 'You shall not commit murder' and 'Whoever commits murder shall be liable to the court.' But I say to you that everyone who is angry with his brother shall be guilty before the court; and whoever says to his brother, 'You good-for-nothing,' shall be guilty before the supreme court; and whoever says, 'You fool,' shall be guilty enough to go into the fiery hell. Therefore if you are presenting your offering at the altar, and there remember that your brother has something against you, leave your offering there before the altar and go; first be reconciled to your brother, and then come and present your offering. Make friends quickly with your opponent at law while you are with him on the way, so that your opponent

may not hand you over to the judge, and the judge to the officer, and you be thrown into prison. Truly I say to you, you will not come out of there until you have paid up the last cent. You have heard that it was said, 'You shall not commit adultery'; but I say to you that everyone who looks at a woman with lust for her has already committed adultery with her in his heart. If your right eye makes you stumble, tear it out and throw it from you; for it is better for you to lose one of the parts of your body, than for your whole body to be thrown into hell. If your right hand makes you stumble, cut it off and throw it from you; for it is better for you to lose one of the parts of your body, than for your whole body to go into hell. It was said, 'Whoever sends his wife away, let him give her a certificate of divorce'; but I say to you that everyone who divorces his wife, except for the reason of unchastity, makes her commit adultery; and whoever marries a divorced woman commits adultery. Again, you have heard that the ancients were told, 'You shall not make false vows, but shall fulfill your vows to the LORD.' *But I say to you, make no oath at all, either by heaven, for it is the throne of God. or by the earth, for it is the footstool of His feet, or by Jerusalem, for it is the city of the great King. Nor shall you make an oath by your head, for you cannot make one hair white or black. But let your statement be, 'Yes, yes,' or 'No, no'; anything beyond these is of evil."* (Matthew 5:21-37)

— Promises + Swearing?

These verses deserve the closest attention of all readers of the Bible. A right understanding of the doctrines they contain lies at the very root of Christianity. The Lord Jesus here explains more fully the meaning of His words, *"I did not come to abolish but to fulfill."* He teaches us that His gospel magnifies the law and exalts its authority. He shows us that the law, as expounded by Him, was a far more spiritual and heart-searching rule than most of the Jews supposed. And He proves this by selecting three commandments out of the ten as examples of what He means.

He expounds the *sixth commandment*. Many thought that they kept this part of God's law as long as they did not commit actual murder. The Lord Jesus shows, however, that its requirements go much further than this. It condemns all angry and passionate language and especially when used without a cause. Let us pay close attention to this. We may be perfectly innocent of taking life away and yet be guilty of breaking the sixth commandment. *Hatred / disdain to your neighbour is equal to committing suicide.*

He expounds the *seventh commandment.* Many supposed that they kept this part of God's law if they did not actually commit adultery. The Lord Jesus teaches, however, that we may break it in our thoughts, hearts, and imaginations even when our outward conduct is moral and correct. The God with whom we have to do looks far beyond actions. With Him, even a glance of the eye may be a sin.

He expounds the *third commandment.* Many fancied that they kept this part of God's law as long as they did not swear falsely and performed their oaths. The Lord Jesus forbids all vain and light swearing altogether. All swearing by created things, even when God's name is not brought forward, all calling upon God to witness, except on the most solemn occasions, is a great sin.

Now all this is very instructive. It ought to raise very serious reflections in our minds. It calls us loudly to use great searching of heart. And what does it teach?

It teaches us *the exceeding holiness of God.* He is a most pure and perfect Being who sees faults and imperfections where man's eyes often see none. He reads our inward motives. He notes our words and thoughts as well as our actions. He *desires truth in the innermost being.* Oh! that men would consider this part of God's character more than they do! There would be no room for pride and self-righteousness and carelessness if they only saw God *as He is.*

It teaches us *the exceeding ignorance of man in spiritual things.* There are thousands and ten thousands of professing Christians, it may be feared, who know no more of the requirements of God's law than the most ignorant Jews. They know the letter of the Ten Commandments well enough. They fancy, like the young ruler, *"All these things I have kept from my youth."* They never dream that it is possible to break the sixth and seventh commandments if they do not break them by outward act or deed. And so they live on satisfied with themselves and quite content with their little bit of religion. Happy indeed are those who really understand God's law!

It teaches us *our exceeding need of the Lord Jesus Christ's atoning blood to save us.* What man or woman upon earth can ever stand before such a God as this and plead "not guilty"? Who is there that has ever grown to years of discretion and not broken the commandments thousands of times? *There is none righteous, not even one.* Without a mighty Mediator, everyone would be condemned in the judgment. Ignorance of the real meaning of the law is one plain reason why so many do not value the gospel and content themselves with a little formal Christianity. They do not see the strictness and holiness of God's Ten Commandments. If they did, they would never rest until they were safe in Christ.

In the last place, this passage teaches us *the exceeding importance of avoiding all occasions of sin.* If we really desire to be holy, we must take heed to our ways, that we offend not with our tongues. We must be ready to make up after quarrels and disagreements lest they gradually lead on to greater evils. *The beginning of strife is like letting out water.* We must labor to crucify our flesh and mortify our members to make any sacrifice and endure any bodily inconvenience rather than sin. We must keep our lips as it were with a bridle and exercise an hourly strictness over our words. Let men call us precise, if they will, for so doing. Let them say, if they please, that we are "too particular." We need not be moved. We are merely doing as our Lord Jesus Christ bids us, and, if this is the case, we have no cause to be ashamed.

Matthew 5:38-48

"You have heard that it was said, 'An eye for an eye, and a tooth for a tooth.' But I say to you, do not resist an evil person; but whoever slaps you on your right cheek, turn the other to him also. If anyone wants to sue you and take your shirt, let him have your coat also. Whoever forces you to go one mile, go with him two. Give to him who asks of you, and do not turn away from him who wants to borrow from you. You have heard that it was said,

'You shall love your neighbor and hate your enemy.' But I say to you, love your enemies and pray for those who persecute you, so that you may be sons of your Father who is in heaven; for He causes His sun to rise on the evil and the good, and sends rain on the righteous and the unrighteous. For if you love those who love you, what reward do you have? Do not even the tax collectors do the same? If you greet only your brothers, what more are you doing than others? Do not even the Gentiles do the same? Therefore you are to be perfect, as your heavenly Father is perfect." (Matthew 5:38-48)

You have here our Lord Jesus Christ's rules for our conduct one towards another. He that would know how he ought to feel and act towards his fellow men should often study these verses. They deserve to be written in letters of gold. They have extorted praise even from the enemies of Christianity. Let us pay attention to what they contain.

The Lord Jesus forbids everything resulting from an unforgiving and revengeful spirit. A readiness to resent injuries – a quickness in taking offense – a quarrelsome and contentious disposition – a keenness in asserting our rights – all, all are contrary to the mind of Christ. The world may see no harm in these habits of mind. But they do not correspond to the character of the Christian. Our Master says, *Do not resist an evil person.*

The Lord Jesus admonishes us to have a spirit of universal love and charity. We ought to put away all malice. We ought to return good for evil and blessing for cursing. We ought to love even our enemies. Moreover, we are not to love in word only but also in deed. We are to deny ourselves and take trouble in order to be kind and courteous. If any man *"forces you to go one mile, go with him two."* We are to put up with much and bear much, rather than hurt another or give offense. In all things we are to be unselfish. Our thought must never be, "How do others behave to me?" but "What would Christ have me to do?"

A standard of conduct like this may seem, at first sight, extravagantly high. But we must never content ourselves with aiming at one lower.

We must observe the two weighty arguments by which our Lord backs up this part of His instruction. They deserve serious attention.

For one thing, *if we do not aim at the spirit and temper which are here recommended, we are not yet children of God. Our Father who is in heaven* is kind to all. He sends rain on good and on evil alike. He causes *His sun* to shine on all without distinction. A son should be like his father. But where is our likeness to our Father in heaven if we cannot show mercy and kindness to everybody? Where is the evidence that we are new creatures if we lack charity? It is altogether lacking. We must yet *be born again* (John 3:7).

For another thing, *if we do not aim at the spirit and temper here recommended, we are manifestly still of the world.* Even those who have no religion can *love those who love them.* They can do good and show kindness when their affection or interest moves them. But a Christian ought to be influenced by higher principles than these. Do we flinch from the test? Do we find it impossible to do good to our enemies? If that be the case, we may be sure we have yet to be converted. As yet we have not *received . . . the Spirit who is from of God* (1 Corinthians 2:12).

There is much in all this which calls loudly for solemn reflection. There are few passages of Scripture so calculated to raise in our minds humbling thoughts. *We have here a lovely picture of the Christian as he ought to be.* We cannot look at it without painful feelings. We must all allow that it differs widely from the Christian as he is. Let us carry away from it two general lessons.

In the first place, *if the spirit of these eleven verses was more continually remembered by true believers, they would recommend Christianity to the world far more than they do.* We must not allow ourselves to suppose that the least words in this passage are trifling and of small importance. They are not so. It is attention to the spirit of this passage which makes our religion beautiful. It is the neglect of the things which it contains by which our religion is deformed. Unfailing courtesy, kindness, tenderness, and consideration for others are some of the greatest ornaments to the character of the child of God. The world can understand these things even if it cannot understand doctrine. There is no religion in rudeness, roughness, bluntness, and incivility. The perfection of practical

Christianity consists in attending to the little duties of holiness as well as to the great.

In the second place, *if the spirit of these eleven verses had more dominion and power in the world, how much happier the world would be than it is.* Who does not know that quarrelings, strifes, selfishness, and unkindness cause half the miseries by which mankind is visited? Who can fail to see that nothing would so much tend to increase happiness as the spread of Christian love such as is here recommended by our Lord? Let us all remember this. Those who fancy that true religion has any tendency to make men unhappy are greatly mistaken. It is the absence of it that does this and not the presence. True religion has the directly contrary effect. It tends to promote peace, charity, kindness, and goodwill among men. The more men are brought under the teaching of the Holy Spirit, the more they will love one another and the happier they will be.

Matthew Chapter 6

Guidance to giving + for prayer

Matthew 6:1-8

"Beware of practicing your righteousness before men to be noticed by them; otherwise you have no reward with your Father who is in heaven. So when you give to the poor, do not sound a trumpet before you, as the hypocrites do in the synagogues and in the streets, so that they may be honored by men. Truly I say to you, they have their reward in full. But when you give to the poor, do not let your left hand know what your right hand is doing, so that your giving will be in secret; and your Father who sees what is done in secret will reward you. When you pray, you are not to be like the hypocrites; for they love to stand and pray in the synagogues and on the street corners so that they may be seen by men. Truly I say to you, they have their reward in full. But you, when you pray, go into your inner room, close your door and pray to your Father who is in secret, and your Father who sees what is done in secret will reward you. And when you are pray-ing, do not use meaningless repetition as the Gentiles do, for they suppose they will be heard for their many words. So do not be like them; for your Father knows what you need before you ask Him." (Matthew 6:1-8)

IN THIS PART OF THE SERMON ON THE MOUNT the Lord Jesus gives us instruction on two subjects. One is that of giving to the poor. The other is that of prayer. Both were subjects to which the Jews attached great importance. Both in themselves deserve the serious attention of all professing Christians.

Observe that our Lord takes it for granted *that all who call themselves His disciples will give to the poor.* He assumes as a matter of course that they will think it a solemn duty to give according to their means to relieve the needs of others. The only point He handles is the *manner* in which the duty should be done. This is a weighty lesson. It condemns the selfish stinginess of many in the matter of giving money. How many are rich towards themselves but poor towards God! How many never give a farthing to do good to the bodies and souls of men! And have such people any right to be called Christians in their present state of mind? It may be well doubted. A giving Savior should have giving disciples.

Observe again that our Lord takes it for granted *that all who call themselves His disciples will pray.* He assumes this also as a matter of course. He only gives directions as to the best way of praying. This is another lesson which deserves to be continually remembered. It teaches plainly that prayerless people are not genuine Christians. It is not enough to join in the prayers of the congregation on Sundays or attend the prayer of a family on weekdays. There must be private prayer also. Without this we may be outward members of Christ's church but we are not living members of Christ.

But what are the rules laid down for our guidance about giving to the poor and praying? They are few and simple, but they contain much matter for thought.

In giving, *everything like excessive display is to be abhorred and avoided.* We are not to give as if we wanted everybody to see how liberal and charitable we are and desired the praise of our fellow men. We are to shun everything like *display.* We are to give quietly and make as little noise as possible about our charities. We are to aim at the spirit of the proverbial saying, *"Do not let your left hand know what your right hand is doing."*

In praying, *the principal object to be sought is to be alone with God.* We should endeavor to find some place where no mortal eye sees us and where we can pour out our hearts with the feeling that no one is looking at us but God. This is a rule which many find it very difficult to follow. The poor man and the servant often find it almost impossible to be really alone. But it is a rule which we must all make great efforts to obey. Necessity, in such cases, is often the mother of invention. When a person has a real desire to find some place where he can be in secret with his God, he will generally find a way.

In all our duties, whether giving or praying, the great thing to be kept in mind is *that we are dealing with a heart-searching and all-knowing God.* Everything like formality, affectation, or mere bodily service is abominable and worthless in God's sight. He takes no account of the quantity of money we give or the quantity of words we use. The one thing at which His all-seeing eye looks is the nature of our motives and the state of our hearts. *Our Father sees what is done in secret.*

May we all remember these things. Here lies a rock on which many are continually making spiritual shipwreck. They flatter themselves that all must be right with their souls if they only perform a certain amount of religious duties. They forget that God does not regard the quantity but the quality of our service. His favor is not to be bought, as many seem to suppose, by the formal repetition of a number of words or the self-righteous payment of a sum of money to a charitable institution. Where are our hearts? Are we doing all, whether we give or pray, *as to the Lord, and not to men*? Do we realize the eye of God? Do we simply and solely desire to please Him *who sees what is done in secret* and by whom *actions are weighed* (1 Samuel 2:3)? Are we sincere? These are the sorts of questions with which we should daily ply our souls.

Matthew 6:9-15 *How to Pray*

"Pray, then, in this way: 'Our Father who is in heaven, Hallowed be Your name. Your kingdom come. Your will be done, on earth as it is in heaven. Give us this day our daily bread. And forgive us our debts, as we also have forgiven our debtors. And do not lead us into temptation, but deliver us from the evil one. For Yours is the kingdom and the power and the glory forever. Amen.' For if you forgive others for their transgressions, your heavenly Father will also forgive you. But if you do not forgive others, then your Father will not forgive your transgressions." (Matthew 6:9-15)

Perhaps no part of Scripture is so well known as this. Its words are familiar wherever Christianity is found. Thousands and tens of thousands who never saw a Bible or heard the pure gospel are acquainted with "Our Father" and "the Lord's Prayer." Happy would it be for the world if this prayer was as well known in the spirit as it is in the letter!

Perhaps no part of Scripture is so *full* and so *simple* at the same time as this. It is the first prayer which we learn to offer up when we are little children. Here is its simplicity. It contains the germ of everything which the most advanced saint can desire. Here is its fullness. The more we ponder every word it contains, the more we shall feel, "this prayer is of God."

The Lord's Prayer consists of ten parts or sentences. There is one declaration of the Being to whom we pray. There are three prayers respecting His name, His kingdom, and His will. There are four prayers respecting our daily needs, our sins, our weakness, and our dangers. There is one profession of our feeling towards others. There is one concluding ascription of praise. In all these parts we are taught to say *we* and *our*. We are to remember others as well as ourselves. On each of these parts a volume might be written. We must content ourselves at present with taking up sentence by sentence and marking out the direction in which each sentence points.

The first sentence declares to whom we are to pray. "*Our Father who is in heaven.*" We are not to cry to saints and angels, but to the everlasting Father, the Father of spirits, the Lord of heaven and earth. We call Him Father in the lowest sense, as our Creator; as Paul told the Athenians, *In Him we live and move and exist, . . . we also are His children* (Acts 17:28). We call Him Father in the highest sense, as the Father of our Lord Jesus Christ, reconciling us to Himself through the death of His Son (Colossians 1:20-22). We profess that which the Old Testament saints only saw dimly, if at all – we profess to be His children by faith in Christ and to *have received a spirit of adoption as sons by which we cry out, "Abba! Father!"* (Romans 8:15). This, we must never forget, is the sonship that we must desire if we would be saved. Without faith in Christ's blood and union with Him, it is vain to talk of trusting in the fatherhood of God.

The second sentence is *a petition respecting God's name*. *"Hallowed be Your name."* By the *name* of God we mean all those attributes under which He is revealed to us – His power, wisdom, holiness, justice, mercy, and truth. By asking that they may be *hallowed*, we mean that they may be made known and glorified. The glory of God is the first thing that God's children should desire. It is the object of one of our Lord's own prayers – *"Father, glorify Your name"* (John 12:28). It is the purpose for which the world was created. It is the end for which the saints are called and converted. It is the chief thing we should seek, that *in all things God may be glorified* (1 Peter 4:11).

The third sentence is *a petition concerning God's kingdom*. *"Your kingdom come."* By His *kingdom* we mean first the kingdom of *grace* which God sets up and maintains in the hearts of all living members of Christ by His Spirit and Word. But we mean chiefly the kingdom of *glory* which shall one day be set up when Jesus shall come the second time, and *"all will know [Him], from the least to the greatest of them."* This is the time when sin and sorrow and Satan shall be cast out of the world. It is the time when the Jews shall be converted, and the fullness of the Gentiles shall come in (Romans 11:25), and a time that is above all things to be desired. It therefore fills a foremost place in the Lord's Prayer. We ask that which is expressed in the words of the burial service, "that it may please you to hasten your kingdom."

The fourth sentence is *a petition concerning God's will. "Your will be done, on earth as it is in heaven."* We here pray that God's laws may be obeyed by men as perfectly, readily, and unceasingly as they are by angels in heaven. We ask that those who now obey not His laws may be taught to obey them, and that those who do obey them may obey them better. Our truest happiness is perfect submission to God's will, and it is the highest charity to pray that all mankind may know it, obey it, and submit to it.

The fifth sentence is *a petition respecting our own daily needs. "Give us this day our daily bread."* We are here taught to acknowledge our entire dependence on God for the supply of our daily necessities. As Israel required daily manna, so we require daily *bread*. We confess that we are poor, weak, and needy creatures and beseech Him who is our

Maker to take care of us. We ask for *bread* as the simplest of our needs, and in that word we include all that our bodies require.

The sixth sentence is *a petition respecting our sins.* "*Forgive us our debts.*" We confess that we are sinners and need daily grants of pardon and forgiveness. This is a part of the Lord's Prayer which deserves especially to be remembered. It condemns all self-righteousness and self-justifying. We are instructed here to keep up a continual habit of confession at the throne of grace, and a continual habit of seeking mercy and remission. Let this never be forgotten. We need daily to *wash [our] feet* (John 13:10).

The seventh sentence is *a profession respecting our own feelings towards others.* We ask our Father to "*forgive us our debts, as we also have forgiven our debtors.*" This is the only profession in the whole prayer, and the only part on which our Lord comments and dwells when He has concluded the prayer. The plain object of it is to remind us that we must not expect our prayers for forgiveness to be heard if we pray with malice and spite in our hearts towards others. To pray in such a frame of mind is mere formality and hypocrisy. It is even worse than hypocrisy. It is as much as saying, "Do not forgive me at all." Our prayer is nothing without charity. We must not expect to be forgiven if we cannot forgive.

The eighth sentence is *a petition respecting our weakness.* "*Do not lead us into temptation.*" It teaches us that we are liable, at all times, to be led astray and fall. It instructs us to confess our infirmity and beseech God to hold us up and not allow us to run into sin. We ask Him who orders all things in heaven and earth to restrain us from going into that which would injure our souls, and to never allow us to be tempted above that which we are able to bear (1 Corinthians 10:13).

The ninth sentence is *a petition respecting our dangers.* "*Deliver us from evil.*" We are here taught to ask God to deliver us from the evil that is in the world, the evil that is within our own hearts, and not least from that Evil One, the devil. We confess that so long as we are in the body, we are constantly seeing, hearing, and feeling the presence of evil. It is about us, within us, and around us on every side. And we entreat

Him, who alone can preserve us, to be continually delivering as from its power (John 17:15).

The last sentence is *an ascription of praise. "Yours is the kingdom and the power and the glory forever."* We declare in these words our belief that the kingdoms of this world are the rightful property of our Father, that to Him alone belongs all power, and that He alone deserves to receive all glory. And we conclude by offering to Him the profession of our hearts, that we give Him all honor and praise, and rejoice that He is King of Kings and Lord of Lords.

And now let us all examine ourselves and see whether we really desire to have the things which we are taught to ask for in the Lord's Prayer. Thousands, it may be feared, repeat these words daily as a form, but never consider what they are saying. They care nothing for the *glory*, the *kingdom*, or the *will* of God. They have no sense of dependence, sinfulness, weakness, or danger. They have no love or charity towards their enemies. And yet they repeat the Lord's Prayer! These things ought not to be so. May we resolve that by God's help our hearts shall go together with our lips! Happy is he who can really call God his Father through Jesus Christ his Savior, and can therefore say a heartfelt "Amen" to all that the Lord's Prayer contains.

Worldliness **Matthew 6:16-24** *Fasting + Prayer*

> *"Whenever you fast, do not put on a gloomy face as the hypo-crites do, for they neglect their appearance so that they will be noticed by men when they are fasting. Truly I say to you, they have their reward in full. But you, when you fast, anoint your head and wash your face so that your fasting will not be noticed by men, but by your Father who is in secret; and your Father who sees what is done in secret will reward you. Do not store up for yourselves treasures on earth, where moth and rust destroy, and where thieves break in and steal. But store up for yourselves treasures in heaven, where neither moth nor rust destroys, and where thieves do not break in or steal; for where your treasure is,*

*there your heart will be also. The eye is the lamp of the body; so
then if your eye is clear, your whole body will be full of light. But
if your eye is bad, your whole body will be full of darkness. If then
the light that is in you is darkness, how great is the darkness! No
one can serve two masters; for either he will hate the one and love
the other, or he will be devoted to one and despise the other. You
cannot serve God and wealth."* (Matthew 6:16-24)

There are three subjects brought before us in this part of our Lord's
Sermon on the Mount. These three are fasting, worldliness, and singleness of purpose in religion.

Fasting, or occasional abstinence from food in order to bring the
body into subjection to the spirit, is a practice frequently mentioned in
the Bible and generally in connection with prayer. David fasted when
his child was sick. Daniel fasted when he sought special light from God.
Paul and Barnabas fasted when they appointed elders. Esther fasted
before going in to Ahasuerus. It is a subject about which we find no
direct command in the New Testament. It seems to be left to everyone's
discretion whether they will fast or not. There is great wisdom in this.
Many a poor man never has enough to eat, and it would be an insult
to tell him to fast. Many a sickly person can hardly be kept well with
the closest attention to diet, and could not fast without bringing on
illness. It is a matter in which everyone must be persuaded in his own
mind and not be hasty to condemn others who do not agree with him.
One thing only must never be forgotten. Those who fast should do it
quietly, secretly, and without excessive display. Let them not *be noticed
by men* to fast. Let them not fast to man, but to God.

Worldliness is one of the greatest dangers that troubles man's soul.
It is no wonder that we find our Lord speaking strongly about it. It is a
treacherous, harmful, enticing, and powerful enemy. It seems so innocent
to pay close attention to our business! It seems so harmless to seek our
happiness in this world so long as we keep clear of open sins! Yet here
is a rock on which many make shipwreck to all eternity. They *store up
treasures on earth* and forget to *store up treasures in heaven.* May we all
remember this! Where are our hearts? What do we love best? Are our

chief affections on things in earth or things in heaven? Life or death depends on the answer we can give to these questions. If our treasure is earthly, our hearts will be earthly also. *Where your treasure is, there your heart will be also.*

Singleness of purpose is one great secret of spiritual prosperity. If our eyes do not see distinctly, we cannot walk without stumbling and falling. If we attempt to work for two different masters, we are sure to give satisfaction to neither. It is just the same with respect to our souls. We cannot serve Christ and the world at the same time. It is vain to attempt it. The thing cannot be done. The ark and Dagon will never stand together. God must be king over our hearts. His law, His will, and His precepts must receive our first attention. Then, and not until then, everything in our inward man will fall into its right place. Unless our hearts are so ordered, everything will be in confusion. *Your whole body will be full of darkness.*

Let us learn from our Lord's instruction about fasting *the great importance of cheerfulness in our religion.* Those words, *anoint your head and wash your face,* are full of deep meaning. They should teach us to aim at letting men see that we find Christianity makes us happy. Never let us forget that there is no religion in looking sad and gloomy. Are we dissatisfied with Christ's wages and Christ's service? Surely not! Then let us not look as if we were.

Let us learn from our Lord's caution about worldliness *what immense need we all have to watch and pray against an earthly spirit.* What are the vast majority of professing Christians around us doing? They are storing up treasures on earth. There can be no mistake about it. Their tastes, their ways, and their habits tell a fearful tale. They are not storing up treasures in heaven. Oh! let us all beware that we do not sink into hell by paying excessive attention to treasures on earth. Open transgression of God's law slays its thousands, but worldliness its tens of thousands.

Let us learn from our Lord's words about the "single eye," *the true secret of the failures* which so many Christians seem to make in their religion. There are failures in all quarters. There are thousands in our churches uncomfortable, ill at ease, and dissatisfied with themselves, and they hardly know why. The reason is revealed here. They are trying to keep in with both sides. They are endeavoring to please God and please man, to serve Christ and serve the world at the same time. Let us not commit this mistake. Let us be decided, thorough-going, and uncompromising followers of Christ. Let our motto be that of Paul: *One thing I do* (Philippians 3:13). Then we shall be happy Christians. We shall feel the sun shining on our faces. Heart, head, and conscience will all be full of light. *Decision* is the secret of happiness in religion. Be decided for Christ, and *your whole body will be full of light.*

Matthew 6:25-34
God our Provider

"For this reason I say to you, do not be worried about your life, as to what you will eat or what you will drink; nor for your body, as to what you will put on. Is not life more than food, and the body more than clothing? Look at the birds of the air, that they do not sow, nor reap nor gather into barns, and yet your heavenly Father feeds them. Are you not worth much more than they? And who of you by being worried can add a single hour to his life? And why are you worried about clothing? Observe how the lilies of the field grow; they do not toil nor do they spin, yet I say to you that not even Solomon in all his glory clothed himself like one of these. But if God so clothes the grass of the field, which is alive today and tomorrow is thrown into the furnace, will He not much more clothe you? You of little faith! Do not worry then, saying, 'What will we eat?' or 'What will we drink?' or 'What will we wear for clothing?' For the Gentiles eagerly seek all these things; for your heavenly Father knows that you need all these things. But seek first His kingdom and His righteousness, and all these things will be added to you. So do not worry about tomorrow; for tomorrow will care for itself. Each day has enough trouble of its own." (Matthew 6:25-34)

These verses are a striking example of the combined wisdom and compassion of our Lord Jesus Christ's teaching. He knows the heart of a man. He knows that we are all ready to turn off warnings against worldliness by the argument that we cannot help being anxious about the things of this life. Have we not our families to provide for? Must not our bodily needs be supplied? How can we possibly get through life if we think first of our souls? The Lord Jesus foresaw such thoughts and furnished an answer.

He forbids us to keep up an anxious spirit about the things of this world. Three times over He says, *"Do not be worried"* or *"Do not worry."* About life, about food, about clothing, about tomorrow – *"do not be worried."* Be not over-careful. Be not over-anxious. Prudent provision for the future is right. *Wearing, corroding, and self-tormenting anxiety is wrong.*

He reminds us of the providential care that God continually takes of everything that He has created. Has He given us life? Then He will surely not let us lack anything necessary for its maintenance. Has He given us a body? Then He will surely not let us die for lack of clothing. He who calls us into being will doubtless find food to feed us.

He points out the uselessness of over-anxiety. Our life is entirely in God's hand. All the care in the world will not make us continue a minute beyond the time which God has appointed. We shall not die until our work is done.

He sends us to the birds of the air for instruction. They make no provision for the future. *They do not sow, nor reap.* They lay up no stores against time yet to come. They do not *gather into barns.* They literally live from day to day on what they can pick up by using the instinct God has put in them. They ought to teach us that no man doing his duty in the station to which God has called him shall ever be allowed to come to poverty.

He bids us to observe the flowers of the field. Year after year they are decked with the brightest colors without the slightest labor or exertion on their part. *They do not toil, nor do they spin.* God, by His almighty power, clothes them with beauty every season. The same God is the Father of all believers. Why should they doubt that He is able to provide them with clothing as well, just as the lilies *of the field*? He who takes thought for perishable flowers will surely not neglect the bodies in which dwell immortal souls.

He suggests to us that anxiety about the things of this world is most unworthy of a Christian. One great feature of heathenism is living for the present. Let the heathen, if he will, be anxious. He knows nothing of a Father in heaven. But let the Christian, who has clearer light and knowledge, give proof of it by his faith and contentment. When bereaved of those whom we love, we are not to *grieve as do the rest who have no hope.* When tried by the cares of this life, we are not to be over-anxious as if we had no God and no Christ.

He offers us a gracious promise as a remedy against an anxious spirit. He assures us that if we *seek first* and foremost to have a place in the kingdom of grace and glory, everything that we really need in this world shall be given to us. It shall be *added* over and above our heavenly inheritance. *God causes all things to work together for good to those who love God. No good thing does He withhold from those who walk uprightly* (Romans 8:28; Psalm 84:11).

Last of all, He seals up all His instruction on this subject by *laying down one of the wisest maxims. Tomorrow will care for itself. Each day has enough trouble of its own.* We are not to carry cares before they come. We are to attend to today's business and leave tomorrow's anxieties until tomorrow dawns. We may die before tomorrow. We know not what may happen tomorrow. This only we may be assured of, that if tomorrow brings a cross, He who sends it can and will send grace to bear it.

In all this passage there is a treasury of golden lessons. Let us seek to use them in our daily life. Let us not only read them but also turn them into practical account. Let us watch and pray against worry and an over-anxious spirit. It deeply affects our happiness. Half our miseries are caused by imagining things that we think are coming upon us. Half the things that we expect to come upon us never come at all. Where is our faith? Where is our confidence in our Savior's words? We may well take shame to ourselves when we read these verses and then look into our hearts. But this we may be sure of, that David's words are true: *I have been young and now I am old, yet I have not seen the righteous forsaken or his descendants begging bread* (Psalm 37:25).

Matthew Chapter 7

Matthew 7:1-11

Interactions ē man + God.

"*Do not judge so that you will not be judged. For in the same way you judge, you will be judged; and by your standard of measure, it will be measured to you. Why do you look at the speck that is in your brother's eye, but do not notice the log that is in your own eye? Or how can you say to your brother, 'Let me take the speck out of your eye,' and behold, the log is in your own eye? You hypocrite, first take the log out of your own eye, and then you will see clearly to take the speck out of your brother's eye. Do not give what is holy to dogs, and do not throw your pearls before swine, or they will trample them under their feet, and turn and tear you to pieces. Ask, and it will be given to you; seek, and you will find; knock and it will be opened to you. For everyone who asks receives, and he who seeks finds, and to him who knocks it will be opened. Or what man is there among you who, when his son asks for a loaf, will give him a stone? Or if he asks for a fish, he will not give him a snake, will he? If you then, being evil, know how to give good gifts to your children, how much more will your Father who is in Heaven give what is good to those who ask him!*"
(Matthew 7:1-11)

THE FIRST PORTION OF THESE VERSES is one of those passages of Scripture which we must be careful not to strain beyond its proper meaning. It is frequently abused and misapplied by the enemies of true religion. *It is possible to press the words of the Bible so far that they yield not medicine but poison.*

Our Lord does not mean that it is wrong, under any circumstances, to pass an unfavorable judgment on the conduct and opinions of others. We ought to have *decided opinions*. We are to *examine everything carefully*. We are to *test the spirits*. Nor yet does He mean that it is wrong to reprove the sins and faults of others until we are perfect and faultless ourselves. Such an interpretation would contradict other parts of Scripture. It would make it impossible to condemn error and false doctrine. It would bar anyone from attempting the office of a minister or a judge. The earth would be *given into the hand of the wicked* (Job 9:24). Heresy would flourish, and wrongdoing would abound.

Verses 1-5. *What our Lord means to condemn is a censorious and fault-finding spirit.* A readiness to blame others for trifling offenses or matters of indifference – a habit of passing rash and hasty judgments – a disposition to magnify the errors and infirmities of our neighbors and make the worst of them – this is what our Lord forbids. This was common among the Pharisees, and it has always been common from their day down to the present time. We must all watch against it. We should *believe all things*, and *hope all things* about others – and be very slow to find fault. This is Christian charity (1 Corinthians 13:7).

Verse 6. The second lesson contained in this passage is *the importance of exercising discretion as to the person with whom we speak on the subject of religion.* Everything is beautiful in its place and season. Our zeal is to be tempered by a prudent consideration of times, places, and people. *"Do not reprove a scoffer,"* says Solomon, *"or he will hate you"* (Proverbs 9:8). It is not everybody to whom it is wise to open our minds and hearts on spiritual matters. There are many, who from violent tempers or openly profligate habits, are utterly incapable of valuing the things of the gospel. They will even fly into a passion and run into greater excesses of sin if you try to do good to their souls. To name the name of Christ to such people is truly to *throw your pearls before swine.* It does them not good, but rather harm. It rouses all their corruption and makes them angry. In short, they are like the Jews at Corinth (Acts 18:6), or like Nabal, of whom it is written that he was *such a worthless man that no one can speak to him* (1 Samuel 25:17)!

This is a lesson which it is peculiarly difficult to use in the proper way. The right application of it needs great wisdom. We are most of us far more likely to err on the side of over-caution than of over-zeal. We are generally far more disposed to remember the *time to be silent* than the *time to speak*. It is a lesson, however, which ought to stir up a spirit of self-inquiry in all our hearts. By our moroseness and irritability of temper, do we ourselves ever prevent our friends from giving us good advice? By our pride and impatient contempt of counsel, have we ever obliged others to say nothing? Have we ever turned against our kind advisers and silenced them by our angry passion? Alas! we may well fear that we have erred in this matter.

Verses 7-11. The last lesson contained in this passage is *the duty of prayer and the rich encouragements there are to pray.* There is a beautiful connection between this lesson and that which goes before it. Would we know when to be silent and when to speak? When to bring forward *holy* things and produce our *pearls*? We must pray. This is a subject to which the Lord Jesus evidently attaches great importance. The language that He uses is a plain proof of this. He employs three different words to express the idea of prayer: *Ask. Seek. Knock.* He holds out the broadest, fullest promise to those who pray. *"Everyone who asks receives."* He illustrates God's readiness to hear our prayers by an argument drawn from the notorious practice of parents on earth. *Evil* and selfish as they are by nature, they do not neglect the needs of their children. Much more will a God of love and mercy attend to the cries of those who are His children by grace.

Let us take special notice of these words of our Lord about prayer. Few of His sayings, perhaps, are so well known and so often repeated as this. The poorest and most unlearned can tell you that "if we do not seek, then we shall not find." But what is the good of *knowing* it if we do not *use* it? *Knowledge which is not improved and well employed will only increase our condemnation at the last day.*

Do we know anything of this asking, seeking, and knocking? Why should we not? There is nothing so simple and plain as praying – if a man really has a desire to pray. Sadly, there is nothing which men are so slow to do as sincere, secret praying. They will use many of the *forms*

Procrastination t prayer

59

of religion, attend many ordinances, and do many things that are right before they will do this. And yet without this, no soul can be saved.

Do we ever really pray? If not, we shall at last be without excuse before God unless we repent. We shall not be condemned for not doing what we could not have done or not knowing what we could not have known. But we shall find that one main reason why we are lost is this – that we never asked that we might be saved.

Do we indeed pray? Then let us pray on and not faint. It is not lost labor. It is not useless. It will bear fruit after many days. That promise has never yet failed: *Everyone who asks receives.*

Relationship c Man
Path of Christianity + Following God.

Matthew 7:12-20

"In everything, therefore, treat people the same way you want them to treat you, for this is the Law and the Prophets. Enter through the narrow gate; for the gate is wide and the way is broad that leads to destruction, and there are many who enter through it. For the gate is small and the way is narrow that leads to life, and there are few who find it. Beware of the false prophets, who come to you in sheep's clothing, but inwardly are ravenous wolves. You will know them by their fruits. Grapes are not gathered from thorn bushes nor figs from thistles, are they? So every good tree bears good fruit, but the bad tree bears bad fruit. A good tree cannot produce bad fruit, nor can a bad tree produce good fruit. Every tree that does not bear good fruit is cut down and thrown into the fire. So then, you will know them by their fruits." (Matthew 7:12-20)

In this part of the Sermon on the Mount our Lord begins to draw His discourse to a conclusion. The lessons He enforces here are broad, general, and full of the deepest wisdom. Let us review them in succession.

Verse 12. *Jesus lays down a general principle for our guidance in all doubtful questions between man and man.* We are to do to others as we would have others do unto us. We are not to deal with others as others deal with us. This is mere selfishness and heathenism. <u>We are to deal with others as we would like others to deal with us.</u> This is real Christianity.

This is a golden rule indeed! It does not merely forbid all petty malice and revenge, all cheating and taking advantage of others. It does much more. *It settles a hundred difficult points, which in a world like this are continually arising between man and man.* It prevents the necessity of laying down endless little rules for our conduct in specific cases. It sweeps the whole debatable ground with one mighty principle. It shows us a balance and measure by which everyone may see at once what his duty is.

Is there a thing which we would not like our neighbor to do unto us? Then let us always remember that this is the thing which we ought not to do unto him. Is there a thing which we would like him to do unto us? Then this is the very thing which we ought to do unto him. *How many intricate questions would be decided at once if this rule were honestly used!*

Verses 13-14. In the second place, *our Lord gives us a general caution against the way of the many in religion.* It is not enough to think as others think and do as others do. It must not satisfy us to follow the fashion and swim with the stream of those among whom we live. He tells us that the way that leads to everlasting life is *narrow*, and *few travel in it.* He tells us that the way that leads to everlasting destruction is *broad and full of travelers. There are many who enter through it.*

[handwritten margin notes: Path to salvation is simple and straight forward but path to destruct Destruction is broad and many.]

These are fearful truths! They ought to raise great searchings of heart in the minds of all who hear them. "Which way am I going? By what road am I traveling?" In one or another of the two ways here described, every one of us may be found. May God give us an honest, self-inquiring spirit and show us what we are!

We may well tremble and be afraid if our religion is that of the multitude. If we can say no more than this, that we go where others go, and worship where others worship, and hope we shall do as well as others at last, we are literally pronouncing our own condemnation. What is this but being in the "broad way"? What is this but being in the road whose end is *destruction*? Our religion at present is not saving religion.

We have no reason to be discouraged and cast down if the religion we profess is not popular and few agree with us. We must remember the words of our Lord Jesus Christ in this passage: *"The gate is small and the way is narrow."* Repentance and faith in Christ and holiness of life have never been fashionable. The true flock of Christ has always been small. It must not move us to find that we are reckoned singular, peculiar, bigoted, and narrow-minded. This is "the narrow way." Surely it is better to enter into life eternal with a *few*, than to go to *destruction* with a great company.

Verses 15-20. In the last place, *the Lord Jesus gives us a general warning against false teachers in the church.* We are to *beware of the false prophets.* The connection between this passage and the preceding one is striking. Do we want to keep clear of this "broad way"? Then we must beware of false prophets. They will arise. They began in the days of the apostles. Even then, the *seeds of error* were sown. They have appeared continually ever since. We must be prepared for them and be on our guard.

This is a warning that is much needed. There are thousands who seem ready to believe anything in religion if they hear it from an ordained minister. They forget that clergymen may err as much as laymen. They are not infallible. Their teaching must be weighed in the balance of Holy Scripture. They are to be followed and believed only so long as their doctrine agrees with the Bible, but not a minute longer. We are to test them *by their fruits. Sound doctrine* and *holy living* are the marks of true prophets. Let us remember this. Our ministers' mistakes will not excuse our own. *"If a blind man guides a blind man, both will fall into a pit."*

What is the best safeguard against false teaching? Beyond all doubt, it is the regular study of the Word of God with prayer for the teaching of the Holy Spirit. The Bible was given to be a lamp to our feet and a light to our path (Psalm 119:105). The man who reads it aright will never be allowed greatly to err. It is neglect of the Bible which makes so many a prey to the first false teacher whom they hear. They would have us believe that they are not learned and do not pretend to have decided opinions. The plain truth is that they are lazy and idle about reading the Bible and do not like the trouble of thinking for themselves. Nothing supplies false prophets with followers so much as *spiritual sloth under a cloak of humility.*

May we all bear in mind our Lord's warning! The world, the devil, and the flesh are not the only dangers in the way of the Christian. There remains another yet, and that is the false prophet – the wolf in sheep's clothing. Happy is he who prays over his Bible and knows the difference between truth and error in religion! There is a difference, and we are meant to know it and use our knowledge.

Matthew 7:21-29

"Not everyone who says to me, 'Lord, Lord,' will enter the kingdom of heaven, but he who does the will of my Father who is in heaven will enter. Many will say to Me on that day, 'Lord, Lord, did we not prophesy in Your name, and in Your name cast out demons, and in Your name perform many miracles?' And then I will declare to them, 'I never knew you; depart from Me, you who practice lawlessness.' Therefore everyone who hears these words of Mine and acts on them, may be compared to a wise man who built his house on the rock. And the rain fell, and the floods came, and the winds blew and slammed against that house; and yet it did not fall, for it had been founded on the rock. Everyone who hears these words of Mine and does not act on them, will be like a foolish man who built his house on the sand. The rain fell, and the floods came, and the winds blew and slammed against that house; and it fell—and great was its fall." When Jesus had finished these words, the crowds were amazed at His teaching; for He was teaching them as one having authority, and not as their scribes. (Matthew 7:21-29)

The Lord Jesus winds up the Sermon on the Mount by a passage of heart-piercing application. He turns from false *prophets* to false *professors*, from unsound *teachers* to unsound *hearers*. Here is a word for all. May we have grace to apply it to our own hearts!

Verses 21-23. The first lesson here is *the uselessness of a mere outward profession of Christianity.* Not everyone who says, *"Lord, Lord,"* shall enter the kingdom of heaven. Not all who *profess* and *call* themselves Christians shall be saved.

Let us take notice of this. It requires far more than most people seem to think necessary to save a soul. We may be baptized in the name of Christ and boast confidently in our ecclesiastical privileges. We may possess head-knowledge and be quite satisfied with our own state before God. We may even be preachers and teachers of others and *perform many miracles* in connection with our church. But all this time are we practically doing the will of our Father in heaven? Do we truly repent – truly believe on Christ – and live holy and humble lives? If not, in spite of all our privileges and profession, we shall miss heaven at last and be forever cast away! We shall hear those dreadful words, *"I never knew you; depart from Me, you who practice lawlessness."*

The day of judgment will reveal strange things. The *hopes* of many who were thought great Christians while they lived will be utterly confounded. The rottenness of their religion will be exposed and put to shame before the whole world. It will then be proved that to be saved means something more than "making a profession." We must make a *practice* of our Christianity as well as a *profession.* Let us often think of *that great day.* Let us often judge ourselves so that we will not be judged and condemned by the Lord. Whatever else we are, let us aim at being *real, true,* and *sincere.*

Verses 24-27. The second lesson here is *a striking picture of two classes of professing Christian hearers:* those who hear and *do nothing* and those who *do* as well as hear. Both classes are placed before us and their histories traced to their respective ends.

The man who hears Christian teaching and practices what he hears is like *a wise man who built his house on the rock.* He does not content himself with listening to exhortations to repent, believe in Christ, and live a holy life. He actually repents. He actually believes. He actually ceases to do evil, learns to do well, abhors that which is sinful, and cleaves to that which is good. He is a *doer* as well as a hearer (James 1:22).

And what is the result? In the time of trial, his religion does not fail him. The floods of sickness, sorrow, poverty, disappointments, and bereavements beat upon him in vain. His soul stands unmoved. His faith does not give way. His spiritual comforts do not utterly forsake him. His religion may have cost him trouble in time past. His *foundation* may have been obtained with much labor and many tears. To discover his own saving interest in Christ may have required many a day of earnest seeking and many an hour of wrestling in prayer. But his labor has not been thrown away. He now reaps a rich reward. The religion that can stand *trial* is the true religion.

The man who hears Christian teaching and never gets beyond hearing is like *a foolish man who built his house on the sand*. He satisfies himself with *listening* and *approving*, but he goes no further. He flatters himself, perhaps, that all is right with his soul because he has feelings, and convictions, and desires of a spiritual kind. In these he rests. He never really breaks off from sin and casts aside the spirit of the world. He never really lays hold of Christ. He never really takes up the cross. He is a *hearer* of truth but nothing more. *How not to be a Christian.*

And what is the end of this man's religion? It breaks down entirely under the first flood of tribulation! It fails him completely, like a summer-dried fountain, when his need is the sorest. It leaves its possessor high and dry like a wreck on a sand bank, a scandal to the church, a byword to the infidel, and a misery to himself. Most true is it that what costs little is worth little! A religion which costs us nothing and consists of nothing but hearing sermons will always prove at last to be a useless thing.

Verses 28-29. So ends the Sermon on the Mount. Such a sermon never was preached before. Such a sermon has never been preached since. Let us see that it has a lasting influence on our own souls. It is addressed to us as well as to those who first heard it. We are those who shall have to give account of its heart-searching lessons. It is no light matter what we think of them. The word that Jesus has spoken *is what will judge [us] at the last day* (John 12:48).

Matthew Chapter 8

Matthew 8:1-15

When Jesus came down from the mountain, large crowds followed Him. And a leper came to Him and bowed down before Him, and said, "Lord, if You are willing, You can make me clean." Jesus stretched out His hand and touched him, saying, "I am willing; be cleansed." And immediately his leprosy was cleansed. And Jesus said to him, "See that you tell no one; but go, show yourself to the priest and present the offering that Moses commanded, as a testimony to them." And when Jesus entered Capernaum, a centurion came to Him, imploring Him, and saying, "Lord, my servant is lying paralyzed at home, fearfully tormented." Jesus said to him, "I will come and heal him." But the centurion said, "Lord, I am not worthy for You to come under my roof, but just say the word, and my servant will be healed. For I also am a man under authority, with soldiers under me; and I say to this one, 'Go!' and he goes, and to another, 'Come!' and he comes, and to my slave, 'Do this!' and he does it." Now when Jesus heard this, He marveled and said to those who were following, "Truly I say to you, I have not found such great faith with anyone in Israel. I say to you that many will come from east and west, and recline at the table with Abraham, Isaac and Jacob in the kingdom of heaven; but the sons of the kingdom will be cast out into the outer darkness; in that place there will be weeping and gnashing of teeth." And Jesus said to the centurion, "Go; it shall be done for you as you have believed." And the servant was healed that very moment. When Jesus came into Peter's home, He saw his mother-in-law lying sick in bed with a fever.

He touched her hand, and the fever left her; and she got up and waited on Him. (Matthew 8:1-15)

THE EIGHTH CHAPTER OF MATTHEW'S GOSPEL is full of our Lord's miracles. No less than five are specially recorded. There is a beautiful fitness in this. It was fitting that the greatest sermon ever preached should be immediately followed by mighty proof that the preacher was the Son of God. Those who heard the Sermon on the Mount would be obliged to confess that, as *never has a man spoken the way this man speaks,* so also no man has ever done such works.

The verses we have now read contain three great miracles. A leper is healed with a touch. A paralyzed person is made well by a word. A woman sick with a fever is restored in a moment to health and strength. On the face of these three miracles, we may read three striking lessons. Let us examine them and lay them to heart.

Let us learn, for one thing, *how great is the power of our Lord Jesus Christ.* Leprosy is the most fearful disease by which man's body can be afflicted. He that has it is like one dead while he lives. It is a disease regarded by physicians as incurable (2 Kings 5:7). Yet Jesus says, *"Be cleansed." And immediately his leprosy was cleansed.* To heal a person of paralysis without even seeing him, by only speaking a word, is to do that which our minds cannot even conceive. Yet Jesus commands and at once it is done. To give a woman prostrate with a fever not merely relief but also strength to do work in an instant would baffle the skill of all the physicians on earth. Yet Jesus *touched* Peter's mother-in-law and *she got up and waited on Him.* These are the doings of one who is almighty. There is no escape from the conclusion. This was *the finger of God* (Exodus 8:19).

Behold here a broad foundation for the faith of a Christian! We are told in the gospel to come to Jesus, to believe on Jesus, and to live the life of faith in Jesus. We are encouraged to lean on Him, to cast all our care on Him, and to rest all the weight of our souls on Him. We may do so without fear. He can bear all. He is a strong rock. He is almighty. It was a fine saying of an old saint, "My faith can sleep sound on no other pillow than Christ's omnipotence." He can give life to the dead. He can give power to the weak. He can *increase power* to *him who lacks might*. Let us trust Him and not be afraid. *The world is full of snares. Our hearts are weak. But with Jesus nothing is impossible.*

Let us learn, for another thing, *the mercy and compassion of our Lord Jesus Christ.* The circumstances of the three cases we are now considering were all different. He *heard* the leper's pitiful cry, *"Lord, if You are willing, You can make me clean."* He was *told* of the centurion's servant, but He never saw him. He *saw* Peter's mother-in-law *lying sick in bed with a fever,* and we are not told that she spoke a word. Yet in each case the heart of the Lord Jesus was one and the same. In each case He was quick to show mercy and ready to heal. Each poor sufferer was tenderly pitied and each effectually relieved.

Behold here another strong foundation for our faith! Our Great High Priest is very gracious. He can *sympathize with our weaknesses.* He is never tired of doing us good. He knows that we are a weak and feeble people in the midst of a weary and troublesome world. He is as ready to bear with us and help us as He was eighteen hundred years ago. It is as true of Him now as it was then, that He *does not despise any* (Job 36:5). No heart can feel for us so much as the heart of Christ can.

Let us learn, in the last place, *what a precious thing is the grace of faith.* We know little about the centurion described in these verses. His name, his nation, and his history are all hidden from us. But one thing we know, and that is that he believed. *"Lord,"* he says, *"I am not worthy for You to come under my roof, but just say the word, and my servant will be healed."* He believed, let us remember, when scribes and Pharisees were unbelievers. He believed, though born a Gentile, when Israel was blinded. And our Lord pronounced upon him the commendation which has been read all over the world from that time to this: *"Truly I say to you, I have not found such great faith with anyone in Israel."*

Let us lay firm hold on this lesson. It deserves to be remembered. To believe Christ's power and willingness to help, and to make a practical use of our belief, is a rare and precious gift. Let us be ever thankful if we have it. To be willing to come to Jesus as helpless, lost sinners and commit our souls into His hands is a mighty privilege. Let us ever bless God if this willingness is ours, for it is His gift. Such faith is better than all other gifts and knowledge in the world. Many a poor converted heathen who knows nothing but that he is sick of sin and trusts in Jesus shall sit down in heaven, while many learned English scholars are rejected forevermore. Blessed indeed are those who believe!

What do we each know of this faith? This is the great question. Our learning may be small, but do we believe? Our opportunities of giving and working for Christ's cause may be few, but do we believe? We may neither be able to preach, nor write, nor argue for the gospel, but do we believe? May we never rest until we can answer this question! Faith in Christ appears a small and simple thing to the children of this world. They see in it nothing great or grand. But faith in Christ is most precious in God's sight, and like most precious things, is rare. By it true Christians live. By it they stand. By it they overcome the world. Without this faith no one can be saved.

Matthew 8:16-27

When evening came, they brought to Him many who were demon-possessed; and He cast out the spirits with a word, and healed all who were ill. This was to fulfill what was spoken through Isaiah the prophet: "He Himself took our infirmities and carried away our diseases." Now when Jesus saw a crowd around Him, He gave orders to depart to the other side of the sea. Then a scribe came and said to Him, "Teacher, I will follow You wherever You go." Jesus said to him, "The foxes have holes and the birds of the air have nests, but the Son of Man has nowhere to lay His head." Another of the disciples said to Him, "Lord, permit me first to go and bury my father." But Jesus said to him, "Follow Me, and allow the dead to bury their own dead." When He got into the boat, His disciples followed Him. And behold, there arose a great storm on the sea, so that the boat was being covered with the waves; but Jesus Himself was asleep. And they came to Him and woke Him, saying, "Save us, Lord; we are perishing!" He

*said to them, "Why are you afraid, you men of little faith?" Then
He got up and rebuked the winds and the sea, and it became
perfectly calm. The men were amazed, and said, "What kind
of a man is this, that even the winds and the sea obey Him?"*
(Matthew 8:16-27)

In the first part of these verses we see a striking example of *our Lord's
wisdom in dealing with those who professed a willingness to be His disciples.* The passage throws so much light on a subject frequently misunderstood in these days that it deserves more than ordinary attention.

A certain scribe offers to follow our Lord wherever He goes. It was a
remarkable offer when we consider the class to which the man belonged
and the time at which it was made. But the offer receives a remarkable
answer. It is not directly accepted nor yet flatly rejected. Our Lord only
makes the solemn reply, *"The foxes have holes and the birds of the air
have nests, but the Son of Man has nowhere to lay His head."*

Another follower of our Lord next comes forward and asks to be
allowed to *bury his father* before going any further in the path of a
disciple. The request seems, at first sight, a natural and lawful one. But
it draws from our Lord's lips a reply no less solemn than that already
referred to: *"Follow Me, and allow the dead to bury their own dead."*

There is something deeply impressive in both these sayings. They
ought to be well weighed by all professing Christians. They teach us
plainly that people who show a desire to come forward and profess themselves to be true disciples of Christ should be warned plainly to "count
the cost" before they begin. Are they prepared to endure hardship? Are
they ready to carry the cross? If not, they are not yet fit to begin. They
teach us plainly that there are times when a Christian must literally
give up all for Christ's sake, and when even such duties as attending to
a parent's funeral must be left to be performed by others. Such duties
some will always be ready to attend to, and at no time can they be put
in comparison with the greater duty of preaching the gospel and doing
Christ's work in the world.

It would be well for the churches of Christ if these sayings of our
Lord were more remembered than they are. It may well be feared that

the lesson they contain is too often overlooked by the ministers of the gospel, and that thousands are admitted to full communion who are never warned to count the cost. Nothing, in fact, has done more harm to Christianity than the practice of filling the ranks of Christ's army with every volunteer who is willing to make a little profession and talk fluently of his experience. It has been painfully forgotten that numbers alone do not make strength, and that there may be a great quantity of mere outward religion while there is very little real grace. Let us all remember this. Let us keep back nothing from young professors and inquirers after Christ. Let us not enlist them on false pretenses. Let us tell them plainly that there is a crown of glory at the end. But let us tell them no less plainly that there is a daily cross in the way.

In the latter part of these verses we learn that *true saving faith is often mingled with much weakness and infirmity.* It is a humbling lesson but a very wholesome one.

We are told of our Lord and His disciples crossing the Sea of Galilee in a boat. A storm arises, and the boat is in danger of being filled with water by the waves that are beating over it. Meanwhile, our Lord is asleep. The frightened disciples wake Him and cry to Him for help. He hears their cry and stills the water with a word, so that *it became perfectly calm.* At the same time, He reproves the anxiety of His disciples. *"Why are you afraid, you men of little faith?"*

What a vivid picture we have here of the hearts of thousands of believers! How many have faith and love enough to forsake all for Christ's sake and follow Him wherever He goes, and yet are full of fear in the hour of trial! How many have grace enough to turn to Jesus in every trouble, crying, *"Save us, Lord,"* and yet not grace enough to lie still and believe in the darkest hour that all is well! Truly, believers have reason indeed to *clothe themselves with humility.*

Let the prayer, *"Lord, increase our faith!"* always form part of our daily petitions. *We never perhaps know the weakness of our faith until we are placed in the furnace of trial and anxiety.* Blessed and happy is that person who finds by experience that his faith can stand the fire and that he can say with Job, *"Though He slay me, I will hope in Him"* (Job 13:15).

We have great reason to thank God that Jesus, our Great High Priest, is very compassionate and tenderhearted. He knows our frame. He considers our infirmities. He does not cast off His people because of defects. He pities even those whom He reproves. The prayer even of *little faith* is heard and gets an answer.

Matthew 8:28-34

When He came to the other side into the country of the Gadarenes, two men who were demon-possessed met Him as they were coming out of the tombs. They were so extremely violent that no one could pass by that way. And they cried out, saying, "What business do we have with each other, Son of God? Have You come here to torment us before the time?" Now there was a herd of many swine feeding at a distance from them. The demons began to entreat Him, saying, "If You are going to cast us out, send us into the herd of swine." And He said to them, "Go!" And they came out and went into the swine, and the whole herd rushed down the steep bank into the sea and perished in the waters. The herdsmen ran away, and went to the city and reported everything, including what had happened to the demoniacs. And behold, the whole city came out to meet Jesus; and when they saw Him, they implored Him to leave their region. (Matthew 8:28-34)

The subject of these seven verses is deep and mysterious. The casting out of a devil is here described with special fullness. It is one of those passages which throws strong light on a dark and difficult point.

Let us settle it firmly in our minds that *there is such a being as the devil*. It is a dreadful truth and one too much overlooked. There is an unseen spirit ever near us, of mighty power and full of endless malice against our souls. From the beginning of creation he has labored to injure man. Until the Lord comes the second time and binds him, he will never cease to tempt and practice mischief. In the days when our

Lord was upon earth, it is clear that he had a peculiar power over the bodies of certain men and women as well as over their souls. Even in our own times there may be more of this bodily possession than some suppose, though it seems in far less degree than when Christ came in the flesh. But that the devil is ever near us in spirit and ever ready to ply our hearts with temptations ought never to be forgotten.

Let us, in the next place, settle it firmly in our minds that *the power of the devil is limited.* Mighty as he is, there is One mightier still. Keenly set as his will is on doing harm in the world, he can only work by permission. These very verses show us that the evil spirits know they can only go to and fro and ravage the earth until the time allowed them by the Lord of Lords. *"Have you come here to torment us,"* they say, *"before the time?"* Their very petition shows us that they could not even hurt one of the Gadarene swine unless Jesus the Son of God allowed them. *"If You are going to cast us out,"* they say, *"send us into the herd of swine."*

Let us, in the next place, settle it in our minds that *our Lord Jesus Christ is man's great deliverer from the power of the devil.* He can redeem us not only *from all our iniquity* and *from this present evil age,* but also from the devil. It was prophesied of old that He would bruise the serpent's head. He began to bruise that head when he was born of the Virgin Mary. He triumphed over that head when He died upon the cross. He showed His complete dominion over Satan by *healing all who were oppressed by the devil* when He was upon earth (Acts 10:38). Our great remedy in all the assaults of the devil is to cry to the Lord Jesus and to seek His help. He can break the chains that Satan casts around us and set us free. He can cast out every devil that plagues our hearts as surely as in the days of old. It would be miserable indeed to know that there is a devil ever near us if we did not also know that Christ was able to *save forever . . . since He always lives to make intercession for [us]* (Hebrews 7:25).

Let us not leave this passage without observing *the painful worldliness of the Gadarenes,* among whom this miracle of casting out a devil was wrought. They besought the Lord Jesus *to leave their region.* They had no heart to feel for anything but the loss of their swine. They cared not that two fellow creatures with immortal souls were freed from Satan's bondage. They cared not that there stood among them One greater than the devil, Jesus the Son of God. They cared for nothing but that their swine were drowned and *their hope of profit was gone.* They ignorantly regarded Jesus as one who stood between them and their profits, and they only wished to be rid of Him.

There are only too many like these Gadarenes. There are thousands who care not one jot for Christ or Satan, so long as they can make a little more money and have a little more of the good things of this world. From this spirit may we be delivered! Against this spirit may we ever watch and pray! It is very common. It is awfully infectious. Let us recollect every morning that we have souls to be saved, and that we shall one day die and after that be judged. Let us beware of loving the world more than Christ. Let us beware of hindering the salvation of others because we fear that the increase of true religion may diminish our gains or give us trouble.

Matthew Chapter 9

Call to action - Jesus our saviour + Deliverer.

Matthew 9:1-13

Getting into a boat, Jesus crossed over the sea and came to His own city. And they brought to Him a paralytic lying on a bed. Seeing their faith, Jesus said to the paralytic, "Take courage, son; your sins are forgiven." And some of the scribes said to themselves, "This fellow blasphemes." And Jesus knowing their thoughts said, "Why are you thinking evil in your hearts? Which is easier, to say, 'Your sins are forgiven,' or to say, 'Get up, and walk'? But so that you may know that the Son of Man has authority on earth to forgive sins"—then He said to the paralytic, "Get up, pick up your bed and go home." And he got up and went home. But when the crowds saw this, they were awestruck, and glorified God, who had given such authority to men. As Jesus went on from there, He saw a man called Matthew, sitting in the tax collector's booth; and He said to him, "Follow Me!" And he got up and followed Him. Then it happened that as Jesus was reclining at the table in the house, behold, many tax collectors and sinners came and were dining with Jesus and His disciples. When the Pharisees saw this, they said to His disciples, "Why is your Teacher eating with the tax collectors and sinners?" But when Jesus heard this, He said, "It is not those who are healthy who need a physician, but those who are sick. But go and learn what this means: 'I desire compassion, and not sacrifice,' for I did not come to call the righteous, but sinners." (Matthew 9:1-13)

LET US NOTICE, in the first part of this passage, *our Lord's knowledge of men's thoughts.* There were certain scribes who found fault with the words Jesus spoke to a man sick who was paralyzed. They said secretly among themselves, *"This fellow blasphemes."* They probably supposed that no one knew what was going on in their minds. They had yet to learn that the Son of God could read hearts and discern spirits. Their malicious thought was publicly exposed. They were put to open shame.

There is an important lesson for us in this. *All things are open and laid bare to the eyes of Him with whom we have to do* (Hebrews 4:13). Nothing can be concealed from Christ. What do we think of in private when no man sees us? What do we think of in church when we seem so grave and serious? What are we thinking of at this moment, while these words pass under our eyes? Jesus knows. Jesus sees. Jesus records. Jesus will one day call us to give account. It is written that *according to my gospel, God will judge the secrets of men through Jesus Christ* (Romans 2:16). Surely we ought to be very humble when we consider these things. We ought to thank God daily that the blood of Christ can cleanse from all sin. We ought often to cry, *Let the words of my mouth, and the meditation of my heart be acceptable in Your sight* (Psalm 19:14).

Let us notice, in the second place, *the wonderful call of the apostle Matthew to be Christ's disciple.* We find the man, who afterwards was the first to write a Gospel, sitting at the tax collector's booth. We see him absorbed in his worldly calling and possibly thinking of nothing but money and gain. But suddenly the Lord Jesus calls on him to follow Him and become His disciple. At once Matthew obeys. He *hastened and did not delay* to keep Christ's commandment (Psalm 119:60). He rises and follows Him.

Let it be a fixed principle in our religion that *with Christ nothing is impossible.* He can take a tax collector and make him an apostle. He can change any heart and make all things new. Let us never despair of anyone's salvation. Let us pray on, and speak on, and work on to do good to souls, even to the souls of the worst. *The voice of the LORD is powerful* (Psalm 29:4). When He says by the power of the Spirit, *"Follow Me,"* He can make the hardest and most sinful obey.

Let us observe *Matthew's decision.* He waited for nothing. He did not tarry to *find time* (Acts 24:25). And he reaped in consequence a great reward. He wrote a book which is known all over the earth. He became a blessing to others as well as blessed in his own soul. He left a name behind him which is better known than the names of princes and kings. The richest man of the world is soon forgotten when he dies. But as long as the world stands, millions will know the name of Matthew the tax collector.

Let us notice, in the last place, *our Lord's precious declaration about His own mission.* The Pharisees found fault with Him because He allowed tax collectors and sinners to be in His company. In their proud blindness they fancied that a teacher sent from heaven ought to have no dealings with such people. They were wholly ignorant of the grand design for which the Messiah was to come into the world – to be a Savior, the Great Physician, a healer of sin-sick souls. And they drew from our Lord's lips a rebuke accompanied by the blessed words, *"I did not come to call the righteous, but sinners."*

Let us make sure that we thoroughly *understand* the doctrine that these words contain. The first thing needful in order to have an interest in Christ is to feel deeply our own corruption and to be willing to come to Him for deliverance. We are not to keep away from Christ, as many ignorantly do, because we feel bad and wicked and unworthy. We are to remember that sinners are those He came into the world to save, and that if we feel ourselves such, it is well. Happy is he who really comprehends that one principal qualification for coming to Christ is a deep sense of sin!

Finally, if by the grace of God we really understand the glorious truth that sinners are those whom Christ came to call, let us take heed that we *never forget it.* Let us not dream that true Christians can ever attain such a state of perfection is this world as not to need the mediation and intercession of Jesus. Sinners we are in the day we first come to Christ. Poor needy sinners we continue to be for as long as we live, drawing all the grace we have every hour out of Christ's fullness. Sinners we shall find ourselves in the hour of our death, and shall die as much indebted to Christ's blood as on the day we first believed.

[handwritten margin notes: Sinners by nature. Seek Christ in all seasons.]

Faith in God an his power.

Matthew 9:14-26

Then the disciples of John came to Him, asking, "Why do we and the Pharisees fast, but Your disciples do not fast?" And Jesus said to them, "The attendants of the bridegroom cannot mourn as long as the bridegroom is with them, can they? But the days will come when the bridegroom is taken away from them, and then they will fast. But no one puts a patch of unshrunk cloth on an old garment; for the patch pulls away from the garment, and a worse tear results. Nor do people put new wine into old wineskins; otherwise the wineskins burst, and the wine pours out and the wineskins are ruined; but they put new wine into fresh wineskins, and both are preserved." While He was saying these things to them, a synagogue official came and bowed down before Him, and said, "My daughter has just died; but come and lay Your hand on her, and she will live." Jesus got up and began to follow him, and so did His disciples. And a woman who had been suffering from a hemorrhage for twelve years, came up behind Him and touched the fringe of His cloak; for she was saying to herself, "If I only touch His garment, I will get well." But Jesus turning and seeing her said, "Daughter, take courage; your faith has made you well." At once the woman was made well. When Jesus came into the official's house, and saw the flute-players and the crowd in noisy disorder, He said, "Leave; for the girl has not died, but is asleep." And they began laughing at Him. But when the crowd had been sent out, He entered and took her by the hand, and the girl got up. This news spread throughout all that land.
(Matthew 9:14-26)

Let us notice in this passage *the gracious name by which the Lord Jesus speaks of Himself.* He calls Himself *the bridegroom.*

What the bridegroom is to the bride, the Lord Jesus is to the souls of all who believe in Him. He loves them with a deep and everlasting love. He takes them into union with Himself. They are "one with Christ and Christ in them." He pays all their debts to God. He supplies

80

all their daily needs. He sympathizes with them in all their troubles. He bears with all their infirmities and does not reject them for a few weaknesses. He regards them as part of Himself. Those who persecute and injure them are persecuting Him. The glory that He has received from His Father they will one day share with Him, and where He is, there shall they be. Such are the privileges of all true Christians. They are the Lamb's wife (Revelation 19:7). Such is the portion to which faith admits us. By it God joins our poor sinful souls to one precious husband; and those whom God thus joins together shall never be put asunder. Blessed indeed are those who believe!

Let us notice, in the next place, *what a wise principle the Lord Jesus lays down for the treatment of young disciples*. There were some who found fault with our Lord's followers because they did not fast as John the Baptist's disciples did. Our Lord defends His disciples with an argument full of deep wisdom. He shows that there would be a lack of fitness in their fasting so long as He, their Bridegroom, was with them. But He does not stop there. He goes on to show by two parables that young beginners in the school of Christianity must be dealt with gently. They must be taught as they are able to bear. They must not be expected to receive everything at once. To neglect this rule would be as unwise as to *put new wine into old wineskins* or to put *a patch of unshrunk cloth on an old garment*.

There is a mine of deep wisdom in this, which all would do well to remember in the spiritual teaching of those who are young in experience. We must be careful not to attach an excessive importance to the lesser things of religion. We must not be in a hurry to require a minute conformity to one rigid rule in "things indifferent," until the first principles of repentance and faith have been thoroughly learned. To guide us in this matter, we have great need to pray for grace and Christian common sense. Tact in dealing with young disciples is a rare gift, but a very useful one. To know what to insist upon as absolutely necessary from the outset – and what to reserve as a lesson to be learned when the learner has come to more perfect knowledge – is one of the highest attainments of a teacher of souls.

Let us notice, in the next place, *what encouragement our Lord gives to the humblest faith.* We read in this passage that a woman severely afflicted with disease came behind our Lord in the crowd *and touched the fringe of His cloak*, in the hope that by so doing she would be healed. She said not a word to obtain help. She made no public confession of faith. But she had confidence that if she could only "touch His cloak," she would be made well. And so it was. There lay hidden in that act of hers a seed of precious faith which obtained our Lord's commendation. She was made whole at once and returned home in peace. To use the words of a good old writer, "She came trembling and went back triumphing."

Let us store up in our minds this history. It may perhaps help us mightily in some hour of need. Our faith may be feeble. Our courage may be small. Our grasp of the gospel and its promises may be weak and trembling. But, after all, the grand question is, do we really trust in Christ alone? Do we look to Jesus, and only to Jesus, for pardon and peace? If this be so, it is well. If we may not touch His cloak, we can touch His heart. Such faith saves the soul. Weak faith is less comfortable than strong faith. Weak faith will carry us to heaven with far less joy than full assurance. But weak faith gives an interest in Christ as surely as strong faith. He that only touches the hem of Christ's cloak shall never perish.

In the last place, let us notice in this passage *our Lord's almighty power.* He restores to life one who was dead. How wonderful that sight must have been! Who that has ever seen the dead can forget the stillness, the silence, and the coldness when the breath has left the body? Who can forget the dreadful feeling that a mighty change has taken place and a mighty gulf been placed between ourselves and the departed? But behold! our Lord goes to the chamber where the dead lies and calls the spirit back to its earthly tabernacle. The pulse once more beats. The eyes once more see. The breath once more comes and goes. The official's daughter is once more alive and restored to her father and mother. This was omnipotence indeed! None could have done this but He who first created man and has all power in heaven and earth.

This is the kind of truth we never can know too well. The more clearly we see Christ's power, the more likely we are to realize gospel peace. Our position may be trying. Our hearts may be weak. The world may be difficult to journey through. Our faith may seem too small to carry us home. But let us take courage when we think on Jesus and not be cast down. Greater is He that is for us than all those who are against us. Our Savior can raise the dead. Our Savior is almighty.

Matthew 9:27-38

As Jesus went on from there, two blind men followed Him, crying out, "Have mercy on us, Son of David!" When He entered the house, the blind men came up to Him, and Jesus said to them, "Do you believe that I am able to do this?" They said to Him, "Yes, Lord." Then He touched their eyes, saying, "It shall be done to you according to your faith." And their eyes were opened. And Jesus sternly warned them: "See that no one knows about this!" But they went out and spread the news about Him throughout all that land. As they were going out, a mute, demon-possessed man was brought to Him. After the demon was cast out, the mute man spoke; and the crowds were amazed, and were saying, "Nothing like this has ever been seen in Israel." But the Pharisees were saying, "He casts out the demons by the ruler of the demons." Jesus was going through all the cities and villages, teaching in their synagogues and proclaiming the gospel of the kingdom, and healing every kind of disease and every kind of sickness. Seeing the people, He felt compassion for them, because they were distressed and dispirited like sheep without a shepherd. Then He said to His disciples, "The harvest is plentiful, but the workers are few. Therefore beseech the Lord of the harvest to send out workers into His harvest." (Matthew 9:27-38)

There are four lessons in this passage which deserve close attention. Let us notice them each in succession.

Let us notice, in the first place, that *strong faith in Christ may sometimes be found where it might least have been expected.* Who would have thought that two blind men would have called our Lord the *Son of David*? They could not, of course, have seen the miracles that He did. They could only know Him by common report. But the eyes of their understanding were enlightened, even if their bodily eyes were dark. They saw the truth which the scribes and Pharisees could not see. They saw that Jesus of Nazareth was the Messiah. They believed that He was able to heal them.

An example like this shows us that *we must never despair of anyone's salvation merely because he lives in a position unfavorable to his soul.* Grace is stronger than circumstances. The life of religion does not depend merely upon outward advantages. The Holy Spirit can give faith and keep faith in active exercise without book-learning, without money, and with little opportunity to attend a good church. Without the Holy Spirit a man may know all mysteries and live in the full blaze of the gospel and yet be lost. We shall see many strange sights at the last day. Poor cottagers will be found to have believed in the son of David, while rich men, full of university learning, will prove to have lived and died like the Pharisees in hardened unbelief. Many that are last will be first, and the first last (Matthew 20:16).

Let us notice, in the next place, that *our Lord Jesus Christ has had great experience with disease and sickness.* He *was going through all the cities and villages* doing good.

He was an eyewitness of all the ills that flesh is heir to. He saw ailments of every kind, sort, and description. He was brought in contact with every form of bodily suffering. None were too loathsome for Him to attend to. None were too frightful for Him to cure. He was a healer of *every kind of disease and every kind of sickness.*

There is much comfort to be drawn from this fact. We are each dwelling in a poor frail body. We never know what quantity of suffering we may have to watch as we sit by the bedside of dear relatives and friends. We never know what racking complaint we ourselves may have to submit to before we lie down and die. But let us arm ourselves beforehand with the precious thought that Jesus is specially fitted to be the sick man's friend. That Great High Priest to whom we must apply for pardon and peace with God is eminently qualified to sympathize with an aching body as well as to heal an ailing conscience. The eyes of

Him who is King of Kings often used to look with pity on the diseased. The world cares little for the sick and often keeps aloof from them. But the Lord Jesus cares specially for the sick. He is the first to visit them and say, *"I stand at the door and knock."* Happy are they who hear His voice and let Him in!

Let us notice, in the next place, *our Lord's tender concern for neglected souls.* He saw multitudes of people when He was on earth, scattered about *like sheep without a shepherd*, and He was moved with compassion. He saw them neglected by those who, for the time, ought to have been teachers. He saw them ignorant, hopeless, helpless, dying, and unfit to die. The sight moved Him to deep pity. That loving heart could not see such things and not feel.

Now what are our feelings when we see such a sight? This is the question that should arise in our minds. There are many such to be seen on every side. There are millions of idolaters and heathen on earth, millions of deluded Muslims, and millions of superstitious Roman Catholics. There are thousands of unsaved Protestants near our own doors. Do we feel tenderly concerned about their souls? Do we deeply pity their spiritual destitution? Do we long to see that destitution relieved? These are serious questions and ought to be answered. It is easy to sneer at missions to the heathen and those who work for them. But the man who does not feel for the souls of all unconverted people can surely not have *the mind of Christ* (1 Corinthians 2:16).

Let us notice, in the last place, that *there is a solemn duty incumbent on all Christians who would do good to the unconverted part of the world.* They are to pray for more men to be raised up to work for the conversion of souls. It seems as if it was to be a daily part of our prayers. *"Therefore beseech the Lord of the harvest to send out workers into His harvest."*

If we know anything of prayer, let us make it a point of conscience never to forget this solemn charge of our Lord's. Let us settle it in our minds that it is one of the surest ways of doing good and stemming evil. Personal working for souls is good. Giving money is good. But praying is best of all. By prayer we reach Him without whom work and money are alike in vain. We obtain the aid of the Holy Spirit. Money can hire workers. Universities can give learning. Congregations may elect.

Bishops may ordain. But the Holy Spirit alone can make ministers of the gospel and raise up lay workmen in the spiritual harvest who need not be ashamed. Never, never may we forget that if we would do good to the world, our first duty is to pray!

Matthew Chapter 10

Power to Preach
Spread the News

Matthew 10:1-15

Jesus summoned His twelve disciples and gave them authority over unclean spirits, to cast them out, and to heal every kind of disease and every kind of sickness. Now the names of the twelve apostles are these: The first, Simon, who is called Peter, and Andrew his brother; and James the son of Zebedee, and John his brother; Philip and Bartholomew; Thomas and Matthew the tax collector; James the son of Alphaeus, and Thaddaeus; Simon the Zealot, and Judas Iscariot, the one who betrayed Him. These twelve Jesus sent out after instructing them: "Do not go in the way of the Gentiles, and do not enter any city of the Samaritans; but rather go to the lost sheep of the house of Israel. And as you go, preach, saying, 'The kingdom of heaven is at hand.' Heal the sick, raise the dead, cleanse the lepers, cast out demons. Freely you received, freely give. Do not acquire gold, or silver, or copper for your money belts, or a bag for your journey, or even two coats, or sandals, or a staff; for the worker is worthy of his support. And whatever city or village you enter, inquire who is worthy in it, and stay at his house until you leave that city. As you enter the house, give it your greeting. If the house is worthy, give it your blessing of peace. But if it is not worthy, take back your blessing of peace. Whoever does not receive you, nor heed your words, as you go out of that house or that city, shake the dust off your feet. Truly I say to you, it will be more tolerable for the land of Sodom and Gomorrah in the day of judgment than for that city." (Matthew 10:1-15)

THIS CHAPTER IS ONE OF PECULIAR SOLEMNITY. Here is the record of the first ordination that ever took place in the church of Christ. The Lord Jesus chooses and sends forth the twelve apostles. Here is an account of the first charge ever delivered to newly ordained Christian ministers. The Lord Jesus Himself delivers it. Never was there so important an ordination. Never was there so solemn a charge!

There are three lessons which stand out prominently on the face of the first fifteen verses of this chapter. Let us take them in order.

We are taught, in the first place, that *all ministers are not necessarily saved men.* We see our Lord choosing a Judas Iscariot to be one of His apostles. We cannot doubt that He who knew all hearts knew well the characters of the men whom He chose. And He includes in the list of apostles one who was a traitor!

We shall do well to bear in mind this fact. Ordination does not confer the saving grace of the Holy Spirit. Ordained men are not necessarily converted. We are not to regard them as infallible either in doctrine or in practice. We are not to make popes or idols of them and insensibly put them in Christ's place. We are to regard them as *men of the same nature* as ourselves, liable to the same infirmities and daily requiring the same grace. We are not to think it impossible for them to do very bad things or to expect them to be above the reach of harm from flattery, covetousness, and the world. We are to prove their teaching by the Word of God and follow them so far as they follow Christ, but no further. Above all, we ought to pray for them, that they may be successors not of Judas Iscariot, but of James and John. It is a dreadful thing to be a minister of the gospel! Ministers need many prayers.

We are taught, in the next place, that *the great work of a minister of Christ is to do good.* He is sent to seek *lost sheep* – to proclaim glad tidings – to relieve those who are suffering – to diminish sorrow – and to increase joy. His life is meant to be one of giving rather than receiving.

This is a high standard and a very peculiar one. Let it be well weighed and carefully examined. It is plain, for one thing, that the life of a faithful minister of Christ cannot be one of ease. He must be ready to spend body and mind, and time and strength in the work of His calling. Laziness and frivolity are bad enough in any profession, but worst of all in that of a watchman for souls. It is plain, for another thing, that the position of the ministers of Christ is not that which ignorant people sometimes ascribe to them and which they unhappily sometimes claim for themselves. They are not so much ordained to rule as to serve. They are not intended so much to have dominion over the church as to supply its needs and serve its members (2 Corinthians 1:24). Happy would it be for the cause of true religion if these things were better understood! Half the diseases of Christianity have arisen from mistaken notions about the pastor's role!

We are taught, in the last place, that *it is a most dangerous thing to neglect the offers of the gospel.* It shall prove *more tolerable for the land of Sodom and Gomorrah* in the judgment day than for those who have heard Christ's truth and not received it.

This is a doctrine fearfully overlooked and one that deserves serious consideration. Men are sadly apt to forget that it does not require great open sins to be committed in order to ruin a soul forever. They have only to go on hearing without believing, listening without repenting, going to church without going to Christ, and by and by they will find themselves in hell! We shall all be judged according to our light. We shall have to give account of our use of religious privileges. To hear of the "great salvation" and yet neglect it is one of the worst sins man can commit (John 16:9).

What are we doing ourselves with the gospel? This is the question everyone who reads this passage should put to his conscience. Let us assume that we are decent and respectable in our lives, correct and moral in all the relations of life, and regular in our formal attendance of church. It is all well, so far as it goes. But is this all that can be said of us? Are we really receiving the love of the truth? Is Christ dwelling in our hearts by faith? If not, we are in fearful danger. We are far more guilty than the men of Sodom who never heard the gospel at all. We may awake to find that in spite of our regularity, morality, and correctness, we have lost our souls for all eternity. It will not save us to have lived in the full sunshine of Christian privileges and to have heard the gospel faithfully preached every week. There must be experimental acquaintance with Christ. There must be personal reception of His truth.

can be empty vessels

89

There must be vital union with Him. We must become His servants and disciples. Without this, the preaching of the gospel only adds to our responsibility, increases our guilt, and will finally sink us more deeply into hell. These are hard sayings. But the words of Scripture which we have read are plain and unmistakable. They are all true.

How to conduct yourself under Persecution

Matthew 10:16-23

"Behold, I send you out as sheep in the midst of wolves; so be shrewd as serpents and innocent as doves. But beware of men, for they will hand you over to the courts and scourge you in their synagogues; and you will even be brought before governors and kings for My sake, as a testimony to them and to the Gentiles. But when they hand you over, do not worry about how or what you are to say; for it will be given to you in that hour what you are to say. For it is not you who speak, but it is the Spirit of your Father who speaks in you. Brother will betray brother to death, and a father his child; and children will rise up against parents and cause them to be put to death. You will be hated by all because of My name, but it is the one who has endured to the end who will be saved. But whenever they persecute you in one city, flee to the next; for truly I say to you, you will not finish going through the cities of Israel until the Son of Man comes." (Matthew 10:16-23)

The truths contained in these verses should be pondered by all who try to do good in the world. To the selfish man who cares for nothing but his own ease or comfort, there may seem to be little in them. To the minister of the gospel and to everyone who seeks to save souls, these verses ought to be full of interest. No doubt there is much in them which applies specially to the days of the apostles. But there is much also which applies to all times.

We see, for one thing, that *those who would do good to souls must be moderate in their expectations.* They must not think that universal success will attend their labors. They must reckon on meeting with much opposition. They must make up their minds to *be hated*, persecuted, and ill-used, and that too by their nearest relations. They will often find themselves like *sheep in the midst of wolves.*

Let us bear this in mind continually. Whether we preach or teach or visit from house to house, whether we write or give counsel, or whatever we do, let it be a settled principle with us not to expect more than Scripture and experience warrant. Human nature is far more wicked and corrupt than we think. The power of evil is far greater than we suppose. It is vain to imagine that everybody will see what is good for them and believe what we tell them. It is expecting what we shall not find, and it will only end in disappointment. Happy is that laborer for Christ who knows these things at his first starting out and has not learned them by bitter experience! Here lies the secret cause why many have turned back who once seemed full of zeal to do good. They began with extravagant expectations. They did not count the cost. They fell into the mistake of the great German Reformer who confessed he forgot at one time that "old Adam was too strong for young Melancthon."

We see, for another thing, that *those who would do good have need to pray for wisdom, good sense, and a sound mind.* Our Lord tells His disciples to be *shrewd as serpents and innocent as doves.* He tells those who, when they are persecuted in one place, may lawfully *flee to the next.*

There are few of our Lord's instructions which it is so difficult to use rightly as this. There is a line marked out for us between two extremes, but one that it requires great judgment to define. To avoid persecution by holding our tongues and keeping our religion entirely to ourselves is one extreme. We are not to err in that direction. To court persecution and thrust our religion upon everyone we meet without regard to place, time, or circumstances is another extreme. In this direction also we are warned not to err any more than in the other. Truly we may say, *Who is adequate for these things?* We have need to cry to the only wise God for wisdom.

The extreme into which most men are liable to fall in the present day is that of silence, cowardice, and letting others alone. Our so-called prudence is apt to degenerate into a compromising line of conduct or downright unfaithfulness. We are only too ready to suppose that it is of no use trying to speak of Christ to people. We excuse ourselves from efforts to benefit their souls by saying it would be indiscreet, or inexpedient, or would give needless offense, or would even do positive harm. Let us all watch and be on our guard against this spirit. Laziness and the devil are often the true explanations of it. To give way to it is pleasant to flesh and blood, no doubt, and saves us much trouble. But those who give way to it often throw away great opportunities of usefulness.

On the other hand, it is impossible to deny that there is such a thing as a righteous and holy zeal which is *not in accordance with knowledge*. It is quite possible to create much needless offense, commit great blunders, and stir up much opposition which might have been avoided by a little prudence, wise management, and exercise of judgment. Let us all take heed that we are not guilty in this respect. We may be sure there is such a thing as Christian wisdom, which is quite distinct from jesuitical deception or carnal policy. This wisdom let us seek. Our Lord Jesus does not require us to throw aside our common sense when we undertake to work for Him. There will be offense enough connected with our religion, do what we will; but let us not increase it without cause. Let us strive to *be careful how [we] walk, not as unwise men but as wise* (Ephesians 5:15).

It is to be feared that believers in the Lord Jesus do not sufficiently pray for the spirit of knowledge, judgment, and a sound mind. They are apt to fancy that if they have grace, they have all they need. They forget that a gracious heart should pray that it may be full of wisdom as well as of the Holy Spirit (Acts 6:3). Let us all remember this: great grace and common sense are perhaps one of the rarest combinations. That they may go together, the life of David and the ministry of the apostle Paul are striking proofs. In this, however, as in every other respect, our Lord Jesus Christ Himself is our most perfect example. None were ever so faithful as He. But none were ever so truly wise either. Let us make Him our pattern and walk in His steps.

Matthew 10:24-33

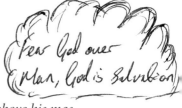

"A disciple is not above his teacher, nor a slave above his master. It is enough for the disciple that he become like his teacher, and the slave like his master. If they have called the head of the house Beelzebul, how much more will they malign the members of his household! Therefore do not fear them, for there is nothing concealed that will not be revealed, or hidden that will not be known. What I tell you in the darkness, speak in the light; and what you hear whispered in your ear, proclaim upon the housetops. Do not fear those who kill the body but are unable to kill the soul; but rather fear Him who is able to destroy both soul and body in hell. Are not two sparrows sold for a cent? And yet not one of them will fall to the ground apart from your Father. But the very hairs of your head are all numbered. So do not fear; you are more valuable than many sparrows. Therefore everyone who confesses Me before men, I will also confess him before My Father who is in heaven. But whoever denies Me before men, I will also deny him before My Father who is in heaven."
(Matthew 10:24-33)

To do good to souls in this world is very hard. All who try it find this out by experience. It needs a large stock of courage, faith, patience, and perseverance. Satan will fight vigorously to maintain his kingdom. Human nature is desperately wicked. To do harm is easy. To do good is hard.

The Lord Jesus knew this well when He sent forth His disciples to preach the gospel for the first time. He knew what was before them if they did not. He took care to supply them with a list of encouragements in order to cheer them when they felt cast down. Weary missionaries abroad, or fainting ministers at home – disheartened teachers of schools, and desponding visitors of districts would do well to study often the ten verses we have just read. Let us notice what they contain.

Those who try to do good to souls must not expect to fare better than their great Master. A disciple is not above his teacher, nor a slave above his master. The Lord Jesus was slandered and rejected by those whom

He came to benefit. There was no error in His teaching. There was no defect in His method of imparting instruction. Yet many hated Him and called Him Beelzebul. Few believed Him and cared for what He said. Surely we have no right to be surprised if we, whose best efforts are mingled with much imperfection, are treated in the same way as Christ. If we let the world alone, it will probably let us alone. But if we try to do it spiritual good, it will hate us as it did our Master.

Those who try to do good must look forward with patience to the day of judgment. There is nothing concealed that will not be revealed, or hidden that will not be known. They must be content in this present world to be misunderstood, misrepresented, vilified, slandered, and abused. They must not cease to work because their motives are mistaken and their characters fiercely assailed. They must remember continually that all will be set right at the last day. The secrets of all hearts shall then be revealed. *He will bring forth your righteousness as the light and your judgment as the noonday* (Psalm 37:6). The purity of their intentions, the wisdom of their labors, and the rightfulness of their cause shall at last be made manifest to all the world. Let us work on steadily and quietly. Men may not understand us and may vehemently oppose us. But the day of judgment draws near. We shall be righted at last. The Lord, when He comes again, *will both bring to light the things hidden in the darkness and disclose the motives of men's hearts; and then each man's praise will come to him from God* (1 Corinthians 4:5).

Those who try to do good must fear God more than man. Man can hurt the body, but there his enmity must stop. He can go no further. God *is able to destroy both soul and body in hell.* We may be threatened with the loss of character, property, and all that makes life enjoyable if we go on in the path of Christian duty. We must not heed such threats when our course is plain. Like Daniel and the three Hebrew young men, we must submit to anything rather than displease God and wound our consciences. The anger of man may be hard to bear, but the anger of God is much harder. The fear of man does indeed bring a snare, but we must make it give way to the expulsive power of a stronger principle – even the fear of God. It was a fine saying of good Colonel Gardiner's: "I fear God, and therefore there is none else that I need fear."

Those who try to do good must keep before their minds the providential care of God over them. Nothing can happen in this world without His permission. There is no such thing in reality as chance, accident, or luck. *The very hairs of your head are all numbered.* The path of duty may sometimes lead them into great danger. Health and life may seem to be in peril if they go forward. Let them take comfort in the thought that all around them is in God's hand. Their bodies, their souls, and their characters are all in His safekeeping. No disease can seize them – no hand can hurt them unless He allows. They may say boldly to every fearful thing they meet with, *"You would have no authority over Me, unless it had been given you from above."*

In the last place, *those who try to do good should continually remember the day when they will meet their Lord to receive their final portion. If they would have Him own them and confess them before His Father's throne, they must not be ashamed to own and confess Him before the* men of this world. To do it may cost us much. It may bring on us laughter, mockery, persecution, and scorn. But let us not be laughed out of heaven. Let us recollect the great and dreadful day of account and not be afraid to show men that we love Christ and want them to know and love Him also.

Let these encouragements be treasured up in the hearts of all who labor in Christ's cause, whatever their position may be. The Lord knows their trials and has spoken these things for their comfort. He cares for all His believing people, but for none so much as those who work for His cause and try to do good. May we seek to be of that number. Every believer may do something if he tries. There is always something for everyone to do. May we each have an eye to see it and a will to do it.

call to

A Matyr for Christ.

Matthew 10:34-42

"Do not think that I came to bring peace on the earth; I did not come to bring peace, but a sword. For I came to set a man against his father, and a daughter against her mother, and a daughter-in-law against her mother-in-law; and a man's enemies will be

*the members of his household. He who loves father or mother
more than Me is not worthy of Me; and he who loves son or
daughter more than Me is not worthy of Me. And he who does
not take his cross and follow after Me is not worthy of Me. He
who has found his life will lose it, and he who has lost his life for
My sake will find it. He who receives you receives Me, and he who
receives Me receives Him who sent Me. He who receives a prophet
in the name of a prophet shall receive a prophet's reward; and
he who receives a righteous man in the name of a righteous man
shall receive a righteous man's reward. And whoever in the name
of a disciple gives to one of these little ones even a cup of cold
water to drink, truly I say to you, he shall not lose his reward."*
(Matthew 10:34-42)

In these verses the Lord winds up His first charge to those whom He
sends forth to make known His gospel. He declares three great truths
which form a fitting conclusion to the whole discourse.

In the first place, He bids us remember that *His gospel will not cause
peace and agreement wherever it comes. "I did not come to bring peace,
but a sword."* The object of His first coming on earth was not to set up
a millennial kingdom in which all would be of one mind, but rather
to bring in the gospel, which would lead to strifes and divisions. We
have no right to be surprised if we see this continually fulfilled. We are
not to think it strange if the gospel rends asunder families and causes
estrangement between the nearest relations. It is sure to do so in many
cases because of the deep corruption of man's heart. So long as one man
believes and another remains unbelieving, so long as one is resolved
to keep his sins and another desirous to give them up, the result of the
preaching of the gospel must needs be division. For this the gospel is
not to blame, but the heart of man.

There is a deep truth in all this which is constantly forgotten and
overlooked. Many talk vaguely about unity, harmony, and peace in the
church of Christ as if they were things that we ought always to expect,
and for the sake of which everything ought to be sacrificed. Such people
would do well to remember the words of our Lord. No doubt unity

and peace are mighty blessings. We ought to seek them, pray for them, and give up everything in order to obtain them, excepting truth and a good conscience. But it is an idle dream to suppose that the churches of Christ will enjoy much of unity and peace before the millennium comes.

In the second place, our Lord tells us *that true Christians must make up their minds to accept trouble in this world.* Whether we are ministers or hearers, whether we teach or are taught, it makes little difference. We must carry "a cross." We must be content to lose even life itself for Christ's sake. We must submit to the loss of man's favor, we must endure hardships, and we must deny ourselves in many things, or we shall never reach heaven at last. So long as the world, the devil, and our own hearts are what they are, these things must be so.

We shall find it most useful to remember this lesson ourselves and to impress it upon others. Few things do so much harm in religion as exaggerated expectations. People look for a degree of worldly comfort in Christ's service which they have no right to expect, and not finding what they look for, are tempted to give up religion in disgust. Happy is he who thoroughly understands that though Christianity holds out a crown in the end, it brings also a cross in the way.

In the last place, our Lord cheers us by saying *that the least service done to those who work for His cause is observed and rewarded by God.* He that gives a believer so little as *a cup of cold water to drink* in the name of a disciple will in no way lose his reward.

There is something very beautiful in this promise. It teaches us that the eyes of the great Master are ever upon those who labor for Him and try to do good. They seem perhaps to work on unnoticed and disregarded. The proceedings of preachers, missionaries, teachers, and visitors of the poor may appear very trifling and insignificant compared to the movements of kings and parliaments, and of armies and statesmen. But they are not insignificant in the eyes of God. He takes notice of who opposes His servants and who helps them. He observes who is kind to them, as Lydia was to Paul – and who throws difficulties in their way, as Diotrephes did to John. All their daily experience is recorded as they labor on in His harvest. All is written down in the great book of His remembrance and will be brought to light at the last day. The chief butler forgot Joseph when he was restored to his place. But the Lord Jesus never forgets any of His people. He will say to many who little expect it in the resurrection morning, *"I was hungry, and you gave Me something to eat; I was thirsty, and you gave Me something to drink"* (Matthew 25:35).

Let us ask ourselves, as we close the chapter, in what light do we regard Christ's work and Christ's cause in the world? Are we helpers of it or hinderers? Do we in any way aid the Lord's prophets and righteous men? Do we assist His *little ones*? Do we impede His laborers or do we cheer them on? These are serious questions. They do well and wisely who give the *cup of cold water* whenever they have opportunity. They do better still who work actively in the Lord's vineyard. May we all strive to leave the world a better world than it was when we were born! This is to have the mind of Christ. This is to find out the value of the lessons this wonderful chapter contains.

Matthew Chapter 11

Matthew 11:1-15

When Jesus had finished giving instructions to His twelve disciples, He departed from there to teach and to preach in their cities. Now when John, while imprisoned, heard of the works of Christ, he sent word by his disciples and said to Him, "Are You the Expected One, or shall we look for someone else?" Jesus answered and said to them, "Go and report to John what you hear and see: the blind receive sight and the lame walk, the lepers are cleansed and the deaf hear, the dead are raised up, and the poor have the gospel preached to them. And blessed is he who does not take offense at Me." As these men were going away, Jesus began to speak to the crowds about John, "What did you go out into the wilderness to see? A reed shaken by the wind? But what did you go out to see? A man dressed in soft clothing? Those who wear soft clothing are in kings' palaces! But what did you go out to see? A prophet? Yes, I tell you, and one who is more than a prophet. This is the one about whom it is written, 'Behold, I send My messenger ahead of You, who will prepare Your way before You.' Truly I say to you, among those born of women there has not arisen anyone greater than John the Baptist! Yet the one who is least in the kingdom of heaven is greater than he. From the days of John the Baptist until now the kingdom of heaven suffers violence, and violent men take it by force. For all the prophets and the Law prophesied until John. And if you are willing to accept it, John himself is Elijah who was to come. He who has ears to hear, let him hear." (Matthew 11:1-15)

THE FIRST THING THAT DEMANDS OUR ATTENTION in this passage is *the message which John the Baptist sends to our Lord Jesus Christ. He sent word by his disciples and said to Him, "Are You the Expected One, or shall we look for someone else?"*

This question did not arise from doubt or unbelief on the part of John. We do that holy man injustice if we interpret it in such a way. Suppose it was put for the benefit of his disciples, to give them an opportunity of hearing from Christ's own lips the evidence of His divine mission. No doubt John the Baptist felt that his own ministry was ended. Something within him told him that he would never come forth from Herod's prison house but would surely die. He remembered the ignorant jealousies that had already been shown by his disciples towards the disciples of Christ. He took the most likely course to dispel those jealousies forever. He sent his followers to *hear and see* for themselves.

The conduct of John the Baptist in this matter affords a striking example to ministers, teachers, and parents when they draw near to the end of their course. Their chief concern should be for the souls of those they are going to leave behind them. Their great desire should be to persuade them to cleave to Christ. The death of those who have guided and instructed us on earth ought always to have this effect. It should make us lay hold more firmly on Him who dies no more, *continues forever*, and *holds His priesthood permanently* (Hebrews 7:24).

The second thing that demands our notice in this passage is *the high testimony which our Lord bears to the character of John the Baptist*. No mortal man ever received such commendation as Jesus here bestows on His imprisoned friend. *"Among those born of women there has not arisen anyone greater than John the Baptist!"* In time past John had boldly confessed Jesus before men as the Lamb of God. Now Jesus openly declares John to be more than a prophet.

There were some, no doubt, who were disposed to think lightly of John the Baptist, partly from ignorance of the nature of his ministry and partly from misunderstanding the question he had sent to ask. Our Lord Jesus silences such quibblers by the declaration He makes here. He tells them not to suppose that John was a timid, vacillating, unstable man, *a reed shaken by the wind*. If they thought so, they were

efforts of John

utterly mistaken. He was a bold, unflinching witness to the truth. He tells them not to suppose that John was at heart a worldly man, fond of king's courts and delicate living. If they thought so, they greatly erred. He was a self-denying preacher of repentance who would risk the anger of a king rather than not reprove his sins. In short, He would have them know that John was *more than a prophet.* He was one to whom God had given more honor than to all the Old Testament prophets. They indeed prophesied of Christ but died without seeing Him. John not only prophesied of Him but also saw Him face to face. They foretold that the days of the Son of Man would certainly come and the Messiah would appear. John was an actual eyewitness of those days and an honored instrument in preparing men for them. To them it was given to predict that Messiah would be *led as a sheep to slaughter* and *cut off.* To John it was given to point to Him and say, *"Behold, the Lamb of God who takes away the sin of the world!"* *Prophesies will always come to pass.*

There is something very beautiful and comforting to true Christians in this testimony which our Lord bears to John. It shows us the tender interest which our great Head feels in the lives and characters of all His members. It shows us what honor He is ready to put on all the work and labor that they go through in His cause. It is a sweet foretaste of the confession which He will make of them before the assembled world when He presents them faultless at the last day before His Father's throne.

Do we know what it is to work for Christ? Have we ever felt cast down and dispirited as if we were doing no good and no one cared for us? Are we ever tempted to feel, when laid aside by sickness or withdrawn by providence, *"I have toiled in vain, I have spent My strength for nothing"*? Let us meet such thoughts by the recollection of this passage. Let us remember there is One who daily records all we do for Him and sees more beauty in His servants' work than His servants do themselves. The same tongue which bore testimony to John in prison will bear testimony to all His people at the last day. He will say, *"Come, you who are blessed of my Father, inherit the kingdom prepared for you from the foundation of the world."* And then shall His faithful witnesses discover, to their wonder and surprise, that there never was a word spoken on their Master's behalf which does not receive a reward.

Great reward for those who prophecy to Christ

Faith + Belief
lies True Salvation **Matthew 11:16-24**

"But to what shall I compare this generation? It is like children
sitting in the market places, who call out to the other children,
and say, 'We played the flute for you, and you did not dance;
we sang a dirge, and you did not mourn.' For John came nei-
ther eating nor drinking, and they say, 'He has a demon!' The
Son of Man came eating and drinking, and they say, 'Behold, a
gluttonous man and a drunkard, a friend of tax collectors and
sinners!' Yet wisdom is vindicated by her deeds." Then He began
to denounce the cities in which most of His miracles were done,
because they did not repent. "Woe to you, Chorazin! Woe to you,
Bethsaida! For if the miracles had occurred in Tyre and Sidon
which occurred in you, they would have repented long ago in
sackcloth and ashes. Nevertheless I say to you, it will be more
tolerable for Tyre and Sidon in the day of judgment than for
you. And you, Capernaum, will not be exalted to heaven, will
you? You will descend to Hades; for if the miracles had occurred
in Sodom which occurred in you, it would have remained to
this day. Nevertheless I say to you that it will be more tolerable
for the land of Sodom in the day of judgment, than for you."
(Matthew 11:16-24)

These sayings of the Lord Jesus were called forth by the state of the
Jewish nation when He was upon earth. But they speak loudly to us
also, as well as to the Jews. They throw great light on some parts of
the natural man's character. They teach us the perilous state of many
immortal souls in the present day.

The first part of these verses shows us *the unreasonableness of many*
unconverted men in the things of religion. The Jews in our Lord's time
found fault with every teacher whom God sent among them. First came
John the Baptist preaching repentance – an austere man, a man who
withdrew himself from society and lived an ascetic life. Did this satisfy
the Jews? No! They found fault and said, *"He has a demon!"* Then came
Jesus the Son of God, preaching the gospel, living as other men lived,

and practicing none of John the Baptist's peculiar austerities. And did this satisfy the Jews? No! They found fault again and said, *"Behold, a gluttonous man and a drunkard, a friend of tax collectors and sinners!"* In short, they were as perverse and hard to please as "contrary children."

It is a mournful fact that there are always thousands of professing Christians just as unreasonable as these Jews. They are equally perverse and equally hard to please. Whatever we teach and preach, they find fault with. Whatever be our manner of life, they are dissatisfied. Do we tell them of salvation by grace and justification by faith? At once they cry out against our doctrine as licentious and antinomian. Do we tell them of the holiness which the gospel requires? At once they exclaim that we are too strict, too precise, and overly righteous. Are we cheerful? They accuse us of excessive frivolity. Are we overly serious? They call us gloomy and sour. Do we keep aloof from balls and races and plays? They denounce us as puritanical, exclusive, and narrow-minded. Do we eat and drink and dress like other people, and attend to our worldly callings and go into society? They sneeringly insinuate that they see no difference between us and those who make no religious profession at all, and that we are not better than other men. What is all this but the conduct of the Jews all over again? *"We played the flute for you, and you did not dance; we sang a dirge, and you did not mourn."* He who spoke these words knew the hearts of men.

The plain truth is that true believers must not expect unconverted men to be satisfied either with their faith or their practice. If they do, they expect what they will not find. They must make up their minds to hear objections, quibblings, and excuses, however holy their own lives may be. Well says Quesnel, "Whatever measures good men take, they will never escape the censures of the world. The best way is not to be concerned at them." After all, what says the Scripture? *The mind set on the flesh is hostile toward God. A natural man does not accept the things of the Spirit of God* (Romans 8:7; 1 Corinthians 2:14). This is the explanation of the whole matter.

The second part of these verses shows us *the exceeding wickedness of willful impenitence.* Our Lord declares that it shall be more tolerable for Tyre, Sidon, and Sodom in the day of judgment than for those towns where people had heard His sermons and seen His miracles but had not repented.

There is something very solemn in this saying. Let us look at it well. Let us think for a moment what dark, idolatrous, immoral, and profligate places Tyre and Sidon must have been. Let us call to mind the unspeakable wickedness of Sodom. Let us remember that the cities named by our Lord – Chorazin, Bethsaida, and Capernaum – were probably no worse than other Jewish towns, and at all events, were far better than Tyre, Sidon, and Sodom. And then let us observe that the people of Chorazin, Bethsaida, and Capernaum are to be in the lowest hell because they heard the gospel and yet did not repent, because they had great religious advantages and did not use them. How dreadful this sounds!

Surely these words ought to make the ears of everyone tingle who hears the gospel regularly and yet remains unconverted. How great is the guilt of such a man before God! How great the danger in which he daily stands! Moral and decent and respectable as his life may be, he is actually more guilty than an idolatrous Tyrian or Sidonian or a miserable inhabitant of Sodom. They had no spiritual light; he has, and neglects it. They heard no gospel; he hears, but does not obey it. Their hearts might have been softened if they had enjoyed his privileges. Tyre and Sidon *would have repented*. Sodom *would have remained to this day*. His heart under the full blaze of the gospel remains hard and unmoved. There is but one painful conclusion to be drawn. His guilt will be found greater than theirs at the last day. Most true is the remark of an English bishop: "Among all the aggravations of our sins, there is none more heinous than the frequent hearing of our duty."

May we all think often about Chorazin, Bethsaida, and Capernaum! Let us settle it in our minds that it will never do to be content with merely hearing and liking the gospel. We must go further than this. We must actually repent and be converted. We must actually lay hold on Christ and become one with Him. Until then we are in dreadful danger. It will prove more tolerable to have lived in Tyre, Sidon, and Sodom than to have readily heard the gospel in our free country today yet still died unconverted.

We need Salvation
Salvation through Christ

Matthew 11:25-30

At that time Jesus said, "I praise You, Father, Lord of heaven and earth, that <u>You have hidden these things from the wise and intelligent and have revealed them to infants</u>. Yes, Father, for this way was well-pleasing in Your sight. All things have been handed over to Me by My Father; and no one knows the Son except the Father; nor does anyone know the Father except the Son, and anyone to whom the Son wills to reveal Him. Come to Me, all who are weary and heavy-laden, and I will give you rest. Take My yoke upon you and <u>learn from Me</u>, for I am gentle and humble in heart, and you will find rest for your souls. <u>For My yoke is easy and My burden is light</u>." (Matthew 11:25-30)

There are few passages in the four Gospels more important than this. There are few which contain, in so short a compass, so many precious truths. May God give us an eye to see and a heart to feel their value!

Let us learn, in the first place, *the excellence of a childlike and teachable frame of mind.* Our Lord says to His Father, *"You have hidden these things from the wise and intelligent and have revealed them to infants."*

It is not for us to attempt to explain why some receive and believe the gospel while others do not. The sovereignty of God in this matter is a deep mystery; we cannot fathom it. But one thing, at all events, stands out in Scripture as a great practical truth to be had in everlasting remembrance. Those from whom the gospel is hidden are generally *wise in their own eyes and clever in their own sight.* Those to whom the gospel is revealed are <u>generally humble, simpleminded, and willing to</u> learn. The words of the Virgin Mary are continually being fulfilled: *"He has filled the hungry with good things; and sent away the rich empty-handed"* (Luke 1:53).

Let us watch against pride in every shape – pride of intellect, pride of wealth, pride in our own goodness, pride in our own merits. Few things are as likely to keep a man out of heaven and prevent him from seeing Christ as pride. Let us pray for and cultivate humility. Let us seek to know ourselves aright and to find out our place in the sight of a holy God. The beginning of the way to heaven is to feel that we are on the way to hell and to be willing to be taught of the Spirit. One of the first steps in saving Christianity is to be able to hear the Lord say as He said to Saul, "I will tell you what you must do" (Acts 9:6). There is hardly a sentence of our Lord's so frequently repeated as this: *"He who humbles himself will be exalted"* (Luke 18:14).

Let us learn, in the second place from these verses, *the greatness and majesty of our Lord Jesus Christ.* The language of our Lord on this subject is deep and wonderful. He says, *"All things have been handed over to Me by My Father; and no one knows the Son except the Father; nor does anyone know the Father except the Son, and anyone to whom the Son wills to reveal Him."* We may truly say as we read these words, *Such knowledge is too wonderful for me; it is high, I cannot attain to it.* We see something of the perfect union which exists between the first and second persons of the Trinity. We see something of the immeasurable superiority of the Lord Jesus to all who are nothing more than men. But still, when we have said all this, we must confess that there are heights and depths in this verse which are beyond our feeble comprehension. We can only admire them in the spirit of little children. But the half of them, we must feel, remain untold.

Let us, however, draw from these words the great practical truth that all power and authority in everything that concerns our soul's interests is placed in our Lord Jesus Christ's hands. *All things have been handed over to Him.* He bears the *keys* – to Him we must go for admission into heaven. He is the *Door* – through Him we must enter. He is the *Shepherd* – we must hear His voice and follow Him if we do not want to perish in the wilderness. He is the *Great Physician* – we must apply to Him if we would be healed of the plague of sin. He is the *Bread of Life* – we must feed on Him if we would have our souls satisfied. He is the *Light* – we must walk after Him if we do not want to wander in darkness. He is the *fountain* – we must wash in His blood if we would be cleansed and made ready for the great day of account. Blessed and glorious are these truths! If we have Christ, we have all things (1 Corinthians 3:22).

Let us learn, in the last place from this passage, *the breadth and fullness of the invitations of Christ's gospel.* The last three verses of the chapter which contain this lesson are indeed precious. They meet the trembling sinner who asks, "Will Christ reveal His Father's love to such a one as me?" with the most gracious encouragement. They are verses which deserve to be read with special attention. For eighteen hundred years they have been a blessing to the world and have done good to myriads of souls. There is not a sentence in them which does not contain a mine of thought.

Notice who they are whom Jesus invites. He does not address those who feel themselves righteous and worthy. He addresses *all who are weary and heavy-laden*. It is a wide description. It comprises multitudes in this weary world. All who feel a load on their heart of which they want to sincerely get free, a load of sin or a load of sorrow, a load of anxiety or a load of remorse – all, whoever they may be, and whatever their past lives, are invited to come to Christ.

Notice what a gracious offer Jesus makes. *"I will give you rest. You will find rest for your souls."* How cheering and comforting are these words! Unrest is one great characteristic of the world. Hurry, vexation, failure, and disappointment stare us in the face all the time. But here is hope. There is an ark of refuge for the weary as truly as there was for Noah's dove. There is rest in Christ, rest of conscience, and rest of heart, rest built on pardon of all sin, and rest flowing from peace with God.

Notice what a simple request Jesus makes to the laboring and heavy-laden ones. *"Come to Me. Take My yoke upon you and learn from Me."* He interposes no hard conditions. He speaks nothing of works to be done first and deservingness of His gifts to be established. He only asks us to come to Him just as we are, with all our sins, and to submit ourselves like little children to His teaching. "Go not," He seems to say, "to man for relief. Wait not for help to arise from any other quarter. Just as you are, this very day, come to Me."

Notice what an encouraging account Jesus gives of Himself. He says, *"I am gentle and humble in heart."* How true that is, which the experience of all the saints of God has often proved. Mary and Martha at Bethany, Peter after his fall, the disciples after the resurrection, and Thomas after his cold unbelief all tasted the *meekness and gentleness of Christ.* It is the only place in Scripture where the *heart* of Christ is actually named. It is a saying never to be forgotten.

Notice lastly the encouraging account that Jesus gives of His service. He says, *"My yoke is easy and My burden is light."* No doubt there is a cross to be carried if we follow Christ. No doubt there are trials to be endured and battles to be fought. But the comforts of the gospel far outweigh the cross. Compared to the service of the world and sin, compared to the yoke of Jewish ceremonies and the bondage of human superstition, Christ's service is in the highest sense easy and light. His yoke is no more a burden than feathers are to a bird. His commandments are not grievous. His ways are ways of pleasantness, and all His paths are peace (1 John 5:3; Proverbs 3:17).

And now comes the solemn question: Have we accepted this invitation for ourselves? Have we no sins to be forgiven, no griefs to be removed, no wounds of conscience to be healed? If we have, let us hear Christ's voice. He speaks to us as well as to the Jews. He says, *"Come to Me."* Here is the key to true happiness. Here is the secret of having a happy heart. Everything turns and hinges on an acceptance of this offer of Christ.

May we never be satisfied until we know and feel that we have come to Christ by faith for rest, and do still come to Him for fresh supplies of grace every day! If we have come to Him already, let us learn to cleave to Him more closely. If we have never come to Him yet, let us begin to come today. His word shall never be broken: *"The one who comes to Me I will certainly not cast out"* (John 6:37).

Acknowledge Sabbath + Don't take the law for Granted!

Matthew Chapter 12

Matthew 12:1-13

At that time Jesus went through the grainfields on the Sabbath, and His disciples became hungry and began to pick the heads of grain and eat. But when the Pharisees saw this, they said to Him, "Look, Your disciples do what is not lawful to do on a Sabbath." But He said to them, "Have you not read what David did when he became hungry, he and his companions, how he entered the house of God, and they ate the consecrated bread, which was not lawful for him to eat nor for those with him, but for the priests alone? Or have you not read in the Law, that on the Sabbath the priests in the temple break the Sabbath and are innocent? But I say to you that something greater than the temple is here. But if you had known what this means, 'I desire compassion, and not a sacrifice,' you would not have condemned the innocent. For the Son of Man is Lord of the Sabbath." Departing from there, He went into their synagogue. And a man was there whose hand was withered. And they questioned Jesus, asking, "Is it lawful to heal on the Sabbath?"—so that they might accuse Him. And He said to them, "What man is there among you who has a sheep, and if it falls into a pit on the Sabbath, will he not take hold of it and lift it out? How much more valuable then is a man than a sheep! So then, it is lawful to do good on the Sabbath." Then He said to the man, "Stretch out your hand!" He stretched it out, and it was restored to normal, like the other. (Matthew 12:1-13)

THE ONE GREAT SUBJECT WHICH STANDS OUT PROMINENTLY

in this passage of Scripture is the Sabbath day. It is a subject on which strange opinions prevailed among the Jews in our Lord's time. The Pharisees had added to the teaching of Scripture about it and overlaid the true character of the day with the traditions of men. It is a subject on which diverse opinions have often been held in the churches of Christ, and wide differences exist among men at the present time. Let us see what we may learn about it from our Lord's teaching in these verses.

Let us, in the first place, settle it in our minds as an established principle, that *our Lord Jesus Christ does not do away with the observance of a weekly Sabbath day.* He neither does so here nor elsewhere in the four Gospels. We often find His opinion expressed about the Jewish errors on the subject of the Sabbath. But we do not find a word to teach us that His disciples were not to keep a Sabbath at all.

It is of much importance to observe this. The mistakes that have arisen from a superficial consideration of our Lord's sayings on the Sabbath question are neither few nor small. Thousands have rushed to the hasty conclusion that Christians have nothing to do with the fourth commandment and that it is no more binding on us than the Mosaic law about sacrifices. There is nothing in the New Testament to justify any such conclusion.

The plain truth is that our Lord did not abolish the law of the weekly Sabbath. He only freed it from incorrect interpretations and purified it from man-made additions. He did not tear out of the Decalogue the fourth commandment. He only stripped off the miserable traditions with which the Pharisees had encrusted the day, and by which they had made it not a blessing but a burden. He left the fourth commandment where He found it, a part of the eternal Law of God, of which no jot or tittle was ever to pass away. May we never forget this!

Let us, in the second place, settle it in our minds that *our Lord Jesus Christ allows all works of real necessity and mercy to be done on the Sabbath day.* This is a principle which is abundantly established in the passage of Scripture we are now considering. We find our Lord justifying His disciples for plucking the ears of corn on a Sabbath. It was an act permitted in Scripture (Deuteronomy 23:25). They *became hungry* and in need of food. Therefore, they were not to blame. We find Him maintaining the lawfulness of healing a sick man on the Sabbath day. The man was suffering from disease and pain. In such a case it was no breach of God's commandment to afford relief. We ought never to rest from doing good.

The arguments by which our Lord supports the lawfulness of any work of necessity and mercy on the Sabbath are striking and unanswerable. He reminds the Pharisees, who charged Him and His disciples with breaking the law, how David and his men, for lack of other food, had eaten the consecrated bread out of the tabernacle. He reminds them how the priests in the temple are obliged to do work on the Sabbath by slaying animals and offering sacrifices. He reminds them how even a sheep would be helped out of a pit on the Sabbath rather than allowed to suffer and die by any one of them. Above all, He lays down the great principle that *no ordinance of God is to be pressed so far as to make us neglect the plain duties of charity. "I desire compassion, and not sacrifice."* The first commandment of the law is not to be so interpreted as to make us break the second. The fourth commandment is not to be so explained as to make us unkind and unmerciful to our neighbor. There is deep wisdom in all this. We are reminded of the saying, *"Never has a man spoken the way this man speaks."*

In leaving the subject, let us beware that we are never tempted to take low views of the sanctity of the Christian Sabbath. Let us take care that we do not make our gracious Lord's teaching an excuse for Sabbath profanation. Let us not abuse the liberty which He has so clearly marked out for us and pretend that we do things on the Sabbath from "necessity and mercy," which in reality we do for our own selfish gratification.

There is great reason for warning people on this point. The mistakes of the Pharisee about the Sabbath were in one direction. The mistakes of the Christian are in another. The Pharisee pretended to add to the holiness of the day. The Christian is too often disposed to take away from that holiness and to keep the day in an idle, profane, and irreverent manner. May we all watch our own conduct on this subject. Saving Christianity is closely bound up with Sabbath observance. May we never forget that our great aim should be to *keep the Sabbath day holy.* Works of necessity may be done. *It is lawful to do good* and show mercy. But to give the Sabbath to idleness, pleasure-seeking, or the world is utterly unlawful. It is contrary to the example of Christ and a sin against a plain commandment of God.

Matthew 12:14-21

But the Pharisees went out and conspired against Him, as to how they might destroy Him. But Jesus, aware of this, withdrew from there. Many followed Him, and He healed them all, and warned them not to tell who He was. This was to fulfill what was spoken through Isaiah the prophet: "Behold, My Servant whom I have chosen; My Beloved in whom My soul is well-pleased; I will put My Spirit upon Him, and He shall proclaim justice to the Gentiles. He will not quarrel, nor cry out; nor will anyone hear His voice in the streets. A battered reed He will not break off, and a smoldering wick He will not put out, until He leads justice to victory. And in His name the Gentiles will hope."
(Matthew 12:14-21)

The first thing that demands our notice in this passage is *the desperate wickedness of the human heart* which it exemplifies. Silenced and defeated by our Lord's arguments, the Pharisees plunged deeper and deeper into sin. They *went out and conspired against Him, as to how they might destroy Him.*

What evil had our Lord done that He should be so treated? None, none at all. No charge could be brought against His life – He was holy, harmless, undefiled, and separate from sinners – His days were spent in doing good. No charge could be brought against His teaching – He had proved it to be agreeable to Scripture and reason, and no reply had been made to His proofs. But it mattered little how perfectly He lived or taught. He was hated.

This is human nature appearing in its true colors. The unconverted heart hates God and will show its hatred whenever it dares and has a favorable opportunity. It will persecute God's witnesses. It will dislike all who have anything of God's mind and are renewed after His image. Why were so many of the prophets killed? Why were the names of the apostles cast out as evil by the Jews? Why were the early martyrs slain? Why were John Huss, Jerome of Prague, Ridley, and Latimer burned at the stake? Not for any sins that they had committed and not for any wickedness they had committed. They all suffered because they were godly men. And human nature, unconverted, hates godly men because it hates God.

It must never surprise true Christians if they meet with the same treatment that the Lord Jesus met with. *Do not be surprised, brethren, if the world hates you* (1 John 3:13). It is not the utmost consistency or the closest walk with God that will exempt them from the enmity of the natural man. They need not torture their consciences by fancying that if they were only more faultless and consistent, everybody would surely love them. It is all a mistake. They should remember that there was never but one perfect man on earth and that He was not loved, but hated. It is not the infirmities of a believer that the world dislikes, but his goodness. It is not the remains of the old nature that call forth the world's enmity, but the exhibition of the new. Let us remember these things and be patient. The world hated Christ, and the world will hate Christians.

The second thing which demands our notice in this passage is *the encouraging description of our Lord Jesus Christ's character*, which Matthew draws from the prophet Isaiah. *A battered reed He will not break off, and a smoldering wick He will not put out.*

What are we to understand by the battered reed and smoldering wick? The language of the prophet no doubt is figurative. What is it that these two expressions mean? The simplest explanation seems to be that the Holy Spirit is here describing believers whose grace is at present weak, whose repentance is feeble, and whose faith is small. Towards such people the Lord Jesus Christ will be very tender and compassionate. Weak as the battered reed is, it shall not be broken. Small as the spark of fire may be within the smoldering wick, it shall not be quenched. It is a standing truth in the kingdom of grace that weak grace, weak faith, and weak repentance are all precious in our Lord's sight. Mighty as He is, He *does not despise any* (Job 36:5).

The doctrine here laid down is full of comfort and consolation. There are thousands in every church of Christ to whom it ought to speak peace and hope. There are some in every congregation who hear the gospel and who are ready to despair of their own salvation because their strength seems so small. They are full of fears and despondency because their knowledge, and faith, and hope, and love appear so dwarfish and diminutive. Let them drink comfort out of this text. Let them know that weak faith gives a man as real and true a saving interest in Christ as strong faith, though it may not give him the same joy. There is life in an infant as truly as in a grown-up man. There is fire in a spark as truly as in a burning flame. The least degree of grace is an everlasting possession. It comes down from heaven. It is precious in our Lord's eyes. It shall never be overthrown.

Does Satan make light of the beginnings of repentance towards God and faith towards our Lord Jesus Christ? No indeed! He does not. He has great wrath because he sees his time is short. Do the angels of God think lightly of the first signs of penitence and feeling after God in Christ? No indeed! *There is joy* among them when they behold the sight. Does the Lord Jesus regard no faith and repentance with interest unless they are strong and mighty? No indeed! As soon as that battered reed – Saul of Tarsus – begins to cry to Him, He sends Ananias to him, saying, *"He is praying"* (Acts 9:11). We err greatly if we do not encourage the very first movements of a soul towards Christ. Let the ignorant world scoff and mock, if it will. We may be sure that "battered reeds" and "smoldering wicks" are very precious in our Lord's eyes.

May we all lay these things to heart and use them in time of need both for ourselves and others. It should be a standing maxim in our religion that a spark is better than utter darkness, and little faith is better than no faith at all. *Who has despised the day of small things?* (Zechariah 4:10). It is not despised by Christ. It ought not to be despised by Christians.

Matthew 12:22-37

Then a demon-possessed man who was blind and mute was brought to Jesus, and He healed him, so that the mute man spoke and saw. All the crowds were amazed, and were saying, "This man cannot be the Son of David, can he?" But when the Pharisees heard this, they said, "This man casts out demons only by Beelzebul the ruler of the demons." And knowing their thoughts Jesus said to them, "Any kingdom divided against itself is laid waste; and any city or house divided against itself will not stand. If Satan casts out Satan, he is divided against himself; how then will his kingdom stand? If I by Beelzebul cast out demons, by whom do your sons cast them out? For this reason they will be your judges. But if I cast out demons by the Spirit of God, then the kingdom of God has come upon you. Or how can anyone enter the strong man's house and carry off his property, unless he first binds the strong man? And then he will plunder his house. He who is not with Me is against Me; and he who does not gather with Me scatters. Therefore I say to you, any sin and blasphemy shall be forgiven people, but blasphemy against the Spirit shall not be forgiven. Whoever speaks a word against the Son of Man, it shall be forgiven him; but whoever speaks against the Holy Spirit, it shall not be forgiven him, either in this age or in the age to come. Either make the tree good and its fruit good, or make the tree bad and its fruit bad; for the tree is known by its fruit. You brood of vipers, how can you, being evil, speak what is good? For the mouth speaks out of that which fills the heart. The good man brings out of his good treasure what is good; and the evil man brings out of his evil treasure what is evil. But I tell you that every careless word that people speak, they shall give an accounting for it in the day of judgment. For by your words you will be justified, and by your words you will be condemned."
(Matthew 12:22-37)

This passage of Scripture contains *things hard to understand*. The sin against the Holy Spirit in particular has never been fully explained by the most learned theologians. It is not difficult to show from Scripture what the sin is not. It is difficult to show clearly what it is. We must not be surprised. The Bible would not be the book of God if it had not deep places here and there which man has no line to fathom. Let us rather thank God that there are lessons of wisdom to be gathered even out of these verses which the unlearned may easily understand.

Let us gather from them, in the first place, that *there is nothing too blasphemous for hardened and prejudiced men to say against Christ.* Our Lord casts out a devil, and at once the Pharisees declare that He does it by *the ruler of the demons.*

This was an absurd charge. Our Lord shows that it was unreasonable to suppose that the devil would help to pull down his own kingdom and that Satan would cast out Satan. But there is nothing too absurd and unreasonable for men to say when they are thoroughly set against Christ. The Pharisees are not the only people who have lost sight of logic, good sense, and temper when they have attacked the gospel of Christ.

Strange as this charge may sound, it is one that has often been made against the servants of God. Their enemies have been obliged to confess that they are doing a work and producing a good effect on the world. The results of Christian labor stare them in the face. They cannot deny them. What then shall they say? They say the very thing that the Pharisees said of our Lord: "It is the devil." The early heretics used language of this kind about Athanasius. The Roman Catholics spread reports of this sort about Martin Luther. Such things will be said as long as the world stands.

We must never be surprised to hear of dreadful charges being made against the best of men, without cause. *If they have called the head of the house Beelzebul, how much more will they malign the members of his household!* It is an old device. When the Christian's arguments cannot be answered and the Christian's works cannot be denied, the last resource of the wicked is to try to blacken the Christian's character. If this be our lot, let us bear it patiently. Having Christ and a good conscience, we may be content. False charges will not keep us out of heaven. Our character will be cleared at the last day.

In the second place, let us gather out of these verses *the impossibility of neutrality in religion. "He who is not with Me is against Me; and he who does not gather with Me scatters."*

There are many people in every age of the church who need to have this lesson pressed upon them. They endeavor to steer a middle course in religion. They are not so bad as many sinners, but still they are not saints. They feel the truth of Christ's gospel when it is brought before them, but they are afraid to confess what they feel. Because they have these feelings, they flatter themselves that they are not so bad as others. And yet they shrink from the standard of faith and practice which the Lord Jesus sets up. They are not boldly on Christ's side, and yet they are not openly against Him. Our Lord warns all such that they are in a dangerous position. There are only two parties in religious matters. There are only two camps. There are only two sides. Are we with Christ and working in His cause? If not, we are against Him. Are we doing good in the world? If not, we are doing harm.

The principle here laid down is one which it concerns us all to remember. Let us settle it in our minds that we shall never have peace and do good to others unless we are thorough-going and decided in our Christianity. The way of Gamaliel and Erastus never yet brought happiness and usefulness to anyone, and never will.

In the third place, let us gather from these verses *the exceeding sinfulness of sins against knowledge.* This is a practical conclusion which appears to flow naturally from our Lord's words about the blasphemy against the Holy Spirit. Difficult as these words undoubtedly are, they seem fairly to prove that there are degrees in sin. Offenses arising from ignorance of the true mission of the Son of Man will not be punished so heavily as offenses committed against the noontide light of the dispensation of the Holy Spirit. The brighter the light, the greater the guilt of him who rejects it. The clearer a man's knowledge of the nature of the gospel, the greater his sin if he willfully refuses to repent and believe.

The doctrine here taught is one that does not stand alone in Scripture. Paul says to the Hebrews, *In the case of those who have once been enlightened . . . and then have fallen away, it is impossible to renew them again to repentance. For if we go on sinning willfully after receiving the knowledge of the truth, there no longer remains a sacrifice for sins, but a terrifying expectation of judgment* (Hebrews 6:4-7; 10:26-27). It is a doctrine of which we find mournful proofs in every quarter. The unconverted children of godly parents, the unconverted servants of godly families, and the unconverted members of evangelical congregations are the hardest people on earth to impress. They seem past feeling. The same fire which melts the wax hardens the clay.

It is a doctrine, moreover, that receives dreadful confirmation from the histories of some of those whose last ends were eminently hopeless. Pharaoh, Saul, Ahab, Judas Iscariot, Julian, and Francis Spira are fearful illustrations of our Lord's meaning. In each of these cases there was a combination of clear knowledge and deliberate rejection of Christ. In each there was light in the head but hatred of truth in the heart. And the end of each seems to have been blackness of darkness forever.

May God give us a will to use our knowledge whether it be little or great! May we beware of neglecting our opportunities and leaving our privileges unimproved! Have we light? Then let us live fully up to our light. Do we know the truth? Then let us walk in the truth. This is the best safeguard against the unpardonable sin.

In the last place, let us gather from these verses *the immense importance of carefulness about our daily words.* Our Lord tells us *that every careless word that people speak, they shall give an accounting for it in the day of judgment.* And He adds, *By your words you will be justified, and by your words you will be condemned.*

There are few of our Lord's sayings which are so heart-searching as this. There is nothing, perhaps, to which most men pay less attention than their words. They go through their daily work, speaking and talking without thought or reflection, and seem to imagine that if they do what is right, it matters but little what they say.

But is it so? Are our words so utterly trifling and unimportant? We dare not say so with such a passage of Scripture as this before our eyes. Our words are the evidence of the state of our hearts, as surely as the taste of the water is an evidence of the state of the spring. *For the mouth speaks out of that which fills the heart.* The lips only utter what the mind conceives. Our words will form one subject of inquiry at the day of judgment. We shall have to give account of our sayings as well as our doings. Truly these are very solemn considerations. If there were no other text in the Bible, this passage ought to convince us that we are all *guilty before the Lord* and need a righteousness better than our own, even the righteousness of Christ (Philippians 3:9).

Let us be humble as we read this passage, in the recollection of time past. How many idle, foolish, vain, light, frivolous, sinful, and unprofitable things we have all said! How many words we have used, which, like thistledown, have flown far and wide and sown mischief in the hearts of others that will never die! How often when we have met our friends, "our conversation," to use an old saint's expression, "has only made work for repentance." There is deep truth in the remark of Burkitt, "A profane scoff or atheistical jest may stick in the minds of those that hear it, after the tongue that spoke it is dead. A word spoken is physically transient, but morally permanent." *Death and life*, says Solomon, *are in the power of the tongue* (Proverbs 18:21).

Let us be watchful as we read this passage about words when we look forward to our days yet to come. Let us resolve, by God's grace, to be more careful over our tongues, and more particular about our use of them. Let us pray daily that our *speech always be with grace* (Colossians 4:6). Let us say every morning with holy David, *I will guard my ways that I may not sin with my tongue.* Let us cry with him to the strong One for strength and say, *Set a guard, O LORD, over my mouth; keep watch over the door of my lips.* Well indeed might James say, *If anyone does not stumble in what he says, he is a perfect man* (Psalm 39:1; 141:3; James 3:2).

Matthew 12:38-50

Then some of the scribes and Pharisees said to Him, "Teacher, we want to see a sign from You." But He answered and said to them, "An evil and adulterous generation craves for a sign; and yet no sign will be given to it but the sign of Jonah the prophet; for just as Jonah was three days and three nights in the belly of the sea

*monster, so will the Son of Man be three days and three nights
in the heart of the earth. The men of Nineveh will stand up with
this generation at the judgment, and will condemn it because
they repented at the preaching of Jonah; and behold, something
greater than Jonah is here. The Queen of the South will rise
up with this generation at the judgment and will condemn it,
because she came from the ends of the earth to hear the wisdom
of Solomon; and behold, something greater than Solomon is
here. Now when the unclean spirit goes out of a man, it passes
through waterless places seeking rest, and does not find it. Then
it says, 'I will return to my house from which I came'; and when
it comes, it finds it unoccupied, swept, and put in order. Then
it goes and takes along with it seven other spirits more wicked
than itself, and they go in and live there; and the last state of
that man becomes worse than the first. That is the way it will
also be with this evil generation." While He was still speaking
to the crowds, behold, His mother and brothers were standing
outside, seeking to speak to Him. Someone said to Him, "Behold,
Your mother and Your brothers are standing outside seeking to
speak to You." But Jesus answered the one who was telling Him
and said, "Who is My mother and who are My brothers?" And
stretching out His hand toward His disciples, He said, "Behold
My mother and My brothers! For whoever does the will of My
Father who is in heaven, he is My brother and sister and mother."*
(Matthew 12:38-50)

The beginning of this passage is one of those places which strikingly
illustrates the truth of Old Testament history. Our Lord speaks of the
Queen of the South as a real, true person who had lived and died. He
refers to the story of Jonah and his miraculous preservation in the
whale's belly as undeniable matters of fact. Let us remember this if we
hear men professing to believe the writers of the New Testament and
yet sneering at the things recorded in the Old Testament as if they were
fables. Such men forget that in so doing they pour contempt upon Christ
Himself. The authority of the Old and New Testaments stands or falls

together. The same Spirit inspired men to write of Solomon and Jonah who inspired the evangelists to write of Christ. These are not unimportant points in this day. Let them be well fixed in our minds.

The first practical lesson which demands our attention in these verses is *the amazing power of unbelief.* Notice how the scribes and Pharisees call upon our Lord to show them more miracles. *"Teacher, we want to see a sign from You."* They pretended that they only needed more evidence in order to be convinced and become disciples. They shut their eyes to the many wonderful works which Jesus had already done. It was not enough for them that He had healed the sick, cleansed the lepers, raised the dead, and cast out devils. They were not yet persuaded. They still demanded more proof. They would not see what our Lord plainly pointed at in His reply, that they had no real will to believe. There was evidence enough to convince them, but they had no wish to be convinced.

There are many in the church of Christ who are exactly in the state of these scribes and Pharisees. They flatter themselves that they only require a little more proof to become decided Christians. They fancy that if their reason and intellect could only be met with some additional arguments, they would at once give up all for Christ's sake, take up the cross, and follow Him. But in the meantime they wait. Alas! for their blindness. They will not see that there is abundance of evidence on every side of them. The truth is that they do not want to be convinced.

May we all be on our guard against the spirit of unbelief! It is a growing evil in these latter days. Lack of simple, childlike faith is an increasing feature of the times in every rank of society. The true explanation of a hundred strange things that startle us in the conduct of leading men in churches and states is downright lack of faith. Men who do not believe all that God says in the Bible must necessarily take a vacillating and undecided line on moral and religious questions. *Do not be wise in your own eyes; Fear the Lord and turn away from evil* (Proverbs 3:7).

The second practical lesson which meets us in these verses is *the immense danger of a partial and imperfect religious reformation.* Notice what a dreadful picture our Lord draws of the man to whom the unclean spirit returns after having once left him. How fearful are those words, *I will return to my house from which I came.* How vivid that description:

it finds it unoccupied, swept, and put in order. How tremendous the conclusion: *Then it goes and takes along with it seven other spirits more wicked than itself, and they go in and live there; and the last state of that man becomes worse than the first.* It is a picture most painfully full of meaning. Let us scan it closely and learn wisdom.

It is certain that we have in this picture *the history of the Jewish church and nation* at the time of our Lord's coming. Called as they were at first out of Egypt to be God's peculiar people, they never seem to have wholly lost the tendency to worship idols. Redeemed as they afterwards were from the captivity of Babylon, they never seem to have rendered to God a due return for His goodness. Aroused as they had been by John the Baptist's preaching, their repentance appears to have been only skin-deep. At the time when our Lord spoke, they had become, as a nation, harder and more perverse than ever. The grossness of idol worship had given place to the deadness of mere formality. Seven other spirits worse than the first had taken possession of them. Their last state was rapidly becoming worse than the first. Just forty years and their iniquity came to the full. They madly plunged into a war with Rome. Judea became a very Babel of confusion. Jerusalem was taken. The temple was destroyed. The Jews were scattered over the face of the earth.

Again, it is highly probable that we have in this picture *the history of the whole body of Christian churches.* Delivered as they were from heathen darkness by the preaching of the gospel, they have never really lived up to their light. Revived as many of them were at the time of the Protestant Reformation, they have none of them made a right use of their privileges or *pressed on to maturity.* They have all more or less stopped short and settled on their lees. They have all been too ready to be satisfied with mere external amendments. And now there are painful symptoms in many quarters that the evil spirit has returned to his house and is preparing an outbreak of infidelity and false doctrine, such as the churches have never yet seen. Between unbelief in some quarters and formal superstition in others, everything seems ripe for some fearful manifestation of Antichrist. It may well be feared that the last state of the professing Christian churches will prove worse than the first.

Saddest and worst of all, we have in this picture *the history of many an individual's soul.* There are men who seemed at one time of their lives to be under the influence of strong religious feelings. They reformed their ways. They laid aside many things that are bad. They took up many things that are good. But they stopped there, and went no further, and by and by gave up religion altogether. The evil spirit returned to their hearts and found them empty, swept, and garnished. They are now worse than they ever were before. Their consciences seem seared. Their sense of religious things appears entirely destroyed. They are like men given over to a reprobate mind. One would say it was *impossible to renew them again to repentance.* None prove so hopelessly wicked as those who, after experiencing strong religious convictions, have gone back again to sin and the world.

If we love life, let us pray that these lessons may be deeply impressed on our minds. Let us never be content with a partial reformation of life without thorough conversion to God and mortification of the whole body of sin. It is a good thing to strive to cast sin out of our hearts. But let us take care that we also receive the grace of God in its place. Let us make sure that we not only get rid of the old tenant, the devil, but also have dwelling in us the Holy Spirit.

The last practical lesson which meets us in these verses is *the tender affection with which the Lord Jesus regards His true disciples.* Notice how He speaks of everyone who does the will of His Father in heaven. He says, *He is My brother and sister and mother.* What gracious words these are! Who can conceive the depth of our dear Lord's love towards His relations according to the flesh? It was a pure, unselfish love. It must have been a mighty love, a love that passes man's understanding. Yet here we see that all His believing people are counted as His family. He loves them, feels for them, and cares for them as members of His family, bone of His bone, and flesh of His flesh.

There is a solemn warning here to all who mock and persecute true Christians on account of their religion. They consider not what they are doing. They are persecuting the near relations of the King of Kings. They will find at the last day that they have mocked those whom the judge of all regards as His *brother and sister and mother.*

There is rich encouragement here for all believers. They are far more

123

precious in their Lord's eyes than they are in their own. Their faith may be feeble, their repentance weak, and their strength small. They may be poor and needy in this world. But there is a glorious *whoever* in the last verse of this chapter which ought to cheer them. *Whoever* believes is a near relation of Christ. The elder Brother will provide for him in time and eternity and never let him be cast away. There is not one *little sister* in the family of the redeemed whom Jesus does not remember (Song of Solomon 8:8). Joseph provided richly for all his relatives, and Jesus will provide for His.

Matthew Chapter 13

Matthew 13:1-23

That day Jesus went out of the house and was sitting by the sea. And large crowds gathered to Him, so He got into a boat and sat down, and the whole crowd was standing on the beach. And He spoke many things to them in parables, saying, "Behold, the sower went out to sow; and as he sowed, some seeds fell beside the road, and the birds came and ate them up. Others fell on the rocky places, where they did not have much soil; and immediately they sprang up, because they had no depth of soil. But when the sun had risen, they were scorched; and because they had no root, they withered away. Others fell among the thorns, and the thorns came up and choked them out. And others fell on the good soil and yielded a crop, some a hundredfold, some sixty, and some thirty. He who has ears, let him hear." And the disciples came and said to Him, "Why do You speak to them in parables?" Jesus answered them, "To you it has been granted to know the mysteries of the kingdom of heaven, but to them it has not been granted. For whoever has, to him more shall be given, and he will have abundance; but whoever does not have, even what he has shall be taken away from him. Therefore I speak to them in parables; because while seeing they do not see, and while hearing they do not hear, nor do they understand. In their case the prophecy of Isaiah is being fulfilled, which says, 'You will keep on hearing, but will not understand; You will keep on seeing, but will not perceive; For the heart of this people has become dull, with their ears they scarcely hear, and they have closed their eyes, otherwise they would see with their eyes, hear with their ears,

and understand with their heart and return, and I would heal them.' But blessed are your eyes, because they see; and your ears, because they hear. For truly I say to you that many prophets and righteous men desired to see what you see, and did not see it, and to hear what you hear, and did not hear it. Hear then the parable of the sower. When anyone hears the word of the kingdom and does not understand it, the evil one comes and snatches away what has been sown in his heart. This is the one on whom seed was sown beside the road. The one on whom seed was sown on the rocky places, this is the man who hears the word and immediately receives it with joy; yet he has no firm root in himself, but is only temporary, and when affliction or persecution arises because of the word, immediately he falls away. And the one on whom seed was sown among the thorns, this is the man who hears the word, and the worry of the world and the deceitfulness of wealth choke the word, and it becomes unfruitful. And the one on whom seed was sown on the good soil, this is the man who hears the word and understands it; who indeed bears fruit and brings forth, some a hundredfold, some sixty, and some thirty."
(Matthew 13:1-23)

THE CHAPTER WHICH THESE VERSES BEGIN is remarkable for the number of parables it contains. Seven striking illustrations of spiritual truth are here drawn by the Lord from the book of nature. By so doing He shows us that religious teaching may draw helps from everything in creation. Those who would *find delightful words* should not forget this (Ecclesiastes 12:10).

The parable of the sower, which begins this chapter, is one of those parables which allows a very wide application. It is being continually verified under our own eyes. Wherever the Word of God is preached or expounded and people are assembled to hear it, the sayings of our Lord in this parable are found to be true. It describes what goes on, as a general rule, in all congregations.

Let us learn, in the first place, from this parable, that *the work of the preacher resembles that of the sower.* Like the sower, the preacher must sow good seed if he wants to see fruit. He must sow the pure Word of God and not the traditions of the church or the doctrines of men. Without this his labor will be in vain. He may go to and fro and seem to say much and to work much in his weekly round of ministerial duty. But there will be no harvest of souls for heaven, no living results, and no conversions.

Like the sower, the preacher must be diligent. He must spare no pains. He must use every possible means to make his work prosper. He must patiently *sow beside all waters* and "sow in hope." He must be *ready in season and out of season.* He must not be deterred by difficulties and discouragements. *He who watches the wind will not sow.* No doubt his success does not entirely depend upon his labor and diligence. But without labor and diligence success will seldom be obtained (Isaiah 32:20; 2 Timothy 4:2; Ecclesiastes 11:4).

Like the sower, the preacher cannot give life. He can scatter the seed committed to his charge, but he cannot command it to grow. He may offer the word of truth to a people, but he cannot make them receive it and bear fruit. To give life is God's sovereign prerogative. *It is the Spirit who gives life.* God alone *causes the growth* (John 6:63; 1 Corinthians 3:7).

Let these things sink down into our hearts. It is no light thing to be a real minister of God's Word. To be an idle, formal workman in the church is an easy business. To be a faithful sower is very hard. Preachers ought to be specially remembered in our prayers.

In the next place, let us learn from this passage that *there are various ways of hearing the Word of God without benefit.* We may listen to a sermon with a heart like the hard "wayside" – careless, thoughtless, and unconcerned. Christ crucified may be affectionately set before us, and we may hear of His sufferings with utter indifference as a subject in which we have no interest. Fast as the words fall on our ears, the devil may pluck them away, and we may go home as if we had not heard a sermon at all. Alas! there are many such hearers! It is as true of them as of the idols of old: *They have eyes, but they do not see; they have ears, but they do not hear* (Psalm 135:16-17). Truth seems to have no more effect on their hearts than water on a stone.

We may listen to a sermon with pleasure while the impression produced on us is only temporary and short-lived. Our hearts, like the *rocky ground*, may yield a plentiful crop of warm feelings and good resolutions. But all this time there may be no deeply rooted work in our souls, and the first cold blast of opposition or temptation may cause our seeming religion to wither away. Alas! there are many such hearers! The mere love of sermons is no sign of grace. Thousands of baptized people are like the Jews of Ezekiel's day: *Behold, you are to them like a sensual song by one who has a beautiful voice and plays well on an instrument; for they hear your words but they do not practice them* (Ezekiel 33:32).

We may listen to a sermon and approve of every word it contains and yet get no good from it, in consequence of the absorbing influence of this world. Our hearts, like the "thorny ground," may be choked with a noxious crop of cares, pleasures, and worldly plans. We may really like the gospel and wish to obey it, and yet insensibly give it no chance of bearing fruit by allowing other things to fill a place in our affections and insensibly to fill our whole hearts. Alas! there are many such hearers! They know the truth well. They hope one day to be decided Christians. But they never come to the point of giving up all for Christ's sake. They never make up their minds to *seek first His kingdom* – and so die in their sins.

These are points that we ought to weigh well. We should never forget that there are more ways than one of hearing the Word without profit. It is not enough that we come to hear. We may come and be careless. It is not enough that we are not careless hearers. Our impressions may be only temporary and ready to perish. It is not enough that our impressions are not merely temporary. But they may be continually yielding no result in consequence of our obstinate cleaving to the world. Truly, *the heart is more deceitful than all else and is desperately sick; who can understand it?* (Jeremiah 17:9).

In the last place, let us learn from this parable that *there is only one evidence of hearing the Word rightly.* That evidence is to bear fruit. The fruit here spoken of is the fruit of the Spirit. Repentance towards God, faith towards the Lord Jesus Christ, holiness of life and character, prayerfulness, humility, charity, and spiritual-mindedness – these are the only satisfactory proofs that the seed of God's Word is doing its proper work in our souls. Without such proofs, our religion is vain, however high our profession. It is no better than sounding brass and a tinkling cymbal. Christ has said, *I chose you, and appointed you that you would go and bear fruit* (John 15:16).

There is no part of the whole parable more important than this. We must never be content with a barren orthodoxy and a cold maintenance of correct theological views. We must not be satisfied with clear knowledge, warm feelings, and a decent profession. We must see to it that the gospel we profess to love produces positive *fruit* in our hearts and lives. This is real Christianity. Those words of James should often ring in our ears: *But prove yourselves doers of the word, and not merely hearers who delude themselves* (James 1:22).

Let us not leave these verses without putting to ourselves the important question, "How do we hear?" We live in a Christian country. We go to a place of worship Sunday after Sunday and hear sermons. In what spirit do we hear them? What effect have they upon our characters? Can we point to anything that deserves the name of *fruit*?

We may rest assured that to reach heaven at last, it needs something more than going to church regularly on Sundays and listening to preachers. The Word of God must be received into our hearts and become the mainspring of our conduct. It must produce practical impressions on our inward man that shall appear in our outward behavior. If it does not do this, it will only add to our condemnation in the day of judgment.

Matthew 13:24-43

Jesus presented another parable to them, saying, "The kingdom of heaven may be compared to a man who sowed good seed in his field. But while his men were sleeping, his enemy came and sowed tares among the wheat, and went away. But when the wheat sprouted and bore grain, then the tares became evident also. The slaves of the landowner came and said to him, 'Sir, did you not sow good seed in your field? How then does it have tares?'

And he said to them, 'An enemy has done this!' The slaves said to him, 'Do you want us, then, to go and gather them up?' But he said, 'No; for while you are gathering up the tares, you may uproot the wheat with them. Allow both to grow together until the harvest; and in the time of the harvest I will say to the reapers, "First gather up the tares and bind them in bundles to burn them up; but gather the wheat into my barn."'" He presented another parable to them, saying, "The kingdom of heaven is like a mustard seed, which a man took and sowed in his field; and this is smaller than all other seeds, but when it is full grown, it is larger than the garden plants and becomes a tree, so that the birds of the air come and nest in its branches." He spoke another parable to them, "The kingdom of heaven is like leaven, which a woman took and hid in three pecks of flour until it was all leavened." All these things Jesus spoke to the crowds in parables, and He did not speak to them without a parable. This was to fulfill what was spoken through the prophet: "I will open My mouth in parables; I will utter things hidden since the foundation of the world." Then He left the crowds and went into the house. And His disciples came to Him and said, "Explain to us the parable of the tares of the field." And He said, "The one who sows the good seed is the Son of Man, and the field is the world; and as for the good seed, these are the sons of the kingdom; and the tares are the sons of the evil one; and the enemy who sowed them is the devil, and the harvest is the end of the age; and the reapers are angels. So just as the tares are gathered up and burned with fire, so shall it be at the end of the age. The Son of Man will send forth His angels, and they will gather out of His kingdom all stumbling blocks, and those who commit lawlessness, and will throw them into the furnace of fire; in that place there will be weeping and gnashing of teeth. Then the righteous will shine forth as the sun in the kingdom of their Father. He who has ears, let him hear."
(Matthew 13:24-43)

The parable of the wheat and weeds, which occupies the chief part of these verses, is one of peculiar importance in the present day. (The consideration of the parables of the mustard seed and the leaves is purposely deferred until a future part of the *Exposition*.) It is eminently calculated to correct the extravagant expectations in which many Christians indulge as to the effect of missions abroad and of preaching the gospel at home. May we give it the attention it deserves!

In the first place, this parable teaches us that *good and evil will always be found together in the professing church until the end of the world*. The visible church is set before us as a mixed body. It is a vast *field* in which *wheat* and *weeds* grow side by side. We must expect to find believers and unbelievers, converted and unconverted, *the sons of the kingdom*, and *the sons of the evil one*, all mingled together in every congregation of baptized people.

The purest preaching of the gospel will not prevent this. In every age of the church, the same state of things has existed. It was the experience of the early church Fathers. It was the experience of the Reformers. It is the experience of the best ministers at the present hour. There has never been a visible church or a religious assembly of which the members have been all *wheat*. The devil, that great enemy of souls, has always taken care to sow *tares*.

The most strict and prudent discipline will not prevent this. Episcopalians, Presbyterians, and Independents all alike find it to be so. Do what we will to purify a church, we shall never succeed in obtaining a perfectly pure communion. Tares will be found among the wheat. Hypocrites and deceivers will creep in. And, worst of all, if we are extreme in our efforts to obtain purity, we do more harm than good. We run the risk of encouraging many a Judas Iscariot, and breaking many a bruised reed. In our zeal to *gather up the tares*, we are in danger of *uprooting the wheat with them*. Such zeal is not according to knowledge and has often done much harm. Those who care not what happens to the wheat, provided they can root up the tares, show little of the mind of Christ. And after all, there is deep truth in the charitable saying of Augustine, "Those who are weeds today, may be wheat tomorrow."

Are we inclined to look for the conversion of the whole world by the labors of missionaries and ministers? Let us place this parable before us and beware of such an idea. We shall never see all the inhabitants of earth as the wheat of God in the present order of things. The weeds and wheat will *grow together until the harvest.* The kingdoms of this world will never become the kingdom of Christ, and the millennium will never begin until the King Himself returns.

Are we ever tried by the scoffing argument of the infidel that Christianity cannot be a true religion when there are so many false Christians? Let us call to mind this parable and remain unmoved. Let us tell the infidel that the state of things he scoffs at does not surprise us at all. Our Master prepared us for it eighteen hundred years ago. He foresaw and foretold that His church would be a field containing not only wheat but also tares.

Are we ever tempted to leave one church for another because we see many of its members unconverted? Let us remember this parable and take heed what we do. We shall never find a perfect church. We may spend our lives in migrating from communion to communion and pass our days in perpetual disappointment. Go where we will, and worship where we may, we shall always find tares.

In the second place, the parable teaches us that *there is to be a day of separation between the godly and ungodly members of the visible church at the end of the world.* The present mixed state of things is not to be forever. The wheat and the tares are to be divided at last. The Lord Jesus shall *send forth His angels* in the day of His second advent and gather all professing Christians into two great companies. Those mighty reapers shall make no mistake. They shall discern with unerring judgment between the righteous and the wicked and place everyone in his own lot. The saints and faithful servants of Christ shall receive glory, honor, and eternal life. The worldly, the ungodly, the careless, and the unconverted shall be thrown *into the furnace of fire* and receive shame and everlasting contempt.

There is something peculiarly solemn in this part of the parable. The meaning of it admits of no mistake. Our Lord Himself explains it in words of singular clearness, as if to impress it deeply on our minds. Well may He say at the conclusion, *He who has ears, let him hear.*

Let the ungodly man tremble when he reads this parable. Let him see in its fearful language his own certain doom unless he repents and is converted. Let him know that he is sowing misery for himself if he goes on still in his neglect of God. Let him reflect that his end will be to be gathered among the *bundles* of tares and be burned. Surely such a prospect ought to make a man think. As Baxter truly says, "We must not misinterpret God's patience with the ungodly."

Let the believer in Christ take comfort when he reads this parable. Let him see that there is happiness and safety prepared for him in the great and dreadful day of the Lord. The voice of the archangel and the trumpet of God will proclaim no terror for him. They will summon him to join what he has long desired to see – a perfect church and a perfect communion of saints. How beautiful will the whole body of believers appear when finally separated from the wicked! How fine will the wheat look in the barn of God when the tares are at last taken away! How brightly will grace shine when no longer dimmed by incessant contact with the worldly and unconverted!

The righteous are little known in the present day. The world sees no beauty in them, even as it saw none in their Master. *The world does not know us, because it did not know Him* (1 John 3:1). But the righteous shall one day *shine forth as the sun in the kingdom of their Father.* To use the words of Matthew Henry, "Their sanctification will be perfected, and their justification will be published." *When Christ, who is our life, is revealed, then you also will be revealed with Him in glory* (Colossians 3:4).

Matthew 13:44-50 *Kingdom of Heaven Parables*

"The kingdom of heaven is like a treasure hidden in the field, which a man found and hid again; and from joy over it he goes and sells all that he has and buys that field. Again, the kingdom of heaven is like a merchant seeking fine pearls, and upon finding one pearl of great value, he went and sold all that he had and bought it. Again, the kingdom of heaven is like a dragnet cast into the sea, and gathering fish of every kind; and when it was filled, they drew it up on the beach; and they sat down and gathered the

good fish into containers, but the bad they threw away. So it will be at the end of the age; the angels will come forth and take out the wicked from among the righteous, and will throw them into the furnace of fire; in that place there will be weeping and gnashing of teeth." (Matthew 13:44-50)

The parables of the *treasure hidden in the field* and the *merchant seeking fine pearls* appear intended to convey one and the same lesson. They vary, no doubt, in one striking particular. The *treasure* was found by one who does not seem to have sought it. The *pearl* was found by one who was actually seeking pearls. But the conduct of the finders in both cases was precisely alike. Both *sold all* to make the thing found their own property. And it is exactly at this point that the instruction of both parables agrees.

These two parables are meant to teach us that *men really convinced of the importance of salvation will give up everything to win Christ and eternal life.* What was the conduct of the two men our Lord describes? The one was persuaded that there was a *treasure hidden in the field*, which would amply repay him if he bought the field, however great the price that he might give. The other was persuaded that the *pearl* he had found was so immensely valuable that it would compensate him to purchase it at any cost. Both were convinced that they had found a thing of great value. Both were satisfied that it was worth a great present sacrifice to make this thing their own. Others might wonder at them. Others might think them foolish for paying such a sum of money for the field and pearl. But they knew what they were about. They were sure that they were making a good bargain.

Behold in this single picture *the conduct of a true Christian explained!* He is what he is and does what he does in his religion because he is thoroughly persuaded that it is worthwhile. He comes out from the world. He puts off the old man. He forsakes the vain companions of his past life. Like Matthew, he gives up everything, and, like Paul, he *counts all things to be loss* for Christ's sake. And why? Because he is convinced that Christ will make amends to him for all he gives up. He sees in Christ an endless *treasure*. He sees in Christ a precious *pearl*.

To win Christ he will make any sacrifice. This is true faith. This is the stamp of a genuine work of the Holy Spirit.

Behold in these two parables *the real clue to the conduct of many unconverted people!* They are what they are in religion because they are not fully persuaded that it is worthwhile to be different. They flinch from decision. They shrink from taking up the cross. They halt between two opinions. They will not commit themselves. They will not come forward boldly on the Lord's side. And why? Because they are not convinced that it will compensate them. They are not sure that the *treasure* is before them. They are not satisfied that the *pearl* is worth so great a price. They cannot yet make up their minds to "sell all," that they may win Christ. And so too often they perish everlastingly! When a man will venture nothing for Christ's sake, we must draw the sorrowful conclusion that he does not have the grace of God.

The parable of the net let down into the sea has some points in common with that of the wheat and the tares. It is intended to instruct us on a most important subject: *the true nature of the visible church of Christ.*

The preaching of the gospel was the letting down of a large net into the midst of the sea of this world. The professing church, which it was to gather together, was to be a mixed body. Within the folds of the net there were to be fish of every kind, both good and bad. Within the pale of the church there were to be Christians of various sorts, unconverted as well as converted, false as well as true. The separation of good and bad is sure to come at last, but not before the end of the world. Such was the account which the great Master gave to His disciples of the churches which they were to found.

It is of the utmost importance to have the lessons of this parable deeply engraved on our minds. There is hardly any point in Christianity on which greater mistakes exist than the nature of the visible church. There is none, perhaps, on which mistakes are so perilous to the soul.

Let us learn from this parable that all congregations of professed Christians ought to be regarded as *mixed bodies.* They are all assemblies containing "good fish and bad," converted and unconverted, children of God and children of the world, and ought to be described and addressed as such. To tell all baptized people that they are born again, and have the Spirit, and are members of Christ, and are holy in the face of such a parable as this is utterly unwarrantable. Such a mode of address may flatter and please. It is not likely to profit or save. It is painfully calculated to promote self-righteousness and lull sinners to sleep. It overthrows the plain teaching of Christ and is ruinous to souls. Do we ever hear such doctrine? If we do, let us remember the *net*.

Finally, let it be a settled principle with us to never be satisfied with mere outward church membership. We may be inside the net and yet not be in Christ. The waters of baptism are poured on myriads who are never washed in the water of life. The bread and wine are eaten and drunk by thousands at the Lord's Table who never feed on Christ by faith. Are we converted? Are we among the *good fish*? This is the grand question. It is one which must be answered at last. The net will soon be drawn to shore. The true character of every man's religion will at last be exposed. There will be an eternal separation between the good fish and the bad. There will be a *furnace of fire* for the wicked. Surely, as Baxter says, "These plain words more need belief and consideration than exposition."

Matthew 13:51-58

"Have you understood all these things?" They said to Him, "Yes." And Jesus said to them, "Therefore every scribe who has become a disciple of the kingdom of heaven is like a head of a household, who brings out of his treasure things new and old." When Jesus had finished these parables, He departed from there. He came to His hometown and began teaching them in their synagogue, so that they were astonished, and said, "Where did this man get this wisdom and these miraculous powers? Is not this the carpenter's son? Is not His mother called Mary, and His brothers, James and Joseph and Simon and Judas? And His sisters, are they not all with us? Where then did this man get all these things?" And they took offense at Him. But Jesus said to them, "A prophet is not without honor except in his hometown and in his own

household." And He did not do many miracles there because of their unbelief. (Matthew 13:51-58)

Personal application has been called the "soul" of preaching. A sermon without application is like a letter posted without an address. It may be well written, rightly dated, and duly signed. But it is useless because it never reaches its destination. Our Lord's question is an admirable example of real heart-searching application, *"Have you understood?"*

The mere form of hearing a sermon can profit no man unless he comprehends what it means. He might just as well listen to the blowing of a trumpet or the beating of a drum. He might just as well attend a Roman Catholic service in Latin. His intellect must be set in motion and his heart impressed. Ideas must be received into his mind. He must carry off the seeds of new thoughts. Without this he hears in vain.

It is of great importance to see this point clearly. There is a vast amount of ignorance about it. There are thousands who go regularly to places of worship and think they have done their religious duty, but never carry away an idea or receive an impression. Ask them, when they return home on a Sunday evening, what they have learned, and they cannot tell you a word. Examine them at the end of a year as to the religious knowledge they have attained, and you will find them as ignorant as the heathen.

Let us watch our souls in this matter. Let us take with us to church not only our bodies but also our minds, our reason, our hearts, and our consciences. Let us often ask ourselves, "What have I got from this sermon? What have I learned? What truths have been impressed on my mind?" *Intellect*, no doubt, is not everything in religion. But it does not therefore follow that it is nothing at all. The *heart* is unquestionably the main point. But we must never forget that the Holy Spirit generally reaches the heart through the mind. Sleepy, idle, and inattentive hearers are never likely to be converted.

The second thing which we ought to notice in these verses is *the strange treatment which our Lord received in His own country.* He came to the town of Nazareth where He had been brought up, and *taught in their synagogues.* His teaching, no doubt, was the same as it always was.

Truth hurts

"*Never has a man spoken the way this man speaks.*" But it had no effect on the people of Nazareth. They were *astonished*, but their hearts were unmoved. They said, "*Is not this the carpenter's son? Is not His mother called Mary?*" They despised Him because they were so familiar with Him. *They took offense at Him.* And they drew from our Lord the solemn remark, "*A prophet is not without honor except in his hometown and in his own household.*"

Let us see, in this history, a sad page of human nature unfolded to our view. We are all apt to despise mercies if we are accustomed to them and have them cheap. The Bibles and religious books which are so plentiful, the churches of which we have so abundant a supply, the preaching of the gospel which we hear every week – all, all are liable to be undervalued. It is mournfully true that in religion more than in anything else, familiarity breeds contempt. Men forget that truth is truth, however old and hackneyed it may sound, and despise it because it is old. Alas! by so doing, they provoke God to take it away.

Do we wonder that the relatives, servants, and neighbors of godly people are not always converted? Do we wonder that the parishioners of eminent ministers of the gospel are often their hardest and most impenitent hearers? Let us wonder no more. Let us notice the experience of our Lord at Nazareth and learn wisdom.

Do we ever imagine that if we had only seen and heard Jesus Christ we would have been His faithful disciples? Do we think that if we had only lived near Him and been eyewitnesses of His ways we would not have been undecided, wavering, and halfhearted about religion? If we do, let us think so no longer. Let us observe the people of Nazareth and learn wisdom.

The last thing which we ought to notice in these verses is *the ruinous nature of unbelief.* The chapter ends with the fearful words, *And He did not do many miracles there because of their unbelief.*

Behold in this single word the secret of the everlasting ruin of multitudes of souls! They perish forever because they will not believe. There is nothing else in earth or heaven that prevents their salvation. Their sins, however many, might all be forgiven. The Father's love is ready to receive them. The blood of Christ is ready to cleanse them. The power of the Spirit is ready to renew them. But a great barrier interposes – they will not believe. *"You are unwilling to come to Me,"* says Jesus, *"so that you may have life"* (John 5:40). May we all be on our guard against this accursed sin. It is the old root-sin which caused the fall of man. Cut down in the true child of God by the power of the Spirit, it is ever ready to bud and sprout again. There are three great enemies against which God's children should daily pray: pride, worldliness, and unbelief. Of these three, none is greater than unbelief.

Matthew Chapter 14

Matthew 14:1-12

At that time Herod the tetrarch heard the news about Jesus, and said to his servants, "This is John the Baptist; he has risen from the dead, and that is why miraculous powers are at work in him." For when Herod had John arrested, he bound him and put him in prison because of Herodias, the wife of his brother Philip. For John had been saying to him, "It is not lawful for you to have her." Although Herod wanted to put him to death, he feared the crowd, because they regarded John as a prophet. But when Herod's birthday came, the daughter of Herodias danced before them and pleased Herod, so much that he promised with an oath to give her whatever she asked. Having been prompted by her mother, she said, "Give me here on a platter the head of John the Baptist." Although he was grieved, the king commanded it to be given because of his oaths, and because of his dinner guests. He sent and had John beheaded in the prison. And his head was brought on a platter and given to the girl, and she brought it to her mother. His disciples came and took away the body and buried it; and they went and reported to Jesus. (Matthew 14:1-12)

WE HAVE IN THIS PASSAGE A PAGE OUT OF GOD'S BOOK OF MARTYRS – the history of the death of John the Baptist. The wickedness of King Herod, the bold reproof which John gave him, the consequent imprisonment of the faithful reprover, and the disgraceful circumstances of his death are all written for our learning. *Precious in the sight of the* LORD *is the death of His godly ones* (Psalm 116:15).

The story of John the Baptist's death is told more fully by Mark than by Matthew. For the present it seems sufficient to draw two general lessons from Matthew's narrative and to fasten our attention exclusively upon them.

Let us learn, in the first place from these verses, *the great power of conscience.* King Herod hears of *the news about Jesus* and says to his servants, *"This is John the Baptist; he has risen from the dead."* He remembered his own wicked dealings with that holy man, and his heart failed within him. His heart told him that he had despised his godly counsel and committed a foul and abominable murder. And his heart told him that though he had killed John, there would yet be a reckoning day. He and John the Baptist would yet meet again. Well says Bishop Hall, "A wicked man needs no other tormentor, especially for sins of blood, than his own heart."

There is a conscience in all men by nature. Let this never be forgotten. Fallen, lost, and desperately wicked as we are all born into the world, God has taken care to leave Himself a witness in our bosoms. But it is a poor, blind guide without the Holy Spirit. It can save no one. It leads no one to Christ. It may be seared and trampled underfoot. But there is such a thing as conscience in every man, accusing or excusing him, and Scripture and experience alike declare it (Romans 2:15).

Conscience can make even kings miserable when they have willfully rejected its advice. It can fill the princes of this world with fear and trembling as it did Felix when Paul preached. They find it easier to imprison and behead the preacher than to bind his sermon and silence the voice of his reproof in their own hearts. God's witnesses may be put out of the way, but their testimony often lives and works on long after they are dead. God's prophets live not forever, but their words often survive them (2 Timothy 2:9; Zechariah 1:5).

Let the thoughtless and ungodly remember this and not sin against their consciences. Let them know that their sins *will find them out.* They may laugh, and jest, and mock at religion for a little time. They may cry, "Who is afraid? What is the mighty harm of our ways?" They may depend upon it that they are sowing misery for themselves and will reap a bitter crop sooner or later. Their wickedness will overtake them one day. They will find, like Herod, that it is an evil and bitter thing to sin against God (Jeremiah 2:19).

Let ministers and teachers remember that there is a conscience in men, and work on boldly. Instruction is not always thrown away because it seems to bear no fruit at the time it is given. Teaching is not always in vain, though we fancy that it is unheeded, wasted, and forgotten. There is a conscience in the hearers of sermons. There is a conscience in the children at our schools. Many a sermon and lesson will yet rise again when he who preached or taught it is laying, like John the Baptist, in the grave. Thousands know that we are right and, like Herod, dare not confess it.

Let us learn, in the second place, that *God's children must not look for their reward in this world*. If ever there was a case of godliness unrewarded in this life, it was that of John the Baptist. Think for a moment what a man he was during his short career, and then think to what an end he came. Behold him, who was the prophet of the Highest, and greater than any born of woman, imprisoned like an evildoer! Behold him, cut off by a violent death before the age of thirty-four, the burning light quenched, the faithful preacher murdered for doing his duty – and this to gratify the hatred of an adulterous woman and at the command of a capricious tyrant! Truly there was an event here, if there ever was one in the world, which might make an ignorant man say, "What profit is it to serve God?"

But these are the sorts of things which show us that there will one day be a judgment. The God of the spirits of all flesh shall at last set up a judicial inquest and reward everyone according to his works. The blood of John the Baptist, and James the apostle, and Stephen, and Polycarp, and Huss, and Ridley, and Latimer shall yet be required. It is all written in God's book. *The earth will reveal her bloodshed and will no longer cover her slain* (Isaiah 26:21). The world shall yet know that there is a God who judges the earth. *If you see the oppression of the poor and denial of justice and righteousness in the province, do not be shocked at the sight; for one official watches over another official, and there are higher officials over them* (Ecclesiastes 5:8).

Let all true Christians remember that their best things are yet to come. Let us count it no strange thing if we have sufferings in this present time. It is a season of probation. We are still in school. We are learning patience, gentleness, and meekness which we could hardly learn if we had our good things now. But there is an eternal holiday yet to begin. For this let us wait quietly. It will make amends for all. *For momentary, light affliction is producing for us an eternal weight of glory far beyond all comparison* (2 Corinthians 4:17).

Matthew 14:13-21 *Compassionate father*

Now when Jesus heard about John, He withdrew from there in a boat to a secluded place by Himself; and when the people heard of this, they followed Him on foot from the cities. When He went ashore, He saw a large crowd, and felt compassion for them and healed their sick. When it was evening, the disciples came to Him and said, "This place is desolate and the hour is already late; so send the crowds away, that they may go into the villages and buy food for themselves." But Jesus said to them, "They do not need to go away; you give them something to eat!" They said to Him, "We have here only five loaves and two fish." And He said, "Bring them here to Me." Ordering the people to sit down on the grass, He took the five loaves and the two fish, and looking up toward heaven, He blessed the food, and breaking the loaves He gave them to the disciples, and the disciples gave them to the crowds, and they all ate and were satisfied. They picked up what was left over of the broken pieces, twelve full baskets. There were about five thousand men who ate, besides women and children.
(Matthew 14:13-21)

These verses contain one of our Lord Jesus Christ's greatest miracles, the feeding of *five thousand men besides women and children* with five loaves and two fish. Of all the miracles worked by our Lord, not one is so often mentioned in the New Testament as this. Matthew, Mark, Luke, and John all dwell upon it. It is plain that this event in our Lord's history is intended to receive special attention. Let us give it that attention and see what we may learn.

In the first place, this miracle is *an unanswerable proof of our Lord's divine power*. To satisfy the hunger of more than five thousand people with so small a portion of food as five loaves and two fish would be manifestly impossible without a supernatural multiplication of the food. It was a thing that no magician, impostor, or false prophet would ever have attempted. Such a person might possibly pretend to cure a single sick person, or raise a single dead body – and by jugglery and trickery might persuade weak people that he succeeded. But such a person would never attempt such a mighty work as that which is here recorded. He would know well that he could not persuade ten thousand men, women, and children that they were full when they were hungry. He would be exposed as a cheat and impostor on the spot.

Yet this is the mighty work which our Lord actually performed, and by performing it gave a conclusive proof that He was God. He called that into being which did not before exist. He provided visible, tangible, material food for ten thousand people out of a supply which in itself would not have satisfied fifty. Surely we must be blind if we do not see in this the hand of Him *who gives food to all flesh* and made the world and all that is therein. To *create* is the peculiar prerogative of God.

We ought to lay firm hold on such passages as this. We should treasure up in our minds every evidence of our Lord's divine power. The cold, orthodox, and unconverted man may see little in the story. The true believer should store it in his memory. Let him think of the world, the devil, and his own heart, and learn to thank God that his Savior, the Lord Jesus Christ, is almighty.

In the second place, this miracle is *a striking example of our Lord's compassion toward men*. He saw a great company in a desert place ready to faint from hunger. He knew that many in that company had no true faith and love towards Himself. They followed Him out of fashion and curiosity or some equally low motive (John 6:26). But our Lord had pity upon all. All were relieved. All partook of the food miraculously provided. All were *satisfied*, and none went away hungry. Let us see in this the heart of our Lord Jesus Christ towards sinners. He is as He was of old, *the* LORD, *the* LORD *God, compassionate and gracious, slow to anger, and abounding in lovingkindness and truth* (Exodus 34:6). He does not deal with men according to their sins, or reward them according to their iniquities. He loads even His enemies with benefits. None will be so excuseless as those who are found impenitent at last. The Lord's goodness leads them to repentance (Romans 2:4). In all His dealings with men on earth, He showed himself one that *delights in unchanging love* (Micah 7:18). Let us strive to be like Him. "We ought," says Quesnel, "to have abundance of pity and compassion on diseased souls."

In the last place, this miracle is *a lively emblem of the sufficiency of the gospel to meet the soul-needs of all mankind.* There can be little doubt that all our Lord's miracles have a deep figurative meaning and teach great spiritual truths. But they must be handled reverently and discreetly. Care must be taken that we do not, like many of the church Fathers, see allegories where the Holy Spirit meant none to be seen. But perhaps if there is any miracle which has a manifest figurative meaning in addition to the plain lessons which may be drawn from its surface, it is that which is now before us.

What does this hungry multitude in a desert place represent to us? It is an emblem of *all mankind.* The children of men are a large assembly of perishing sinners, famishing in the midst of a wilderness world, helpless, hopeless, and on the way to ruin. We have all gone astray like lost sheep (Isaiah 53:6). We are by nature far away from God. Our eyes may not be opened to the full extent of our danger. But in reality we are wretched, and miserable, and poor, and blind, and naked (Revelation 3:17). There is but a step between us and everlasting death.

What do these loaves and fish represent, apparently so inadequate to meet the necessities of the case, but by a miracle made sufficient to feed ten thousand people? They are an emblem of *the doctrine of Christ crucified for sinners* as their vicarious substitute, and making atonement by His death for the sin of the world. That doctrine seems to the natural man weakness itself. Christ crucified was to the Jews a stumbling block and to the Greeks foolishness (1 Corinthians 1:23). And yet Christ crucified has proved the bread of God which comes down from heaven and gives life to the world (John 6:33). The story of the cross has amply met the spiritual needs of mankind wherever it has been preached. Thousands of every rank, age, and nation are witnesses that it is *the power of God and the wisdom of God.* They have eaten of it and been *satisfied.* They have found it *meat indeed* and *drink indeed.*

Let us ponder these things well. There are great depths in all our Lord Jesus Christ's recorded dealings upon earth which no one has ever fully fathomed. There are mines of rich instruction in all His words and ways which no one has thoroughly explored. Many passages of the Gospels are like the cloud which Elijah's servant saw (1 Kings 18:44). The more we look at it, the greater it will appear. There is an inexhaustible fullness in Scripture. Other writings seem comparatively threadbare when we become familiar with them. But as to Scripture, the more we read it, the richer we shall find it.

Matthew 14:22-36

Immediately He made the disciples get into the boat and go ahead of Him to the other side, while He sent the crowds away. After He had sent the crowds away, He went up on the mountain by Himself to pray; and when it was evening, He was there alone. But the boat was already a long distance from the land, battered by the waves; for the wind was contrary. And in the fourth watch of the night He came to them, walking on the sea. When the disciples saw Him walking on the sea, they were terrified, and said, "It is a ghost!" And they cried out in fear. But immediately Jesus spoke to them, saying, "Take courage, it is I; do not be afraid." Peter said to Him, "Lord, if it is You, command me to come to You on the water." And He said, "Come!" And Peter got out of the boat, and walked on the water and came toward Jesus. But seeing the wind, he became frightened, and beginning to sink, he cried out, "Lord, save me!" Immediately Jesus stretched out His hand and took hold of him, and said to him, "You of little faith, why did you doubt?" When they got into the boat, the wind stopped. And those who were in the boat worshiped Him, saying,

"You are certainly God's Son." When they had crossed over, they came to land Gennesaret. And when the men of that place rec-ognized Him, they sent word into all that surrounding district and brought to Him all who were sick; and they implored Him that they might just touch the fringe of His cloak; and as many as touched it were cured. (Matthew 14:22-36)

The history contained in these verses is one of singular interest. The miracle here recorded brings out in strong light the character both of Christ and His people. The power and mercy of the Lord Jesus, and the mixture of faith and unbelief in His best disciples, are beautifully illustrated.

We learn, in the first place from this miracle, *what absolute dominion our Savior has over all created things.* We see Him *walking on the sea* as if it was dry land. Those angry waves which tossed the ship of His disciples to and fro obey the Son of God and become a solid floor under His feet. That liquid surface, which was agitated by the least breath of wind, bears up the feet of our Redeemer like a rock. To our poor, weak minds, the whole event is utterly incomprehensible. The picture of two feet walking on the sea is said by Doddridge to have been the Egyptian emblem of an impossible thing. The man of science will tell us that for material flesh and blood to walk on water is a physical impossibility. Enough for us to know that it was done. Enough for us to remember that to Him who created the seas at the beginning, it must have been perfectly easy to walk over their waves whenever He pleased.

There is encouragement here for all true Christians. Let them know that *there is nothing created which is not under Christ's control.* All things serve Him. He may allow His people to be tried for a season and tossed to and fro by storms of trouble. He may be later than they wish in coming to their aid and not draw near until the *fourth watch of the night.* But never let them forget that winds, waves, and storms are all Christ's servants. They cannot move without Christ's permission. *More than the sounds of many waters, than the mighty breakers of the sea, the* LORD *on high is mighty* (Psalm 93:4). Are we ever tempted to cry with Jonah, *The current engulfed me. All your breakers and billows passed over me* (Jonah 2:3). Let us remember they are *His* billows. Let us wait patiently. We may yet see Jesus coming to us and *walking on the sea.*

We learn, in the second place from this miracle, *what power Jesus can bestow on those who believe on Him.* We see Simon Peter coming down out of the ship and walking on the water like his Lord. What a wonderful proof was this of our Lord's divinity! To walk on the sea Himself was a mighty miracle. But to enable a poor weak disciple to do the same was a mightier miracle still.

There is a deep meaning in this part of our history. It shows us what great things our Lord can do for those who hear His voice and follow Him. He can enable them to do things which at one time they would have thought impossible. He can carry them through difficulties and trials which without Him they would never have dared to face. He can give them strength to walk through fire and water unharmed, and to get the better of every foe. Moses in Egypt, Daniel in Babylon, and the saints in Nero's household are all examples of His mighty power. Let us fear nothing if we are in the path of duty. The waters may seem deep. But if Jesus says, "Come," we have no cause to be afraid. *He who believes in Me, the works that I do, he will do also; and greater works than these he will do* (John 14:12).

Let us learn, in the third place from this miracle, *how much trouble disciples bring on themselves by unbelief.* We see Peter walking boldly on the water for a little way. But by and by, when be sees *the wind was contrary,* he is afraid and begins to sink. The weak flesh gets the better of the willing spirit. He forgets the wonderful proofs of his Lord's goodness and power which he had just received. He considered not that the same Savior who had enabled him to walk one step must be able to hold him up forever. He did not reflect that he was nearer to Christ when once on the water than he was when he first left the ship. Fear took away his memory. Alarm confused his reason. He thought of nothing but the winds and waves and his immediate danger, and his faith gave way. *"Lord,"* he cried, *"save me!"*

What a lively picture we have here of the experience of many a believer! How many there are who have faith enough to take the first step in following Christ but not faith enough to go on as they began.

They take fright at the trials and dangers which seem to be in their way. They look at the *enemies* that surround them and the *difficulties* that seem likely to beset their path. They dwell on them more than on Jesus, and at once their feet begin to sink. Their hearts faint within them. Their hope vanishes away. Their comforts disappear. And why is all this? Christ is not altered. Their enemies are not greater than they were. It is just because, like Peter, *they have ceased to look to Jesus, and have given way to unbelief.* They are taken up with thinking about their enemies instead of thinking about Christ. May we lay this to heart and learn wisdom.

Let us learn, in the last place from this miracle, *how merciful our Lord Jesus Christ is to weak believers.* We see Him stretching forth His hand immediately to save Peter as soon as Peter cried to Him. He does not leave him to reap the fruit of his own unbelief and sink in the deep waters. He only seems to consider his trouble and to think of nothing so much as delivering him from it. The only word He utters is the gentle reproof, *"You of little faith, why did you doubt?"*

Behold in this concluding part of the miracle the exceeding gentleness of Christ! He can bear with much and forgive much when He sees true grace in a man's heart. As a mother deals gently with her infant and does not cast him away because of his little waywardness and misbehavior, so does the Lord Jesus deal gently with His people. He loved and pitied them before conversion, and after conversion He loves and pities them still more. He knows their feebleness and bears long with them. He would have us know that doubting does not prove that a man has no faith but only that his faith is small. And even when our faith is small, the Lord is ready to help us. *If I should say, "My foot has slipped," Your lovingkindness, O* LORD, *will hold me up* (Psalm 94:18).

How much there is in all this to encourage men to serve Christ! Where is the man who ought to be afraid to begin running the Christian race with such a Savior as Jesus? If we fall, He will raise us again. If we err, He will bring us back. But His mercy shall never be altogether taken from us. He has said, *"I will never desert you, nor will I ever forsake you,"* and He will keep His word. May we only remember that while we do not despise little faith, we must not sit down content with it. Our prayer must ever be to the Lord, *"Increase our faith!"*

Matthew Chapter 15

Matthew 15:1-9

Then some Pharisees and scribes came to Jesus from Jerusalem and said, "Why do Your disciples break the tradition of the elders? For they do not wash their hands when they eat bread." And He answered and said to them, "Why do you yourselves transgress the commandment of God for the sake of your tradition? For God said, 'Honor your father and mother,' and, 'He who speaks evil of father or mother is to be put to death.' But you say, 'Whoever says to his father or mother, "Whatever I have that would help you has been given to God," he is not to honor his father or his mother.' And by this you invalidated the word of God for the sake of your tradition. You hypocrites, rightly did Isaiah prophesy of you: 'This people honors Me with their lips, But their heart is far away from Me. But in vain do they worship Me, teaching as doctrines the precepts of men.'" (Matthew 15:1-9)

WE HAVE IN THESE VERSES A CONVERSATION between our Lord Jesus Christ and certain scribes and Pharisees. The subject of it may seem, at first sight, of little interest in modern days. But it is not so in reality. The principles of the Pharisees are principles that never die. There are truths laid down here which are of deep importance.

We learn, for one thing, that *hypocrites generally attach great importance to mere outward things in religion.* The complaint of the scribes and Pharisees in this place is a striking case in point. They brought an accusation to our Lord against His disciples. But what was its nature? It was not that they were covetous or self-righteous. It was not that they were untruthful or uncharitable. It was not that they had broken any part of the law of God. But they *break the tradition of the elders. For they do not wash their hands when they eat bread.* They did not observe some rule of mere human authority which some old Jew had invented! This was the head and front of their offense!

Do we see nothing of the spirit of the Pharisees in the present day? Unhappily we see only too much. There are thousands of professing Christians who seem to care nothing about the religion of their neighbors, provided that it agrees in outward matters with their own. Does their neighbor worship according to their particular form? Can he repeat their shibboleth and talk a little about their favorite doctrines? If he can, they are satisfied, though there is no evidence that he is converted. If he cannot, they are always finding fault and cannot speak peaceably of him, though he may be serving Christ better than themselves. Let us beware of this spirit. It is the very essence of hypocrisy. Let our principle be: *The kingdom of God is not eating and drinking, but righteousness and peace and joy in the Holy Spirit* (Romans 14:17).

We learn, for another thing from these verses, *the great danger of attempting to add anything to the Word of God.* Whenever a man takes upon him to make additions to the Scriptures, he is likely to end with valuing his own additions above Scripture itself.

We see this point brought out most strikingly in our Lord's answer to the charge of the Pharisees against His disciples. He says, *"Why do you yourselves transgress the commandment of God for the sake of your tradition?"* He strikes boldly at the whole system of adding anything, as needful to salvation, to God's perfect Word. He exposes the mischievous tendency of the system by an example. He shows how the vaunted traditions of the Pharisees were actually destroying the authority of the fifth commandment. In short, He establishes the great truth which ought never to be forgotten, that there is an inherent tendency in all traditions to make the commandment of God void. The authors of these traditions may have meant no such thing. Their intentions may have been pure. But that there is a tendency in all religious institutions of mere human authority to usurp the authority of God's Word is evidently the doctrine of Christ. It is a solemn remark of Bucer's that "a man is rarely to be found, who pays an excessive attention to human inventions in religion, who does not put more trust in them than in the grace of God."

And have we not seen proof of this truth in the history of the church of Christ? Unhappily we have seen only too much. As Baxter says, "Men think God's laws too many and too strict, and yet make more of their own, and are precise for keeping them." Have we never read how some have exalted canons, rubrics, and ecclesiastical laws above the Word of God, and punished disobedience to them with far greater severity than open sins like drunkenness and swearing? Have we never heard of the extravagant importance which the Church of Rome attaches to monastic vows, vows of celibacy, and keeping feasts and fasts, insomuch that she seems to place them far above family duties and the Ten Commandments? Have we never heard of men who make more ado about eating meat during Lent than about gross impurity of life or murder? Have we never observed in our own land how many seem to make adherence to episcopacy the weightiest matter in Christianity, and to regard "churchmanship," as they call it, as far outweighing repentance, faith, holiness, and the graces of the Spirit?

These are questions which can only receive one sorrowful answer. The spirit of the Pharisees still lives, after eighteen hundred years. The disposition to make the commandment of God void by traditions is to be found among Christians as well as among Jews. The tendency practically to exalt man's inventions above God's Word is still fearfully prevalent. May we watch against it and be on our guard! May we remember that no tradition or man-made institution in religion can ever excuse the neglect of relative duties or justify disobedience to any plain commandment of God's Word.

We learn, in the last place from these verses, that *the religious worship which God desires is the worship of the heart.* We find our Lord establishing this by a quotation from Isaiah: *This people honors Me with their lips, but their heart is far away from Me.*

The heart is the principal thing in the relation of husband and wife, of friend and friend, of parent and child. The heart must be the principal point to which we attend in all the relations between God and our souls. What is the first thing we need in order to be Christians? A new heart. What is the sacrifice God asks us to bring to Him? A broken and a contrite heart. What is the true circumcision? The circumcision of the heart. What is genuine obedience? To obey from the heart. What is saving faith? To believe with the heart. Where ought Christ to dwell? To dwell in our hearts by faith. What is the chief request that Wisdom makes to everyone? *Give me your heart, my son.*

Let us leave the passage with honest self-inquiry as to the state of our own hearts. Let us settle it in our minds that all formal worship of God, whether in public or private, is utterly in vain so long as our hearts are far away from Him. The bended knee, the bowed head, the loud amen, the daily chapter, the regular attendance at the Lord's Table, are all useless and unprofitable so long as our affections are nailed to sin, or pleasure, or money, or the world. The question of our Lord must yet be answered satisfactorily before we can be saved. He says to everyone, *"Do you love Me?"* (John 21:17).

Matthew 15:10-20

After Jesus called the crowd to Him, He said to them, "Hear and understand. It is not what enters into the mouth defiles the man, but what proceeds out of the mouth, this defiles the man." Then the disciples came and said to Him, "Do You know that the Pharisees were offended when they heard this statement?" But He answered and said, "Every plant which My heavenly Father did not plant shall be uprooted. Let them alone; they are blind guides of the blind. And if a blind man guides a blind man, both will fall into a pit." Peter said to Him, "Explain the parable to us." Jesus said, "Are you still lacking in understanding also? Do you not understand that everything that goes into the mouth passes into the stomach, and is eliminated? But the things that proceed out of the mouth come from the heart, and those defile the man. For out of the heart come evil thoughts, murders, adulteries, fornications, thefts, false witness, slanders. These are the things which defile the man; but to eat with unwashed hands does not defile the man." (Matthew 15:10-20)

There are two striking sayings of the Lord Jesus in this passage. One concerns false doctrine. The other concerns the human heart. Both of them deserve the closest attention.

Concerning false doctrine, our Lord declares *that it is a duty to oppose it, that its final destruction is sure, and that its teachers ought to be forsaken.* He says, *"Every plant which My heavenly Father did not plant shall be uprooted. Let them alone."*

It is clear from examination of the passage that the disciples were surprised at our Lord's strong language about the Pharisees and their traditions. They had probably been accustomed from their youth to regard them as the wisest and best of men. They were startled to hear their Master denouncing them as hypocrites and charging them with transgressing the commandment of God. *"Do you know,"* they said, *"that the Pharisees were offended?"* To this question we are indebted for our Lord's explanatory declaration – a declaration which perhaps has never received the notice it deserves.

The plain meaning of our Lord's words is that false doctrine like that of the Pharisees was a plant to which no mercy should be shown. It was a plant which His heavenly Father had not planted, and a plant which it was a duty to root up, whatever offense it might cause. It was no charity to spare it, because it was injurious to the souls of men. It mattered nothing that those who planted it were high in office or learned. If it contradicted the Word of God, it ought to be opposed, refuted, and rejected. His disciples must therefore understand that it was right to resist all teaching that was unscriptural and to "let alone" and forsake all instructors who persisted in it. Sooner or later they would find that all false doctrine will be completely overthrown and put to shame, and nothing shall stand but that which is built on the Word of God.

There are lessons of deep wisdom in this saying of our Lord, which serve to throw light on the duty of many a professing Christian. Let us scan them well and see what they are. It was practical obedience to this saying which produced the blessed Protestant Reformation. Its lessons deserve close attention.

Do we not see here *the duty of boldness in resisting false teaching?* Beyond doubt we do. No fear of giving offense and no dread of ecclesiastical censure should make us hold our peace when God's truth is in peril. If we are true followers of our Lord, we ought to be outspoken and unflinching witnesses against error. "Truth," says Musculus, "must not be suppressed because men are wicked and blind."

Do we not see again *the duty of forsaking false teachers if they will not give up their delusions?* Beyond doubt we do. No false delicacy, no mock humility should make us shrink from leaving the ministrations of any minister who contradicts God's Word. It is at our peril if we submit to unscriptural teaching. Our blood will be on our own heads. To use the words of Whitby, "It never can be right to follow the blind into the ditch."

Do we not see, in the last place, *the duty of patience when we see false teaching abound?* Beyond doubt we do. We may take comfort in the thought that it will not stand long. God Himself will defend the cause of His own truth. Sooner or later every heresy *will be uprooted.* We are not to fight with carnal weapons, but rather wait, preach, protest, and pray. Sooner or later, as Wycliffe said, "the truth shall prevail."

Respecting the heart of man, our Lord declares in these verses that *it is the true source of all sin and defilement.* The Pharisees taught that holiness depended on foods and drinks and on bodily washings and purification. They held that all who observed their traditions on these matters were pure and clean in God's sight, and that all who neglected them were impure and unclean. Our Lord overthrew this miserable doctrine by showing His disciples that the real fountain of all defilement was not outside a man but within him. *"For out of the heart,"* He says, *"come evil thoughts, murders, adulteries, fornications, thefts, false witness, slanders. These are the things which defile the man."* He who would serve God aright needs something far more important than bodily washings. He must seek to have *a clean heart.*

What a dreadful picture we have here of human nature, and drawn too by One who knew what was in man. What a fearful catalogue is this of the contents of our own bosoms! What a horrible list of seeds of evil our Lord has exposed, lying deep down within every one of us, and ready at any time to start into active life! What can the proud and self-righteous say when they read such a passage as this? This is no sketch of the heart of a robber or murderer. It is the true and faithful account of the hearts of all mankind. May God grant that we may ponder it well and learn wisdom!

Let it be a settled resolution with us that *in all our religion the state of our hearts shall be the main thing.* Let it not content us to go to church and observe the forms of religion. Let us look far deeper than this and desire to have a heart that is right in the sight of God (Acts 8:21). The right heart is a heart sprinkled with the blood of Christ, renewed by the Holy Spirit, and purified by faith. Never let us rest until we find within the witness of the Spirit that God has created in us a clean heart and made all things new (Psalm 51:10; 2 Corinthians 5:17).

Finally, let it be a settled resolution with us to *watch over [our] heart[s] with all diligence* all the days of our lives (Proverbs 4:23). Even after renewal they are weak. Even after putting on the new man they are deceitful. Let us never forget that *our chief danger is from within.* The world and the devil combined cannot do us so much harm as our own hearts will if we do not watch and pray. Happy is he who remembers daily the words of Solomon: *He who trusts in his own heart is a fool* (Proverbs 28:26).

Matthew 15:21-28

Jesus went away from there, and withdrew into the district of Tyre and Sidon. And a Canaanite woman from that region came out and began to cry out, saying, "Have mercy on me, Lord, Son of David; my daughter is cruelly demon-possessed." But He did not answer her a word. And His disciples came and implored Him, saying, "Send her away, because she keeps shouting at us." But He answered and said, "I was sent only to the lost sheep of the house of Israel." But she came and began to bow down before Him, saying, "Lord, help me!" And He answered and said, "It is not good to take the children's bread and throw it to the dogs." But she said, "Yes, Lord; but even the dogs feed on the crumbs which fall from their masters' table." Then Jesus said to her, "O

woman, your faith is great; it shall be done for you as you wish."
And her daughter was healed at once. (Matthew 15:21-28)

Another of our Lord's miracles is recorded in these verses. The circumstances which attend it are peculiarly full of interest. Let us take them up in order and see what they are. Every word in these narratives is rich in instruction.

We see, in the first place, that *true faith may sometimes be found where it might have been least expected.* A Canaanite woman cries to our Lord for help on behalf of her daughter. *"Have mercy on me,"* she says, *"Lord, Son of David."* Such a request would have showed great faith had she lived in Bethany or Jerusalem. But when we find that she came from the *district of Tyre and Sidon,* such a request may well fill us with surprise. It ought to teach us that it is grace, not place, which makes people believers. We may live in a prophet's family, like Gehazi, the servant of Elisha, and yet continue impenitent, unbelieving, and fond of the world. We may dwell in the midst of superstition and dark idolatry, like the little maid in Naaman's house, and yet be faithful witnesses for God and His Christ. Let us not despair of anyone's soul merely because his lot is cast in an unfavorable position. It is possible to dwell in the *district of Tyre and Sidon* and yet sit down in the kingdom of God.

We see, in the second place, that *affliction sometimes proves a blessing to a person's soul.* This Canaanite mother no doubt had been severely tried. She had seen her darling child vexed with a devil and been unable to relieve her. But yet that trouble prompted her to seek Christ. Without it she might have lived and died in careless ignorance and never seen Jesus at all. Surely it was good for her that she was afflicted (Psalm 119:71).

Let us pay close attention to this. There is nothing which shows our ignorance so much as our impatience under trouble. We forget that every cross is a message from God and intended to do us good in the end. Trials are intended to make us think, to wean us from the world, to send us to the Bible, and to drive us to our knees. Health is a good thing, but sickness is far better if it leads us to God. Prosperity is a great mercy, but adversity is a greater one if it brings us to Christ. Anything, anything is better than living in carelessness and dying in sin. Better a thousand times be afflicted like the Canaanite mother and like her flee to Christ, than live at ease like the rich *fool* and die at last without Christ and without hope (Luke 12:20).

We see, in the third place, that *Christ's people are often less gracious and compassionate than Christ Himself*. The woman about whom we are reading found small favor with our Lord's disciples. Perhaps they regarded an inhabitant of the district of Tyre and Sidon as unworthy of their Master's help. At any rate they said, *"Send her away."*

There is only too much of this spirit among many who profess and call themselves believers. They are apt to discourage inquirers after Christ instead of helping them forward. They are too ready to doubt the reality of a beginner's grace because it is small, and to treat him as Saul was treated when he first came to Jerusalem after his conversion in *not believing that he was a disciple* (Acts 9:26). Let us beware of giving way to this spirit. Let us seek to have more of the mind that was in Christ. Like Him, let us be gentle, and kind, and encouraging in all our treatment of those who are seeking to be saved. Above all, let us tell men continually that *they must not judge Christ by Christians*. Let us assure them that there is far more in that gracious Master than there is in the best of His servants. Peter, James, and John may say to the afflicted soul, *"Send her away,"* but such a word never came from the lips of Christ. He may sometimes keep us waiting a long time, as He did this woman, but He will never send us away empty.

We see, in the last place, *what encouragement there is to persevere in prayer, both for ourselves and others*. It is hard to conceive a more striking illustration of this truth than we have in this passage. The prayer of this afflicted mother at first seemed entirely unnoticed – Jesus *did not answer her a word*. Yet she persisted. The answer which by and by fell from our Lord's lips sounded discouraging: *"I was sent only to the lost sheep of the house of Israel."* Yet she said, *"Lord, help me!"* The second answer of our Lord was even less encouraging than the first: *"It is not good to take the children's bread and throw it to the dogs."* Yet *hope deferred* did not make her heart sick (Proverbs 13:12). Even then she was not silenced. Even then she finds a plea for some *crumbs* of mercy to be granted to her. And her importunity obtained at last a gracious reward. *"O woman, your faith is great; it shall be done for you as you wish."* That promise has never been broken: *"Seek, and you will find"* (Matthew 7:7).

Let us remember this history *when we pray for ourselves.* We are sometimes tempted to think that we get no good by our prayers and that we may as well give them up altogether. Let us resist the temptation. It comes from the devil. Let us believe and pray on. Against our besetting sins, against the spirit of the world, against the wiles of the devil, let us pray on and not faint. For strength to do duty, for grace to bear our trials, for comfort in every trouble, let us continue in prayer. Let us be sure that *no time is so well-spent in every day as that which we spend upon our knees.* Jesus hears us and in His own good time will give an answer.

Let us remember this history *when we intercede for others.* Have we children whose conversion we desire? Have we relatives and friends about whose salvation we are anxious? Let us follow the example of this Canaanite woman and lay the state of their souls before Christ. Let us name their names before Him night and day and never rest until we have an answer. We may have to wait many a long year. We may seem to pray in vain and intercede without profit. But let us never give up. Let us believe that Jesus is not changed, and that He who heard the Canaanite mother and granted her request will also hear us and one day give us an answer of peace.

Matthew 15:29-39

Departing from there, Jesus went along by the Sea of Galilee, and having gone up on the mountain, He was sitting there. And large crowds came to Him, bringing with them those who were lame, crippled, blind, mute, and many others, and they laid them down at His feet; and He healed them. So the crowd marveled as they saw the mute speaking, the crippled restored, and the lame walking, and the blind seeing; and they glorified the God of Israel. And Jesus called His disciples to Him, and said, "I feel

160

compassion for the people, because they have remained with Me now three days and have nothing to eat; and I do not want to send them away hungry, for they might faint on the way." The disciples said to Him, "Where would we get so many loaves in this desolate place to satisfy such a large crowd?" And Jesus said to them, "How many loaves do you have?" And they said, "Seven, and a few small fish." And He directed the people to sit down on the ground; and He took the seven loaves and the fish; and giving thanks, He broke them and started giving them to the disciples, and the disciples gave them to the people. And they all ate and were satisfied, and they picked up what was left over of the broken pieces, seven large baskets full. And those who ate were four thousand men, besides women and children. And sending away the crowds, Jesus got into the boat and came to the region of Magadan. (Matthew 15:29-39)

The beginning of this passage contains three points which deserve our special attention. For the present, let us dwell exclusively on them.

In the first place, let us remark *how much more pain people take about the relief of their bodily diseases than about their souls.* We read that *large crowds came to Him, bringing with them those who were lame, crippled, blind, mute, and many others.* Many of them, no doubt, had journeyed many miles and gone through great fatigues. Nothing is so difficult and troublesome as to move sick people. But the *hope of being healed* was in sight. Such hope is everything to a sick man.

We know little of human nature if we wonder at the conduct of these people. We need not wonder at all. They felt that health was the greatest of earthly blessings. They felt that pain was the hardest of all trials to bear. There is no arguing against sense. A man feels his strength failing. He sees his body wasting and his face becoming pale. He is sensing that his appetite is leaving him. He knows, in short, that he is ill and needs a physician. Show him a physician within reach who is said never to fail in working cures, and he will go to him without delay.

Let us, however, not forget that *our souls are far more diseased than our bodies,* and learn a lesson from the conduct of these people. Our

↪ Don't forget to heal the Spirit

souls are afflicted with a malady far more deep-seated, far more complicated, and far more hard to cure than any ailment that flesh is heir to. They are in fact plague-stricken by sin. They must be healed, and healed effectually, or perish everlastingly. Do we really know this? Do we feel it? Are we alive to our spiritual disease? Alas! there is but one answer to these questions. The bulk of mankind do not feel it at all. Their eyes are blinded. They are utterly insensible to their danger. For bodily health they crowd the waiting rooms of doctors. For bodily health they take long journeys to find purer air. But for their soul's health they take no thought at all. Happy indeed is that man or woman who has found out his soul's disease! Such a one will never rest until he has found Jesus. Troubles will seem like nothing to him. Life, life, eternal life is at stake. He will count all things loss that he may win Christ and be healed.

In the second place, let us notice *the marvelous ease and power with which our Lord healed all who were brought to Him.* We read that *the crowd marveled as they saw the mute speaking, the crippled restored, and the lame walking, and the blind seeing; and they glorified the God of Israel.*

Behold in these words a lively emblem of our Lord Jesus Christ's power to heal sin-diseased souls! There is no ailment of heart that He cannot cure. There is no form of spiritual complaint that He cannot overcome. The fever of lust, the palsy of the love of the world, the slow consumption of indolence and sloth, the heart-disease of unbelief – all, all give way when He sends forth His Spirit on any one of the children of men. He can put a new song in a sinner's mouth and make him speak with love of that gospel which he once ridiculed and blasphemed. He can open the eyes of a man's understanding and make him see the kingdom of God. He can open the ears of a man and make him willing to hear His voice and follow Him wherever He goes. He can give power to a man who once walked in the broad way that leads unto destruction to walk in the way of life. He can make hands that were once instruments of sin serve Him and do His will. The time of miracles is not yet past. Every conversion is a miracle. Have we ever seen a real instance of conversion? Let us know that we saw in it the hand of Christ. We should have seen nothing really greater if we had seen our Lord making the dumb to speak and the lame to walk when He was on earth.

Would we know what to do if we desire to be saved? Do we feel soul-sick and want a cure? We must just go to Christ by faith and apply to Him for relief. He has not changed. Eighteen hundred years have made no difference in Him. High at the right hand of God He is still the Great Physician. He still *receives sinners*. He is still mighty to heal.

In the third place, let us notice *the abundant compassion of our Lord Jesus Christ*. We read that Jesus summoned His disciples and said, *"I feel compassion for the people."* A great crowd of men and women is always a solemn sight. It should stir our hearts to feel that each is a dying sinner and each has a soul to be saved. No one ever seems to have felt so much when he saw a crowd as Christ did.

It is a curious and striking fact that of all the feelings experienced by our Lord when upon earth, there is none so often mentioned as *compassion*. His joy, His sorrow, His thankfulness, His anger, His wonder, and His zeal are all occasionally recorded. But none of these feelings are so frequently mentioned as *compassion*. The Holy Spirit seems to point out to us that this was the distinguishing feature of His character and the predominant feeling of His mind when He was among men. Thirteen times over – to say nothing of expressions in parables – the Spirit has caused that word *compassion* to be written in the Gospels.

There is something very touching and instructive in this circumstance. Nothing is written by chance in the Word of God. There is a special reason for the selection of every single expression. That word *compassion* no doubt was specially chosen for our profit.

It ought to encourage all who are hesitating about beginning to walk in God's ways. Let them remember that their Savior is full of compassion. He will receive them graciously. He will forgive them freely. He will remember their former iniquities no more. He will abundantly supply all their needs. Let them not be afraid. *Christ's mercy is a deep well of which no one ever found the bottom.*

It ought to comfort the saints and servants of the Lord when they feel weary. Let them call to mind that Jesus is full of compassion. He knows what a world it is in which they live. He knows the body of a man and all its frailties. He knows the devices of their enemy, the devil. And the Lord pities His people. Let them not be cast down. They may feel that weakness, failure, and imperfection are stamped on all they do. But let them not forget that word which says, *His compassions never fail* (Lamentations 3:22).

Matthew Chapter 16

Don't be the Pharisees + Sadducees

Matthew 16:1-12

The Pharisees and Sadducees came up, and testing Jesus, they asked Him to show them a sign from heaven. But He replied to them, "When it is evening, you say, 'It will be fair weather, for the sky is red.' And in the morning, 'There will be a storm today, for the sky is red and threatening.' Do you know how to discern the appearance of the sky, but cannot discern the signs of the times? <u>An evil and adulterous generation seeks after a sign; and a sign will not be given it,</u> except the sign of Jonah." And He left them and went away. And the disciples came to the other side of the sea, but they had forgotten to bring any bread. And Jesus said to them, "Watch out and beware of the leaven of the Pharisees and Sadducees." They began to discuss this among themselves, saying, "He said that because we did not bring any bread." But Jesus, aware of this, said, "You men of little faith, why do you discuss among yourselves that you have no bread? Do you not yet understand or remember the five loaves of the five thousand, and how many baskets full you picked up? Or the seven loaves of the four thousand, and how many large baskets full you picked up? How is it that you do not understand that I did not speak to you concerning bread? But beware of the leaven of the Pharisees and Sadducees." Then they understood that He did not say to beware of the leaven of bread, but of the teaching of the Pharisees and Sadducees. (Matthew 16:1-12)

IN THESE VERSES WE FIND OUR LORD ASSAILED by the untiring

enmity of the Pharisees and Sadducees. As a general rule these two sects were at enmity between themselves. In persecuting Christ, however, they had a common cause. Truly it was *an unholy alliance!* Yet how often we see the same thing in the present day. Men of the most opposite opinions and habits will agree in disliking the gospel and will work together to oppose its progress. *There is no new thing under the sun* (Ecclesiastes 1:9).

The first point in this passage which deserves special notice is *the repetition which our Lord makes of words used by Him on a former occasion.* He says, *"An evil and adulterous generation seeks after a sign; and a sign will not be given it, except the sign of Jonah."* If we turn to the twelfth chapter of this Gospel and the thirty-ninth verse, we shall find that He had said the very same thing once before.

This repetition may seem a trifling and unimportant matter in the eyes of some. But it is not so in reality. It throws light on a subject which has perplexed the minds of many sincere lovers of the Bible, and ought therefore to be specially observed.

This repetition shows us that our Lord was in the habit of saying the same things over again. He did not content Himself with saying a thing once, and afterwards never repeating it. It is evident that it was His custom to bring forward certain truths again and again, and thus to impress them more deeply on the minds of His disciples. He knew the weakness of our memories in spiritual things. He knew that what we hear twice we remember better than what we hear once. He therefore brought out of His treasury old things as well as new.

Now what does all this teach us? It teaches us that we need not be so anxious to harmonize the narratives we read in the four Gospels, as many are disposed to be. It does not follow that the sayings of our Lord which we find the same in Matthew and Luke were always used at the same time, or that the events with which they are connected must necessarily be the same. Matthew may be describing one event in our Lord's life. Luke may be describing another. And yet the words of our Lord on both occasions may have been precisely alike. To attempt to make out the two events to be one and the same because of the sameness of the words used has often led Bible students into great difficulties. It is far safer to hold the view here maintained that at different times our Lord often used the same words.

The second point which deserves special notice in these verses is *the solemn warning which our Lord takes occasion to give to His disciples.* His mind was evidently pained with the false doctrines which He saw among the Jews and the pernicious influence they exercised. He seizes the opportunity to utter a caution. *"Watch out and beware of the leaven of the Pharisees and Sadducees."* Let us pay close attention to what those words contain.

To whom was this warning addressed? To the twelve apostles – to the first ministers of the church of Christ – to men who had forsaken all for the gospel's sake! Even *they* are warned! The best of men are only men, and at any time may fall into temptation. *Let him who thinks he stands take heed that he does not fall.* If we love life and desire to see good days, let us never think that we do not need that hint, *"Watch out and beware."*

Against what does our Lord warn His apostles? Against the *doctrine* of the Pharisees and the Sadducees. The Pharisees, we are frequently told in the Gospels, were self-righteous formalists. The Sadducees were skeptics, freethinkers, and half infidels. Yet even Peter, James, and John must beware of their doctrines! Truly, the best and holiest of believers must well be on their guard!

By what figure does our Lord describe the false doctrines against which He cautions His disciples? He calls them *leaven.* Like leaven, they might seem a small thing compared to the whole body of truth. Like leaven, once admitted they would work secretly and noiselessly. Like leaven, they would gradually change the whole character of the religion with which they were mixed. How much is often contained in a single word! It was not merely the open danger of heresy, but also the *leaven* of which the apostles were to beware.

There is much in all of this that calls loudly for the close attention of all professing Christians. The caution of our Lord in this passage has been shamefully neglected. It would have been well for the church of Christ if the warnings of the gospel had been as much studied as its promises.

Let us then remember that this saying of our Lord's about the *leaven of the Pharisees and Sadducees* was intended for all time. It was not meant only for the generation to which it was spoken. It was meant for the perpetual benefit of the church of Christ. He who spoke it saw with prophetical eye the future history of Christianity. The Great Physician knew well that Pharisee doctrines and Sadducee doctrines would prove the two great wasting diseases of His church until the end of the world. He would have us know that there will always be Pharisees and Sadducees in the ranks of Christians. Their succession shall never fail. Their generation shall never become extinct. Their name may change, but their spirit will always remain. Therefore He cries to us, "*Watch out and beware.*"

Finally, let us make a personal use of this caution by keeping up a holy jealousy over our own souls. Let us remember that we live in a world where Pharisaism and Sadduceeism are continually striving for mastery in the church of Christ. Some want to add to the gospel, and some want to take away from it. Some would bury it, and some would pare it down to nothing. Some would stifle it by heaping on additions, and some would bleed it to death by subtraction from its truths. Both parties agree only in one respect: both would kill and destroy the life of Christianity if they succeeded in having their own way. Against both errors let us watch and pray and stand upon our guard. Let us not add to the gospel to please the Roman Catholic Pharisee. Let us not subtract from the gospel to please the Neologian Sadducee. Let our principle be "the truth, the whole truth, and nothing but the truth" – nothing added to it and nothing taken away.

Matthew 16:13-20

Now when Jesus came into the district of Caesarea Philippi, He was asking His disciples, "Who do people say that the Son of Man is?" And they said, "Some say John the Baptist; and others, Elijah; but still others, Jeremiah, or one of the prophets." He said to them, "But who do you say that I am?" Simon Peter answered,

"You are the Christ, the Son of the living God." And Jesus said to
him, "Blessed are you, Simon Barjona, because flesh and blood
did not reveal this to you, but My Father who is in heaven. I also
say to you that you are Peter, and upon this rock I will build My
church; and the gates of Hades will not overpower it. I will give
you the keys of the kingdom of heaven; and whatever you bind on
earth shall have been bound in heaven, and whatever you loose
on earth shall have been loosed in heaven." Then He warned
the disciples that they should tell no one that He was the Christ.
(Matthew 16:13-20)

There are words in this passage which have led to painful differences
and divisions among Christians. Men have striven and contended about
their meaning until they have lost sight of all charity, and yet failed to
carry conviction to one another's minds. Let it suffice us to glance briefly
at the controverted words and then pass on to more practical lessons.

What then are we to understand when we read that remarkable saying
of our Lord's, *"You are Peter, and upon this rock I will build My church"*?
Does it mean that the apostle Peter himself was to be the foundation
on which Christ's church was to be built? Such an interpretation, to
say the least, appears exceedingly improbable. To speak of an erring,
fallible child of Adam as the foundation of the spiritual temple is very
unlike the ordinary language of Scripture. Above all, no reason can be
given why our Lord should not have said, "I will build My church upon
you," if such had been His meaning, instead of saying, *"Upon this rock*
I will build My church."

The true meaning of "this rock" in this passage appears to be the truth
of our Lord's messiahship and divinity which Peter had just confessed.
It is as though our Lord had said, "You are rightly called by the name
Peter, or stone, for you have confessed that mighty truth on which, as
on a rock, I will build my church."

But what are we to understand when we read the promise which our
Lord makes to Peter, *"I will give you the keys of the kingdom of heaven"*?
Do these words mean that the right of admitting souls to heaven was
to be placed in Peter's hands? The idea is preposterous. Such an office

is the special prerogative of Christ Himself (Revelation 1:18). Do the words mean that Peter was to have any primacy or superiority over the rest of the apostles? There is not the slightest proof that such a meaning was attached to the words in the New Testament times or that Peter had any rank or dignity above the rest of the twelve.

The true meaning of the promise to Peter appears to be that *he was to have the special privilege of first opening the door of salvation both to the Jews and the Gentiles.* This was fulfilled to the letter when he preached on the day of Pentecost to the Jews and visited the Gentile Cornelius at his own house. On each occasion he used *the keys* and threw open the door of faith. And of this he seems to have been sensible himself: *"God,"* he says, *"made a choice among you, that by my mouth the Gentiles would hear the word of the gospel and believe"* (Acts 15:7).

Finally, what are we to understand when we read the words, *"Whatever you bind on earth shall have been bound in heaven, and whatever you loose on earth shall have been loosed in heaven"*? Does this mean that the apostle Peter was to have any power of forgiving sins and absolving sinners? Such an idea is derogatory to Christ's special office as our Great High Priest. It is a power which we never find Peter or any of the apostles at all exercising. They always refer men to Christ.

The true meaning of this promise appears to be that Peter and his brethren, the apostles, were to be *specially commissioned to teach with authority the way of salvation.* As the Old Testament priest declared authoritatively whose leprosy was cleansed, so the apostles were appointed to "declare and pronounce" authoritatively whose sins were forgiven. Besides this, they were to be specially inspired to lay down rules and regulations for the guidance of the church on disputed questions. Some things they were to *bind* or forbid, others they were to *loose* or allow. The decision of the council at Jerusalem, that the Gentiles need not be circumcised, was one example of the exercise of this power (Acts 15:19). But it was a commission specially confined to the apostles. In discharging it they had no successors. With them it began, and with them it expired.

We will leave these controverted words here. Enough perhaps has been said upon them for our personal edification. Let us only remember that in whatever sense men take them, they have nothing to do with the Church of Rome. Let us now turn our attention to points which more immediately concern our own souls.

In the first place, let us admire *the noble confession which the apostle Peter makes in this passage.* He says in reply to our Lord's question, *"Who do people say that the Son of Man is?"* that *"You are the Christ, the Son of the living God."*

At first sight, a careless reader may see nothing very remarkable in these words of the apostle. He may think it extraordinary that they should call forth such strong commendation from our Lord. But such thoughts arise from ignorance and inconsideration. Men forget that it is a widely different thing to believe in Christ's divine mission when we dwell in the midst of professing Christians, and to believe in it when we dwell in the midst of hardened and unbelieving Jews. The glory of Peter's confession lies in this, that he made it when few were with Christ and many were against Him. He made it when the rulers of his own nation, the scribes, and priests, and Pharisees, were all opposed to his Master. He made it when our Lord was in the *form of a bond-servant,* without wealth, without royal dignity, and without any visible marks of a king. To make such a confession at such a time required great faith and great decision of character. The confession itself, as Brentius says, "was an epitome of all Christianity, and a compendium of true doctrine about religion." Therefore it was that our Lord said, *"Blessed are you, Simon Barjona."*

We shall do well to copy that hearty zeal and affection which Peter here displayed. We are perhaps too much disposed to underrate this holy man because of his occasional instability and his thrice-repeated denial of his Lord. This is a great mistake. With all his faults, Peter was a truehearted, fervent, single-minded servant of Christ. With all his imperfections, he has given us a pattern that many Christians would be wise to follow. Zeal like his may have its ebbs and flows and sometimes lack steadiness of purpose. Zeal like his may be ill-directed and sometimes make sad mistakes. But zeal like his is not to be despised. It awakens the sleeping. It stirs the sluggish. It provokes others to exertion. Anything is better than sluggishness, lukewarmness, and apathy in the church of Christ. Happy would it have been for Christendom had there been more Christians like Peter and Martin Luther, and fewer like Erasmus.

In the next place, let us take care that *we understand what our Lord means when He speaks of His church.* The church which Jesus promises to build upon a rock is the blessed company of all believing people. It is not the *visible* church of any one nation, or country, or place. It is the whole body of believers of every age, and tongue, and people. It is a church composed of all who are washed in Christ's blood, clothed in Christ's righteousness, renewed by Christ's Spirit, joined to Christ by faith, and are epistles of Christ in life. It is a church of which every member is baptized with the Holy Spirit and is really and truly holy. It is a church which is one body. All who belong to it are of one heart and one mind, hold the same truths, and believe the same doctrines as necessary to salvation. It is a church which has only one Head. That Head is Jesus Christ Himself. *He is also head of the body* (Colossians 1:18).

Let us beware of mistakes on this subject. Few words are so misunderstood as the word *church.* Few mistakes have so much injured the cause of pure religion. Ignorance on this point has been a fertile source of bigotry, sectarianism, and persecution. Men have wrangled and contended about Episcopal, Presbyterian, and Independent churches as if it were needful to salvation to belong to some particular party, and as if, belonging to that party, we must of course belong to Christ. And all this time they have lost sight of the one true church, outside of which there is no salvation at all. It will matter nothing at the last day where we have worshiped, if we are not found as members of the true church of God's elect.

In the last place, let us notice *the glorious promises our Lord makes to His church.* He says, *"The gates of Hades will not overpower it."* The meaning of this promise is that the power of Satan shall never destroy the people of Christ. He that brought sin and death into the first creation by tempting Eve shall never bring ruin on the new creation by overthrowing believers. The mystical body of Christ shall never perish or decay. Though often persecuted, afflicted, distressed, and brought low, it shall never come to an end. It shall outlive the wrath of pharaohs and Roman emperors. Visible churches, like Ephesus, may come to nothing. But the true church never dies. Like the bush that Moses saw, it may burn, but it shall not be consumed. Every member of it shall be brought safely to glory. In spite of falls, failures, and shortcomings, in spite of the world, the flesh, and the devil – no member of the true church shall ever be cast away (John 10:28).

Matthew 16:21-23

From that time Jesus began to show His disciples that He must go to Jerusalem, and suffer many things from the elders and chief priests and scribes, and be killed, and be raised up on the third day. Peter took Him aside and began to rebuke Him, saying, "God forbid it, Lord! This shall never happen to You." But He turned and said to Peter, "Get behind Me, Satan! You are a stumbling block to Me; for you are not setting your mind on God's interests, but man's." (Matthew 16:21-23)

In the beginning of these verses we find our Lord revealing to His disciples a great and startling truth. That truth was His approaching death upon the cross. For the first time He places before their minds the astounding announcement *that He must go to Jerusalem, and suffer and be killed.* He had not come on earth to take a kingdom, but to die. He had not come to reign and be served, but to shed His blood as a sacrifice and to give His life as a ransom for many.

It is almost impossible for us to conceive how strange and incomprehensible these tidings must have seemed to His disciples. Like most of the Jews, they could form no idea of a *suffering* Messiah. They did not understand that the fifty-third chapter of Isaiah must be literally fulfilled. They did not see that the sacrifices of the law were all meant to point them to the death of the true Lamb of God. They thought of nothing but the second glorious coming of Messiah, which is yet to take place at the end of the world. They thought so much of Messiah's crown that they lost sight of His cross. We shall do well to remember this. A right understanding of this matter throws strong light on the lessons this passage contains.

We learn, in the first place from these verses, that *there may be much spiritual ignorance even in a true disciple of Christ.* We cannot have a clearer proof of this than the conduct of the apostle Peter in this passage. He tries to dissuade our Lord from suffering on the cross. *"God forbid it, Lord!"* he says. *"This shall never happen to You."* He did not see the full purpose of our Lord's coming into the world. His eyes were blinded to the necessity of our Lord's death. He actually did what he could to prevent that death from taking place at all! And yet we know that Peter was a converted man. He really believed that Jesus was the Messiah. His heart was right in the sight of God.

These things are meant to teach us that we must neither regard saved men as infallible because they are saved men, nor yet suppose they have no grace because their grace is weak and small. One brother may possess singular gifts and be a bright and shining light in the church of Christ. But let us not forget that he is a man, and as a man, he is liable to commit great mistakes. Another brother's knowledge may be scanty. He may fail to judge rightly on many points of doctrine. He may err both in word and deed. But has he faith and love towards Christ? Does he hold to the Head? If so, let us deal patiently with him. What he sees not now he may see hereafter. Like Peter, he may now be in the dark, and yet, like Peter, enjoy one day the full light of the gospel.

Let us learn, in the second place from these verses, that *there is no doctrine of Scripture so deeply important as the doctrine of Christ's atoning death.* We cannot have clearer proof of this than the language used by our Lord in rebuking Peter. He addresses him by the dreadful name of *Satan,* as if he was an adversary and was doing the devil's work in trying to prevent His death. He says to him, whom he had so lately called *blessed, "Get behind Me, Satan! You are a stumbling block to Me."* He tells the man whose noble confession He had just commended so highly, *"for you are not setting your mind on God's interests, but man's."* Stronger words than these never fell from our Lord's lips. The error that drew from so loving a Savior such a stern rebuke to such a true disciple must have been a mighty error indeed.

The truth is that our Lord would have us regard the crucifixion as the central truth of Christianity. Right views of His vicarious death and the benefits resulting from it lie at the very foundation of biblical religion. Never let us forget this. On matters of church government and the form of worship, men may differ from us and yet reach heaven in safety. On the matter of Christ's atoning death as the way of peace, there is only one truth. If we are wrong here, we are ruined forever. *Error on many other points is only a skin disease. Error about Christ's death is a disease of the heart.* Here let us take our stand. Let nothing move us from this ground. The sum of all our hopes must be that Christ has died for us (1 Thessalonians 5:10). Give up that doctrine, and we have no solid hope at all.

Matthew 16:24-28

Then Jesus said to His disciples, "If anyone wishes to come after Me, he must deny himself, and take up his cross and follow Me. For whoever wishes to save his life will lose it; but whoever loses his life for My sake will find it. For what will it profit a man if he gains the whole world and forfeits his soul? Or what will a man give in exchange for his soul? For the Son of Man is going to come in the glory of His Father with His angels, and will then repay every man according to his deeds. Truly I say to you, there are some of those who are standing here who will not taste death until they see the Son of Man coming in His kingdom." (Matthew 16:24-28)

In order to see the connection of these verses, we must remember the mistaken impressions of our Lord's disciples as to the purpose of His coming into the world. Like Peter, they could not bear the idea of the crucifixion. They thought that Jesus had come to set up an earthly kingdom. They did not see that He must suffer and die. They dreamed of worldly honors and temporal rewards in their Master's service. They did not understand that true Christians, like Christ, must be made perfect through sufferings. Our Lord corrects these misapprehensions in words of peculiar solemnity, which we shall do well to lay up in our hearts.

Let us learn, in the first place from these verses, that *men must make up their minds to trouble and self-denial if they follow Christ.* Our Lord dispels the fond dreams of His disciples by telling them that His followers must *take up their cross.* The glorious kingdom they were expecting was not about to be set up immediately. They must make up their minds to accept persecution and affliction if they intended to be His servants. They must be content to "lose their lives" if they would have their souls saved.

It is good for us all to see this point clearly. We must not conceal from ourselves that true Christianity brings with it a daily cross in this life, while it offers us a crown of glory in the life to come. The flesh must be daily crucified. The devil must be daily resisted. The world must be daily overcome. There is a warfare to be waged and a battle to be fought. All this is the inseparable accompaniment of true religion. Heaven is not to be won without it. Never was there a truer word than the old saying, "No cross, no crown!" If we never find this out by experience, our souls are in a poor condition.

Let us learn, in the second place from these verses, that *there is nothing so precious as a man's soul.* Our Lord teaches this lesson by asking one of the most solemn questions that the New Testament contains. It is a question so well known and so often repeated, that people often lose sight of its searching character. But it is a question that ought to sound in our ears like a trumpet whenever we are tempted to neglect our eternal interests: *"What will it profit a man if he gains the whole world and forfeits his soul?"*

There can only be one answer to this question. There is nothing on earth, or under the earth, that can make amends to us for the loss of our souls. There is nothing that money can buy, or man can give, to be named in comparison with our souls. The world and all that it contains is temporal. It is all fading, perishing, and passing away. The soul is eternal. That one single word is the key to the whole question. Let it sink down deeply into our hearts. Are we wavering in our religion? Do we fear the cross? Does the way seem too narrow? Let our Master's words ring in our ears, *"What will it profit a man?"* and let us doubt no more.

Let us learn, in the last place, that *the second coming of Christ is the time when His people shall receive their rewards.* *"For the Son of Man is going to come in the glory of His Father with His angels, and will then repay every man according to his deeds."*

There is deep wisdom in this saying of our Lord's when viewed in connection with the preceding verses. He knows the heart of a man. He knows how soon we are ready to be cast down and like Israel of old to become *impatient because of the journey.* He therefore holds out to us a gracious promise. He reminds us that He will come a second time as surely as He came the first time. He tells us that this is the time when His disciples shall receive their good things. There will be glory, honor, and reward in abundance one day for all who have served and loved Jesus. But it is to be in the dispensation of the second advent and not of the first. The bitter must come before the sweet, the cross before the crown. The first advent is the dispensation of the crucifixion. The second advent is the dispensation of the kingdom. We must submit to take part with our Lord in His humiliation if we mean ever to share in His glory.

And now let us not leave these verses without serious self-inquiry as to the matters which they contain. We have heard of the necessity of taking up the cross and denying ourselves. Have we taken it up and are we carrying it daily? We have heard of the value of the soul. Do we live as if we believed it? We have heard of Christ's second advent. Do we look forward to it with hope and joy? Happy is that man who can give a satisfactory answer to these questions.

Matthew Chapter 17

Matthew 17:1-13

*Six days later Jesus took with Him Peter and James and John
his brother, and led them up on a high mountain by themselves.
And He was transfigured before them; and His face shone like
the sun, and His garments became as white as light. And behold,
Moses and Elijah appeared to them, talking with Him. Peter
said to Jesus, "Lord, it is good for us to be here; if You wish, I will
make three tabernacles here, one for You, and one for Moses,
and one for Elijah." While he was still speaking, a bright cloud
overshadowed them, and behold, a voice out of the cloud said,
"This is My beloved Son, with whom I am well-pleased; listen to
Him!" When the disciples heard this, they fell face down to the
ground and were terrified. And Jesus came to them and touched
them and said, "Get up, and do not be afraid." And lifting up
their eyes, they saw no one except Jesus Himself alone. As they
were coming down from the mountain, Jesus commanded them,
saying, "Tell the vision to no one until the Son of Man has risen
from the dead." And His disciples asked Him, "Why then do the
scribes say that Elijah must come first?" And He answered and
said, "Elijah is coming and will restore all things; but I say to you
that Elijah already came, and they did not recognize him, but did
to him whatever they wished. So also the Son of Man is going to
suffer at their hands." Then the disciples understood that He had
spoken to them about John the Baptist.* (Matthew 17:1-13)

THESE VERSES CONTAIN ONE OF THE MOST REMARKABLE

events in our Lord's earthly ministry – the event commonly called the *transfiguration*. The order in which it is recorded is beautiful and instructive. The latter part of the last chapter shows us the cross. Here we are graciously allowed to see something of the coming reward. The hearts which have just been saddened by a plain statement of Christ's sufferings are at once gladdened by a vision of Christ's glory. Let us pay close attention to this. We often lose much by not tracing the connection between chapter and chapter in the Word of God.

There are some mysterious things, no doubt, in the vision here described. It must needs be so. We are yet in the body. Our senses are conversant with physical and material things. Our ideas and perceptions about glorified bodies and dead saints must necessarily be vague and imperfect. Let us content ourselves with endeavoring to mark out the practical lessons which the transfiguration is meant to teach us.

In the first place, we have in these verses a *striking pattern of the glory in which Christ and His people will appear when He comes the second time*. There can be little question that this was one main object of this wonderful vision. It was meant to encourage the disciples by giving them a glimpse of good things yet to come. That face that *shone like the sun* and those clothes that *became as white as light* were intended to give the disciples some idea of the majesty in which Jesus will appear to the world when He comes the second time and all His saints with Him. The corner of the veil was lifted up to show them their Master's true dignity. They were taught that if He did not yet appear to the world in the semblance of a king, it was only because the time for putting on His royal apparel was not yet come. It is impossible to draw any other conclusion from Peter's language when writing on the subject. He says with distinct reference to the transfiguration, *We were eyewitnesses of His majesty* (2 Peter 1:16).

It is good for us to have the coming glory of Christ and His people deeply impressed on our minds. We are sadly apt to forget it. There are few visible indications of it in the world. We see not yet all things put under our Lord's feet. Sin, unbelief, and superstition abound. Thousands are practically saying, *"We do not want this man to reign over us."* It does not yet appear what His people shall be. Their crosses, their tribulations, their weaknesses, and their conflicts are all manifest enough. But there are few signs of their future reward. Let us beware of giving way to doubts in this matter. Let us silence such doubts by reading over the history of the transfiguration. There is laid up for Jesus, and all who believe on Him, such glory as the heart of man never conceived. It is not only promised, but part of it has also actually been seen by three competent witnesses. One of them says, *We saw His glory, glory as of the only begotten from the Father* (John 1:14). Surely that which has been seen may well be believed.

In the second place, we have in these verses *an unanswerable proof of the resurrection of the body and the life after death.* We are told that Moses and Elijah appeared visibly in glory with Christ. They were seen in a bodily form. They were heard talking with our Lord. Fourteen hundred and eighty years had rolled around since Moses died and was buried. More than nine hundred years had passed away since Elijah *went up by a whirlwind to heaven.* Yet here they are seen alive by Peter, James, and John. Let us lay firm hold on this part of the vision. It deserves close attention. We must all feel, if we ever think at all, that the state of the dead is an amazing and mysterious subject. One after another we bury them out of our sight. We lay them in their narrow beds and see them no more, and their bodies become dust. But will they really live again? Shall we really see them again? Will the grave really give back the dead at the last day? These are questions that will occasionally come across the minds of some, in spite of all the plainest statements in the Word of God.

Now we have in the transfiguration the clearest evidence that the dead will rise again. We find two men appearing on earth, in their bodies, who had long been separate from the land of the living; and in them, we have a pledge of the resurrection of all. All who have ever lived upon earth will again be called to life and render up their account. Not one will be found missing. There is no such thing as annihilation. All who have ever fallen asleep in Christ will be found in safe keeping – patriarchs, prophets, apostles, and martyrs – down to the humblest servant of God in our own day. Though unseen to us, they all live to God. *He is not the God of the dead but of the living* (Luke 20:38). Their spirits live as surely as we live ourselves, and they will appear hereafter in glorified bodies as surely as Moses and Elijah on the mountain. These are indeed solemn thoughts! There is a resurrection, and men like Felix may well tremble. There is a resurrection, and men like Paul may well rejoice.

In the last place, we have in these verses *a remarkable testimony to Christ's infinite superiority over all mankind.* This is a point which is brought out strongly by the voice from heaven which the disciples heard. Peter, bewildered by the heavenly vision, and not knowing what to say, proposed to build three tabernacles, one for Christ, one for Moses, and one for Elijah. He seemed in fact to place the Lawgiver and the prophet side by side with his divine Master, as if all three were equal. At once, we are told, the proposal was rebuked in a marked manner. A cloud covered Moses and Elijah, and they were seen no more. A voice at the same time came forth from the cloud, repeating the solemn words spoken at our Lord's baptism: *"This is My beloved Son, with whom I am well-pleased; listen to Him!"*

That voice was meant to teach Peter that there was one there far greater than Moses or Elijah. Moses was a faithful servant of God. Elijah was a bold witness for the truth. But Christ was far above either one of them. He was the Savior to whom the law and the prophets were continually pointing. He was the true prophet whom all were commanded to hear (Deuteronomy 18:15). Moses and Elijah were great men in their day. But Peter and his companions were to remember that in nature, dignity, and office, they were far below Christ. He was the true sun – they were the planets depending daily on His light. He was the root – they were the branches. He was the Master – they were the servants. Their goodness was all derived – His was original and His own. Let them honor Moses and the prophets as holy men. But if they would be saved, they must take Christ alone for their Master and glory only in Him. *"Listen to Him!"*

Let us see in these words a striking lesson to the whole church of Christ. There is a constant tendency in human nature to "hear man." Bishops, priests, deacons, popes, cardinals, councils, Presbyterian preachers, and Independent ministers are continually exalted to a place which God never intended them to fill, and are made practically to usurp the honor of Christ. Against this tendency let us all watch and be on our guard. Let these solemn words of the vision ever ring in our ears: "Listen to Christ."

The best of men are only men at their very best. Patriarchs, prophets, and apostles – martyrs, church Fathers, Reformers, and Puritans – all, all are sinners who need a Savior. They may be holy, useful, and honorable in their place, but they are sinners after all. They must never be allowed to stand between us and Christ. He alone is the Son in whom the Father is well pleased. He alone is sealed and appointed to give the bread of life. He alone has the keys in His hands, "God over all, blessed forever." Let us take heed that we hear His voice and follow Him. Let us value all religious teaching just in proportion as it leads us to Jesus. The sum and substance of saving religion is to listen to Christ.

Matthew 17:14-21 *Little Faith can go very far*

When they came to the crowd, a man came up to Jesus, falling on his knees before Him and saying, "Lord, have mercy on my son, for he is a lunatic and is very ill; for he often falls into the fire and often into the water. I brought him to Your disciples, and they could not cure him." And Jesus answered and said, "You unbelieving and perverted generation, how long shall I be with you? How long shall I put up with you? Bring him here to Me." And Jesus rebuked him, and the demon came out of him, and the boy was cured at once. Then the disciples came to Jesus privately and said, "Why could we not drive it out?" And He said to them, "Because of the littleness of your faith; for truly I say to you, if you have faith the size of a mustard seed, you will say to this mountain, 'Move from here to there,' and it will move; and nothing will be impossible to you. [But this kind does not go out except by prayer and fasting."] (Matthew 17:14-21)

We read in this passage another of our Lord's great miracles. He heals a young man possessed with a devil.

The first thing we see in these verses is *a lively emblem of the dreadful influence sometimes exercised by Satan over the young*. We are told of a certain man's son who was *a lunatic and was very ill*. We are told of the evil spirit pressing him on to the destruction of body and soul. *"He often falls into the fire and often into the water."* It was one of those cases of satanic possession which, however common in our Lord's times, in our own day is rarely seen. But we can easily imagine that when it did occur, it must have been peculiarly distressing to the family of the afflicted. It is painful enough to see the bodies of those we love racked by disease. How much more painful must it have been to see body and mind completely under the influence of the devil. "Out of hell," says Bishop Hall, "there could not be greater misery."

But we must not forget that there are many instances of Satan's spiritual dominion over young people which are quite as painful, in their way, as the case described in this passage. There are thousands of young men who seem to have wholly given themselves up to Satan's temptations and to be led captive at his will. They cast off all fear of God and all respect for His commandments. They serve diverse lusts and pleasures. They run wildly into every excess of riot. They refuse to listen to the advice of parents, teachers, or ministers. They fling aside all regard for health, character, or worldly respectability. They do all that lies in their power to ruin themselves, body and soul, for time and eternity. They are willing bondslaves of Satan. Who has not seen such young men? They are to be seen in town and in country. They are to be found among rich and among poor. Surely such young men give mournful proof that although Satan nowadays seldom has possession of men's bodies, he still exercises a fearful dominion over some men's souls.

Yet even about such young men as these, be it remembered, we must never despair. We must call to mind the almighty power of our Lord Jesus Christ. Bad as this boy's case was, of whom we read in these verses, he was *cured at once* after he was brought to Christ! Parents, teachers, and ministers should go on praying for young men even at their worst. Hard as their hearts seem now, they may yet be softened.

Desperate as their wickedness now appears, they may yet be healed. They may yet repent and be converted, like John Newton, and their last state prove better than their first. Who can tell? Let it be a settled principle with us when we read our Lord's miracles to never despair of the conversion of any soul. *Conversion is a miracle*

In the second place, we see in these verses *a striking example of the weakening effect of unbelief.* The disciples anxiously inquired of our Lord when they saw the devil yielding to his power, *"Why could we not drive it out?"* They received an answer full of the deepest instruction: *"Because of the littleness of your faith."* Would they know the secret of their own sad failure in the hour of need? It was lack of faith.

Let us ponder this point well and learn wisdom. Faith is the key to success in Christian warfare. Unbelief is the sure road to defeat. If we once let our faith languish and decay, all our graces will languish with it. Courage, patience, long-suffering, and hope will soon wither and dwindle away. Faith is the root on which they all depend. The same Israelites who at one time went through the Red Sea in triumph, at another time shrunk from danger, like cowards, when they reached the borders of the promised land. Their God was the same God who had brought them out of the land of Egypt. Their leader was that same Moses who had wrought so many wonders before their eyes. But their faith was not the same. They gave way to shameful doubts of God's love and power. *They were not able to enter because of unbelief* (Hebrews 3:19).

In the last place, we see in these verses that *Satan's kingdom is not to be pulled down without diligence and pains.* This seems to be the lesson of the verse which concludes the passage we are now considering: *"This kind does not go out except by prayer and fasting."* A gentle rebuke to the disciples appears to be implied in the words. Perhaps they had been too much lifted up by past successes. Perhaps they had been less careful in the use of means in their Master's absence than they were under their Master's eye. At any rate, they receive a plain hint from our Lord that the warfare against Satan must never be lightly carried on. They are warned that no victories are to be won easily over the prince of this world. Without fervent prayer and diligent self-mortification, they would often meet with failure and defeat.

The lesson here laid down is one of deep importance. "I would," says Bullinger, "that this part of the Gospel pleased us as much as those parts which concede liberty." We are all apt to contract a habit of doing religious acts in a thoughtless, perfunctory way. Like Israel, puffed up with the fall of Jericho, we are ready to say to ourselves that "the men of Ai" are few (Joshua 7:3); "do not make all the people toil up there." Like Israel, we often learn by bitter experience that spiritual battles are not to be won without hard fighting. The ark of the Lord must never be handled irreverently. God's work must never be carelessly done.

[handwritten margin note: Christians don't rest on your Laurels]

May we all bear in mind our Lord's words to His disciples and make practical use of them. In the pulpit and on the platform, in the Sunday school and in the district, in our use of family prayers and in reading our own Bibles, let us diligently watch our own spirit. Whatever we do, let us *do it with all [our] might* (Ecclesiastes 9:10). It is a fatal mistake to underrate our foes. Greater is He that is for us than he that is against us – but, for all that, he that is against us is not to be despised. He is the prince of this world. He is a strong man armed, keeping his house, who will not *go out* and part with his goods without a struggle. We wrestle not against flesh and blood, but against principalities and powers. We have need to take the whole armor of God, and not only to take it, but to use it too. We may be very sure that those who win most victories over the world, the flesh, and the devil are those who pray most in private and discipline their bodies and make them their slaves (1 Corinthians 9:27).

Matthew 17:22-27

And while they were gathering together in Galilee, Jesus said to them, "The Son of Man is going to be delivered into the hands of men; and they will kill Him, and He will be raised on the third day." And they were deeply grieved. When they came to Capernaum, those who collected the two-drachma tax came to Peter and said, "Does your teacher not pay the two-drachma tax?" He said, "Yes." And when he came into the house, Jesus spoke to him first, saying, "What do you think, Simon? From whom do the kings of the earth collect customs or poll-tax, from their sons or from strangers?" When Peter said, "From strangers," Jesus said to him, "Then the sons are exempt. However, so that we do not offend them, go to the sea and throw in a hook, and take the first fish that comes up; and when you open its mouth, you will find a shekel. Take that and give it to them for you and Me." (Matthew 17:22-27)

These verses contain a circumstance in our Lord's history that is not recorded by any of the evangelists excepting Matthew. A remarkable miracle is worked in order to provide payment of the tax money required for the service of the temple. There are three striking points in the narrative which deserve attentive observation.

Let us observe, in the first place, *our Lord's perfect knowledge of everything that is said and done in this world.* We are told that *those who collected the two-drachma tax came to Peter and said, "Does your teacher not pay the two-drachma tax?" He said, "Yes."* It was evident that our Lord was not present when the question was asked and the answer given. And yet no sooner did Peter come into the house than our Lord asked him, *"What do you think, Simon? From whom do the kings of the earth collect customs or poll-tax?"* He showed that He was as well acquainted with the conversation as if He had been listening or standing by.

There is something unspeakably solemn in the thought that the Lord Jesus knows all things. There is an eye that sees all our daily conduct. There is an ear that hears all our daily words. All things are naked and opened unto the eyes of Him with whom we have to do. Concealment is impossible. Hypocrisy is useless. We may deceive ministers. We may fool our family and neighbors. But the Lord sees us through and through. We cannot deceive Christ.

We ought to endeavor to make practical use of this truth. We should strive to live as in the Lord's sight and, like Abraham, to *walk before [Him]* (Genesis 17:1). Let it be our daily aim to say nothing we would not like Christ to hear, and to do nothing we would not like Christ to see. Let us measure every difficult question as to right and wrong by one simple test: How would I behave if Jesus was standing by my side? Such a standard is not extravagant and absurd. It is a standard that interferes with no duty or relation of life. It interferes with nothing but sin. Happy is he who tries to realize his Lord's presence and to do all and say all as unto Christ.

Let us observe, in the next place, *our Lord's almighty power over all creation*. He makes a fish his paymaster. He makes a voiceless creature bring the tribute money to meet the collector's demand. Well says Jerome, "I know not which to admire most here, our Lord's foreknowledge, or His greatness."

We see here a literal fulfillment of the psalmist's words, *You make him to rule over the works of Your hands; You have put all things under his feet, all sheep and oxen, and also the beasts of the field, the birds of the heavens and the fish of the sea, whatever passes through the paths of the seas* (Psalm 8:6-8).

Here is one among many proofs of the majesty and greatness of our Lord Jesus Christ. He only who first created could at His will command the obedience of all His creatures. *For by Him all things were created, . . . and in Him all things hold together* (Colossians 1:16-17). The believer who goes forth to do Christ's work among the heathen may safely commit himself to his Master's keeping. He serves one who has all power, even over the beasts of the earth. How wonderful the thought that such an almighty Lord should condescend to be crucified for our salvation! How comfortable the thought that when He comes again the second time, He will gloriously manifest His power over all created things to the whole world. *The wolf and the lamb will graze together, and the lion will eat straw like the ox; and dust will be the serpent's food* (Isaiah 65:25).

In the last place, let us observe in these verses *our Lord's willingness to make concessions rather than give offense*. He might justly have claimed exemption from the payment of this tax money. He who was Son of God might fairly have been excused from paying for the maintenance of His Father's house. He who was *greater than the temple* might have shown good cause for declining to contribute to the support of the temple. But our Lord does not do so. He claims no exemption. He desires Peter to pay the money demanded. At the same time He declares His reasons. It was to be done *"so that we do not offend them."* "A miracle is worked," says Bishop Hall, "rather than offend even a tax-collector."

Our Lord's example in this case deserves the attention of all who profess and call themselves Christians. There is deep wisdom in those seven words, *"so that we do not offend them."* They teach us plainly that there are matters in which Christ's people ought to forego their own opinions and submit to requirements which they may not thoroughly approve, rather than give offense and cause *hindrance to the gospel of Christ.* God's rights undoubtedly we ought never to give up, but we may sometimes safely give up our own. It may sound very fine and seem very heroic to be always standing out tenaciously for our rights. But it may well be doubted, with such a passage as this, whether such tenacity is always wise and shows the mind of Christ. There are occasions when it shows more grace in a Christian to submit than to resist.

Let us remember this passage as citizens. We may not like all the political measures of our rulers. We may disapprove of some of the taxes they impose. But the grand question after all is, Will it do any good to the cause of religion to resist the powers that be? Are their measures really injuring our souls? If not, let us hold our peace *"so that we do not offend them."* "A Christian," says Bullinger, "never ought to disturb the public peace for things of mere temporary importance."

Let us remember this passage as members of a church. We may not like every jot and tittle of the forms and ceremonies used in our communion. We may not think that those who rule us in spiritual matters are always wise. But after all, are the points on which we are dissatisfied really of vital importance? Is any great truth of the gospel at stake? If not, let us be quiet *"so that we do not offend them."*

Let us remember this passage as members of society. There may be usages and customs in the circle where our lot is cast which to us, as Christians, are tiresome, useless, and unprofitable. But are they matters of principle? Do they injure our souls? Will it do any good to the cause of religion if we refuse to comply with them? If not, let us patiently submit, lest we cause them to stumble.

Well would it be for the church and the world if these seven words of our Lord had been more studied, pondered, and used! Who can tell the damage that has been done to the cause of the gospel by morbid scrupulosity and conscientiousness falsely so called! May we all remember the example of the great apostle of the Gentiles: *We endure all things so that we will cause no hindrance to the gospel of Christ* (1 Corinthians 9:12).

Matthew Chapter 18

Matthew 18:1-14

At that time the disciples came to Jesus and said, "Who then is greatest in the kingdom of heaven?" And He called a child to Himself and set him before them, and said, "Truly I say to you, unless you are converted and become like children, you will not enter the kingdom of heaven. Whoever then humbles himself as this child, he is the greatest in the kingdom of heaven. And whoever receives one such child in My name receives Me; but whoever causes one of these little ones who believe in Me to stumble, it would be better for him to have a heavy millstone hung around his neck, and to be drowned in the depth of the sea. Woe to the world because of its stumbling blocks! For it is inevitable that stumbling blocks come; but woe to that man through whom the stumbling block comes! If your hand or your foot causes you to stumble, cut it off and throw it from you; it is better for you to enter life crippled or lame, than to have two hands or two feet and be cast into the eternal fire. If your eye causes you to stumble, pluck it out and throw it from you. It is better for you to enter life with one eye, than to have two eyes and be cast into the fiery hell. See that you do not despise one of these little ones, for I say to you that their angels in heaven continually see the face of My Father who is in heaven. [For the Son of Man has come to save that which was lost.] What do you think? If any man has a hundred sheep, and one of them has gone astray, does he not leave the ninety-nine on the mountains and go and search for the one that is straying? If it turns out that he finds it, truly I say to you, he rejoices over it more than over the ninety-nine which have not gone astray. So it is not the will of your Father who is in heaven that one of these little ones perish." (Matthew 18:1-14)

THE FIRST THING THAT WE ARE TAUGHT IN THESE VERSES is *the necessity of conversion, and of conversion manifested by childlike humility.* The disciples came to our Lord with the question, *"Who then is greatest in the kingdom of heaven?"* They spoke as men half-enlightened and full of carnal expectations. They received an answer well calculated to awaken them from their daydream, an answer containing a truth which lies at the very foundation of Christianity: *"Unless you are converted and become like children, you will not enter the kingdom of heaven."*

Let these words sink down deeply into our hearts. Without conversion there is no salvation. We all need an entire change of nature. Of ourselves we have neither faith, nor fear, nor love towards God. We must be born again. Of ourselves we are utterly unfit for dwelling in God's presence. Heaven would be no heaven to us if we were not converted. It is true of all ranks, classes, and orders of mankind. All are born in sin and are children of wrath, and all, without exception, need to be born again and made new creatures. A new heart must be given to us and a new spirit put within us. Old things must pass away, and all things must become new. It is a good thing to be baptized into the Christian church and to attend a good church. But after all, are we converted?

Would we know whether we are really converted? Would we know the test by which we must try ourselves? The surest mark of true conversion is humility. If we have really received the Holy Spirit, we shall show it by a meek and childlike spirit. Like children, we shall think humbly of our own strength and wisdom, and be very dependent on our Father in heaven. Like children, we shall not seek great things in this world; and having food and clothing and the Father's love, we shall be content. Truly this is a heart-searching test! It exposes the unsoundness of many a so-called conversion. It is easy to be a convert from one party to another party, from one sect to another sect, or from one set of opinions to another set of opinions. Such conversions save no one's soul. What we all want is a conversion from pride to humility, from high thoughts of ourselves to lowly thoughts of ourselves, from self-conceit to self-abasement, and from the mind of the Pharisee to the mind of the tax collector. A conversion of this kind we must experience if we hope to be saved. These are the conversions that are wrought by the Holy Spirit.

The next thing that we are taught in these verses is *the great sin of putting stumbling blocks in the way of believers.* The words of the Lord Jesus on this subject are peculiarly solemn. *"Woe to the world because of its stumbling blocks! Woe to that man through whom the stumbling block comes!"*

We put offenses or stumbling blocks in the way of men's souls whenever we do anything to keep them back from Christ, or to turn them out of the way of salvation, or to disgust them with true religion. We may do it directly by persecuting, ridiculing, opposing, or dissuading them from decided service for Christ. We may do it indirectly by living a life inconsistent with our religious profession and by making Christianity loathsome and distasteful by our own conduct. Whenever we do anything of the kind, it is clear from our Lord's words that we commit a great sin.

There is something very fearful in the doctrine here laid down. It ought to stir up within us great searchings of heart. It is not enough that we wish to do good in this world. Are we quite sure that we are not doing harm? We may not openly persecute Christ's servants. But are there none whom we are injuring by our ways and our example? It is dreadful to think of the amount of harm that can be done by one inconsistent professor of religion. He gives a handle to the infidel. He supplies the worldly man with an excuse for remaining undecided. He checks the inquirer after salvation. He discourages the saints. He is, in short, a living sermon on behalf of the devil. The last day alone will reveal the wholesale ruin of souls that offenses have occasioned in the church of Christ. One of Nathan's charges against David was, *"You have given occasion to the enemies of the LORD to blaspheme"* (2 Samuel 12:14).

The next thing that we are taught in these verses is *the reality of future punishment after death.* Two strong expressions are used by our Lord on this point. He speaks of being *cast into the eternal fire.* He speaks of being *cast into the fiery hell.*

The meaning of these words is clear and unmistakable. There is a place of unspeakable misery in the world to come, to which all who die impenitent and unbelieving must ultimately be consigned. There is revealed in Scripture *the fury of a fire* which sooner or later will devour all God's adversaries (Hebrews 10:27). The same sure word which holds out a heaven to all who repent and are converted declares plainly that there will be a hell for all the ungodly.

Let no man deceive us with vain words upon this dreadful subject. Men have arisen in these latter days who profess to deny the eternity of future punishment and repeat the devil's old lie that we *surely will not die* (Genesis 3:4). Let none of their reasonings move us, however plausible they may sound. Let us stand fast in the old paths. The God of love and mercy is also a God of justice. He will surely requite. The flood in Noah's day and the burning of Sodom were meant to show us what He will one day do. No lips have ever spoken so clearly about hell as those of Christ Himself. Hardened sinners will find out, to their cost, that there is such a thing as the *wrath of the Lamb* (Revelation 6:16).

The last thing we are taught in these verses is *the value that God sets on the least and lowest of believers.* "It is not the will of your Father who is in heaven that one of these little ones perish."

These words are meant for the encouragement of all true Christians, and not for little children only. The connection in which they are found with the parable of the hundred sheep and one that went astray seems to place this beyond doubt. They are meant to show us that our Lord Jesus is the Good Shepherd who cares tenderly for every soul committed to His charge. The youngest, the weakest, the sickliest of His flock are as dear to Him as the strongest. They shall never perish. None shall ever pluck them out of His hand. He will lead them gently through the wilderness of this world. He will not overdrive them a single day, lest any die (Genesis 33:13). He will carry them through every difficulty. He will defend them against every enemy. The saying which He spoke shall be literally fulfilled: *"Of those whom You have given Me I lost not one"* (John 18:9). With such a Savior, who needs to fear beginning to be a thorough Christian? With such a Shepherd, who, having once begun, needs to fear being cast away?

Matthew 18:15-20

*"If your brother sins, go and show him his fault in private; if
he listens to you, you have won your brother. But if he does
not listen to you, take one or two more with you, so that by the
mouth of two or three witnesses every fact may be confirmed. If
he refuses to listen to them, tell it to the church; and if he refuses
to listen even to the church, let him be to you as a Gentile and a
tax collector. Truly I say to you, whatever you bind on earth shall
have been bound in heaven; and whatever you loose on earth
shall have been loosed in heaven. Again I say to you, that if two
of you agree on earth about anything that they may ask, it shall
be done for them by My Father who is in heaven. For where two
or three have gathered together in My name, I am there in their
midst."* (Matthew 18:15-20)

These words of the Lord Jesus contain an expression which has been
often misapplied. The command to *listen even to the church* has been so
interpreted as to contradict other passages of God's Word. It has been
falsely applied to the authority of the whole visible church in matters of
doctrine, and so been made an excuse for the exercise of much ecclesiastical tyranny. *But the abuse of Scripture truths must not tempt us
to neglect the use of them.* We must not turn away altogether from any
text because some have perverted it and made it poison.

Let us notice, in the first place, *how admirable are the rules laid down
by our Lord for the healing of differences among brethren.*

If we have unhappily received any injury from a fellow member of
Christ's church, the first step to be taken is to visit him alone and tell
him his fault. He may have injured us unintentionally, as Abimelech
did Abraham (Genesis 21:26). His conduct may need explanation, like
that of the tribes of Reuben, Gad, and Manasseh when they built an
altar as they returned to their own land (Joshua 22:24). At any rate,
this friendly, faithful, and straightforward way of dealing is the most
likely course to win a brother, if he is to be won. *A gentle answer turns*

away wrath, But a harsh word stirs up anger. (Proverbs 15:1). Who can tell but he may say at once, "I was wrong," and make ample reparation?

If, however, this course of proceeding fails to produce any good effect, a second step is to be taken. We are to *take one or two more with us* and tell our brother of his fault in their presence and hearing. Who can tell but his conscience may be stricken when he finds his misconduct made known, and he may be ashamed and repent? If not, we shall at all events have the testimony of witnesses that we did all we could to bring our brother to a right mind, and that he deliberately refused, when appealed to, to make amends.

Finally, if this second course of proceeding proves useless, we are to refer the whole matter to the Christian congregation of which we are members – we are to *tell it to the church.* Who can tell but the heart which has been unmoved by private remonstrances may be moved by the fear of public exposure? If not, there remains but one view to take of our brother's case: we must sorrowfully regard him as one who has shaken off all Christian principles and will be guided by no higher motives than *a Gentile and a tax collector.*

The passage is a beautiful instance of the mingled wisdom and tender consideration of our Lord's teaching. What a knowledge it shows of human nature! Nothing does so much harm to the cause of religion as the quarrels of Christians. No stone should be left unturned and no trouble spared in order to prevent their being dragged before the public. What a delicate thoughtfulness it shows for the sensitiveness of poor human nature! Many a scandalous breach would be prevented if we were more ready to practice the rule of *showing him his fault in private.* Happy would it be for the church and the world if this portion of our Lord's teaching was more carefully studied and obeyed. Differences and divisions there will be, so long as the world stands. But how many of them would be extinguished at once if the course recommended in these verses was tried.

In the second place, let us observe *what a clear argument we have in these verses for the exercise of discipline in a Christian congregation.*

Our Lord commands disagreements between Christians, which cannot be otherwise settled, to be referred to the decision of the Christian assembly to which they belong. *"Tell it,"* He says, *"to the church."* It is evident from this that He intends every congregation of professing Christians to take cognizance of the moral conduct of its members, either by the action of the whole body collectively or of heads and elders to whom its authority may be delegated. It is evident also that He intends every congregation to have the power of excluding disobedient and refractory members from participation in its ordinances. *"If he refuses,"* He says, *"to listen even to the church, let him be to you as a Gentile and a tax collector."* He says not a word about temporal punishment and civil disabilities. Spiritual penalties are the only penalties He permits the church to inflict, and when rightly inflicted, they are not to be lightly regarded. *"Whatever you bind on earth shall have been bound in heaven."* Such appears to be the substance of our Lord's teaching about ecclesiastical discipline.

It is vain to deny that the whole subject is surrounded with difficulties. On no point has the influence of the world weighed so heavily on the action of churches. On no point have churches made so many mistakes – sometimes on the side of sleepy remissness, sometimes on the side of blind severity. No doubt the power of excommunication has been fearfully abused and perverted, and, as Quesnel says, "We ought to be more afraid of our sins than of all the excommunications in the world." Still it is impossible to deny, with such a passage as this before us, that church discipline is according to the mind of Christ, and when wisely exercised, is calculated to promote a church's health and well-being. It can never be right that all sorts of people, however wicked and ungodly, should be allowed to come to the table of the Lord with no one either permitting or forbidding. It is the binding duty of every Christian to use his influence to prevent such a state of things. A perfect communion can never be attained in this world, but purity should be the mark at which we aim. An increasingly high standard of qualification for full church membership will always be found as one of the best evidences of a prosperous church.

Let us observe, in the last place, *what gracious encouragement Christ holds out to those who meet together in His name.* He says, "Where two or three have gathered together in My name, I am there in their midst."

That saying is a striking proof of our Lord's divinity. God alone can be in more places than one at the same time.

There is comfort in these words for all who love to meet together for religious purposes. At every assembly for public worship, at every gathering for prayer and praise, at every missionary meeting, at every Bible reading, the King of Kings is present – Christ Himself attends! We may be often disheartened by the small number who are present on such occasions compared to those who meet for worldly ends. We may sometimes find it hard to bear the taunts and ridicule of an ill-natured world which cries like the enemy of old, *"What are these feeble [people] doing?"* (Nehemiah 4:2). But we have no reason for despondency. We may boldly fall back on these words of Jesus. At all such meetings we have the company of Christ Himself.

There is a solemn rebuke in these words for all who neglect the public worship of God and never attend meetings for any religious purpose. They turn their backs on the society of the Lord of Lords. They miss the opportunity of meeting Christ Himself. It avails nothing to say that the proceedings of religious meetings are marked by weakness and infirmity, or that as much good is gotten by staying at home as going to church. The words of our Lord should silence such arguments at once. Surely men are not wise when they speak contemptuously of any gathering where Christ is present.

May we all ponder these things. If we have met together with God's people for spiritual purposes in times past, let us persevere and not be ashamed. If we have hitherto despised such meetings, let us consider our ways and learn wisdom.

Matthew 18:21-35

Then Peter came and said to Him, "Lord, how often shall my brother sin against me and I forgive him? Up to seven times?" Jesus said to him, "I do not say to you, up to seven times, but up to seventy times seven. For this reason the kingdom of heaven may be compared to a king who wished to settle accounts with his slaves. When he had begun to settle them, one who owed him ten thousand talents was brought to him. But since he did not have the means to repay, his lord commanded him to be sold, along with his wife and children and all that he had, and repayment to be made. So the slave fell down and prostrated himself before him, saying, 'Have patience with me and I will repay you everything.' And the lord of that slave felt compassion and released him and forgave him the debt. But that slave went out and found one of his fellow slaves who owed him a hundred denarii; and he seized him and began to choke him, saying, 'Pay back what you owe.' So his fellow slave fell to the ground and began to plead with him, saying, 'Have patience with me and I will repay you.' But he was unwilling and went and threw him in prison until he should pay back what was owed. So when his fellow slaves saw what had happened, they were deeply grieved and came and reported to their lord all that had happened. Then summoning him, his lord said to him, 'You wicked slave, I forgave you all that debt because you pleaded with me. Should you not also have had mercy on your fellow slave, in the same way that I had mercy on you?' And his lord, moved with anger, handed him over to the torturers until he should repay all that was owed him. My heavenly Father will also do the same to you, if each of you does not forgive his brother from your heart." (Matthew 18:21-35)

In these verses the Lord Jesus deals with a deeply important subject: the forgiveness of injuries. We live in a wicked world, and it is vain to expect that we can escape ill-treatment, however carefully we may behave. To know how to conduct ourselves when we are ill-treated is of great importance to our souls.

In the first place, *the Lord Jesus lays it down as a general rule that we ought to forgive others to the uttermost.* Peter put the question, *"How often shall my brother sin against me and I forgive him? Up to seven times?"* He received for an answer, *"I do not say to you, up to seven times, but up to seventy times seven."*

The rule here laid down must of course be interpreted with

sober-minded qualification. Our Lord does not mean that offenses against the law of the land and the good order of society are to be passed over in silence. He does not mean that we are to allow people to commit thefts and assaults with impunity. All that He means is that we are to exercise a general spirit of mercy and forgiveness towards our brethren. We are to bear much and to put up with much, rather than quarrel. We are to look over much and submit to much, rather than have any strife. We are to lay aside everything like malice, strife, revenge, and retaliation. Such feelings are only fit for heathen. They are utterly unworthy of a disciple of Christ.

What a happy world it would be if this rule of our Lord's was more known and better obeyed! How many of the miseries of mankind are occasioned by disputes, quarrels, lawsuits, and an obstinate tenacity about what men call "their rights!" How many of them might be altogether avoided if men were more willing to forgive and more desirous for peace! Let us never forget that a fire cannot go on burning without fuel. Just in the same way it takes two to make a quarrel. Let us each resolve by God's grace that of these two we will never be one. Let us resolve to return good for evil, and blessing for cursing, and so melt down enmity, and change our foes into friends (Romans 12:20). It was a fine feature in Archbishop Cranmer's character that if you did him an injury, he was sure to be your friend.

In the second place, our Lord supplies us with *two powerful motives for exercising a forgiving spirit.* He tells us a story of a man who owed an enormous sum to his master and had not *the means to repay.* Nevertheless, at the time of reckoning, his master had compassion on him and *forgave him the debt.* He tells us that this very man, after being forgiven himself, refused to forgive a fellow servant a trifling debt. He actually cast him into prison and would not abate a fragment of his demand. He tells us how punishment overtook this wicked and cruel man who, after receiving mercy, ought surely to have shown mercy to others. And finally, he concludes the parable with the impressive words, *"My heavenly Father will also do the same to you, if each of you does not forgive his brother from your heart."*

It is clear from this parable that one motive for forgiving others ought to be the recollection that we all need forgiveness at God's hands ourselves. Day after day we are coming short in many things, leaving undone what we ought to do, and doing what we ought not to do. Day after day we require mercy and pardon. Our neighbors' offenses against us are mere trifles compared with our offenses against God. Surely it adversely suits poor erring creatures like us to be extreme in marking what is done amiss by our brethren or slow to forgive it.

Another motive for forgiving others ought to be the recollection of the day of judgment and the standard by which we shall all be tried in that day. There will be no forgiveness in that day for unforgiving people. Such people would be unfit for heaven. They would not be able to value a dwelling place to which mercy is the only title, and in which mercy is the eternal subject of song. Surely if we intend to stand at the right hand when Jesus sits on the throne of His glory, we must learn, while we are on earth, to forgive.

Let these truths sink down deeply into our hearts. It is a grievous fact that there are few Christian duties so little practiced as that of forgiveness. It is sad to see how much bitterness, unmercifulness, spite, harshness, and unkindness there is among men. Yet there are few duties so strongly enforced in the New Testament Scriptures as this duty is, and few the neglect of which so clearly shuts a man out of the kingdom of God.

Would we give proof that we are at peace with God, washed in Christ's blood, born of the Spirit, and made God's children by adoption and grace? Let us remember this passage. Like our Father in heaven, let us be forgiving. Has any man injured us? Let us this day forgive him. As Leighton says, "We ought to forgive ourselves little, and others much."

Would we do good to the world? Would we have any influence on others and make them see the beauty of true religion? Let us remember this passage. Men who care not for doctrines can still understand a forgiving temper.

Would we grow in grace ourselves and become more holy in all our ways, words, and works? Let us remember this passage. Nothing so grieves the Holy Spirit and brings spiritual darkness over the soul as giving way to a quarrelsome and unforgiving temper (Ephesians 4:30-32).

Matthew Chapter 19

Matthew 19:1-15

When Jesus had finished these words, He departed from Galilee and came into the region of Judea beyond the Jordan; and large crowds followed Him, and He healed them there. Some Pharisees came to Jesus, testing Him and asking, "Is it lawful for a man to divorce his wife for any reason at all?" And He answered and said, "Have you not read that He who created from the beginning made them male and female, and said, 'For this reason a man shall leave his father and mother and be joined to his wife, and the two shall become one flesh'? So they are no longer two, but one flesh. What therefore God has joined together, let no man separate." They said to Him, "Why then did Moses command to give her a certificate of divorce and send her away?" He said to them, "Because of your hardness of heart Moses permitted you to divorce your wives; but from the beginning it has not been this way. And I say to you, whoever divorces his wife, except for immorality, and marries another woman commits adultery." The disciples said to Him, "If the relationship of the man with his wife is like this, it is better not to marry." But He said to them, "Not all men can accept this statement, but only those to whom it has been given. For there are eunuchs who were born that way from their mother's womb; and there are eunuchs who were made eunuchs by men; and there are also eunuchs who made themselves eunuchs for the sake of the kingdom of heaven. He who is able to accept this, let him accept it." Then some children were brought to Him so that He might lay His hands on them and pray; and the disciples rebuked them. But Jesus said, "Let the children alone, and do not hinder them from coming to Me; for the kingdom of heaven belongs to such as these." After laying His hands on them, He departed from there. (Matthew 19:1-15)

IN THESE VERSES WE HAVE THE MIND OF CHRIST declared on two subjects of great moment. One is the relation of husband and wife. The other is the light in which we should regard little children in the matter of their souls.

It is difficult to overrate the importance of these two subjects. The well-being of nations and the happiness of society are closely connected with right views upon them. Nations are nothing but a collection of families. The good order of families depends entirely on keeping up the highest standard of respect for the marriage tie and on the right training of children. We ought to be thankful that on both these points the Lord has pronounced judgment so clearly.

With respect to marriage, our Lord teaches that *the union of husband and wife ought never to be broken off except for the greatest of all causes, namely, actual unfaithfulness.*[1]

In the days when our Lord was upon earth, divorces were permitted among the Jews for the most trifling and frivolous causes. The practice, though tolerated by Moses, had gradually become an enormous abuse and no doubt led to much immorality (Malachi 2:14-16). The remark made by our Lord's disciples shows the deplorably low state of public feeling on the subject. They said, *"If the relationship of the man with his wife is like this, it is better not to marry."* They meant, of course, that if a man may not put away his wife for a slight cause at any time, he had better not marry at all. Such language from the mouths of apostles sounds strange indeed!

Our Lord brings forward a widely different standard for the guidance of His disciples. He first bases His judgment on the original institution of marriage. He quotes the words used in the beginning of Genesis, where the creation of man and the union of Adam and Eve are described, as a proof that no relation should be so highly regarded

---

1   Additionally, we understand that this condition for divorce was only applicable when a newlywed bride was found out to not have been a virgin.

as that of husband and wife. The relation of parent and child may seem very close, but there is one closer still: *A man shall leave his father and mother and be joined to his wife.* He then backs up the quotation by His own solemn words, *"What therefore God has joined together, let no man separate."* And finally He brings in the grave charge of breaking the seventh commandment against marriage contracted after a divorce for light and frivolous causes: *"Whoever divorces his wife, except for immorality, and marries another woman commits adultery."*

It is clear from the whole tenor of the passage that the relationship of marriage ought to be highly reverenced and honored among Christians. It is a relationship which was instituted in Paradise in the time of man's innocence, and it is a chosen figure of the mystical union between Christ and His church. It is a relationship which nothing but death ought to terminate. It is a relationship which is sure to have the greatest influence on those whom it brings together, for happiness or for misery, for good or for evil. Such a relationship ought never to be taken in hand unadvisedly, lightly, or wantonly, but soberly, discreetly, and with due consideration. It is only too true that thoughtlessly entering into marriage is one of the most fertile causes of unhappiness and too often, it may be feared, of sin.

With respect to little children, we find our Lord instructing us in these verses both by word and deed, and both by precept and example. *Then some children were brought to Him so that He might lay His hands on them and pray.* They were evidently tender infants, too young to receive instruction but not too young to receive benefit by prayer. The disciples seem to have thought them beneath their Master's notice and rebuked those who brought them. But this drew forth a solemn declaration from the Lord: *"Let the children alone, and do not hinder them from coming to Me; for the kingdom of heaven belongs to such as these."*

Let us learn from these verses that the Lord Jesus cares tenderly for the souls of little children. It is probable that Satan specially hates them. It is certain that Jesus specially loves them. Young as they are, they are not beneath His thoughts and attention. That mighty heart of His has room for the babe in his cradle as well as for the king on his throne. He regards each one as possessing within his little body an undying principle that will outlive the pyramids of Egypt and see sun and moon quenched at the last day. With such a passage as this before us, we may surely hope well about the salvation of all who die in infancy. *"The kingdom of heaven belongs to such as these."*

Finally, let us draw from these verses *encouragement to attempt great things in the religious instruction of children.* Let us begin from their very earliest years to deal with them as having souls lost to be saved and strive to bring them to Christ. Let us make them acquainted with the Bible as soon as they can understand anything. Let us pray with them, and pray for them, and teach them to pray for themselves. We may rest assured that Jesus looks with pleasure on such endeavors and is ready to bless them. We may rest assured that such endeavors are not in vain. The seed sown in infancy is often found after many days. Happy is that church whose infant members are cared for as much as the oldest communicants! The blessing of Him who was crucified will surely be on that church! He put His hands on little children. He prayed for them.

What Are we willing to give all away to walk with Christ. **Matthew 19:16-22**

And someone came to Him and said, "Teacher, what good thing shall I do that I may obtain eternal life?" And He said to him, "Why are you asking Me about what is good? There is only One who is good; but if you wish to enter into life, keep the commandments." Then he said to Him, "Which ones?" And Jesus said, "You shall not commit murder; You shall not commit adultery; You shall not steal; You shall not bear false witness; Honor your father and mother; and You shall love your neighbor as yourself." The young man said to Him, "All these things I have kept; what am I still lacking?" Jesus said to him, "If you wish to be complete, go and sell your possessions and give to the poor, and you will have treasure in heaven; and come, follow Me." But when the young man heard this statement, he went away grieving, for he was one who owned much property. (Matthew 19:16-22)

These verses detail a conversation between our Lord Jesus Christ and a young man who came to Him to inquire about the way to eternal life. Like every conversation recorded in the Gospels between our Lord and an individual, it deserves special attention. Salvation is an individual business. Everyone who wishes to be saved must have private, personal dealings with Christ about his own soul.

We see for one thing, from the case of this young man, that *a person may have desires for salvation and yet not be saved.* Here is one who in a day of abounding unbelief comes of his own accord to Christ. He comes not to have a sickness healed. He comes not to plead for a child. He comes for his own soul. He opens the conference with the frank question, *"Teacher, what good thing shall I do that I may obtain eternal life?"* Surely we might have thought, "This is a promising case. This is no prejudiced ruler or Pharisee; this is a hopeful inquirer." Yet by and by this very young man *went away grieving*, and we never read a word to show that he was converted!

We must never forget that *good feelings alone in religion are not the grace of God.* We may know the truth intellectually. We may often feel pierced in conscience. We may have religious affections awakened within us, have many anxieties about our souls, and shed many tears. But all this is not conversion. It is not the genuine, saving work of the Holy Spirit.

Unhappily this is not all that must be said on this point. Not only are good feelings alone not grace, but they are also even decidedly dangerous if we content ourselves with them and do not act as well as feel. It is a profound remark of that mighty master on moral questions, Bishop Butler, that passive impressions often repeated gradually lose all their power. Actions often repeated produce a habit in man's mind. Feelings often indulged in, without leading to corresponding actions, will finally exercise no influence at all. *Be True to your word* [Let actions of Forgiveness stay and not often Repeated]

Let us apply this lesson to our own state. Perhaps we know what it is to feel religious fears, wishes, and desires. Let us beware that we do not rest in them. Let us never be satisfied until we have the witness of the Spirit in our hearts, that we are actually born again and are new creatures. Let us never rest until we know that we have really repented and laid hold on the hope set before us in the gospel. It is good to feel. But it is far better to be converted.

We see for another thing, from this young man's case, that *an unconverted person is often profoundly ignorant on spiritual subjects.* Our Lord refers this inquirer to the eternal standard of right and wrong – the moral law. Seeing that he speaks so boldly about "doing," Jesus tries him by a command well calculated to draw out the real state of his heart: *"If you wish to enter into life, keep the commandments."* He even repeats to him the second table of the law. And at once the young man confidently replies, *"All these things I have kept; what am I still lacking?"* So utterly ignorant is he of the spirituality of God's statutes, that he never doubts that he has perfectly fulfilled them. He seems thoroughly unaware that the commandments apply to the thoughts and words as well as to the deeds, and that if God were to enter into judgment with him, *"he could not answer Him once in a thousand times"* (Job 9:3). How dark must his mind have been as to the nature of God's law! How low must his ideas have been as to the holiness which God requires!

It is a sad fact that ignorance like that of this young man is only too common in the church of Christ. There are thousands of baptized people who know no more of the leading doctrines of Christianity than the basest heathen. Tens of thousands fill churches and chapels weekly who are utterly in the dark as to the full extent of man's sinfulness. They cling obstinately to the old notion that in some sort or other their own doings can save them, and when ministers visit them on their deathbeds, they prove as blind as if they had never heard truth at all. So true is it that the *natural man does not accept the things of the Spirit of God, for they are foolishness to him* (1 Corinthians 2:14).

We see in the last place, from this young man's case, that *one idol cherished in the heart may ruin a soul forever.* Our Lord, who knew what was in man, at last shows His inquirer his besetting sin. The same searching voice which said to the Samaritan woman, *"Go, call your husband"* (John 4:16), says to the young man, *"Go and sell your possessions and give to the poor."* At once the weak point in his character is detected. It turns out that with all his wishes and desires after eternal life, there was one thing he loved better than his soul, and that was his money. He cannot stand the test. He is weighed in the balance and found lacking. And the history ends with the sad words, *He went away grieving; for he was one who owned much property.*

We have in this history one more proof of the truth, *The love of money is a root of all sorts of evil* (1 Timothy 6:10). We must place this young man in our memories by the side of Judas, Ananias, and Sapphira, and learn to beware of covetousness. Alas! it is a rock on which thousands are continually making shipwreck. There is hardly a minister of the gospel who could not point to many in his congregation who, humanly speaking, *are not far from the kingdom of God.* But they never seem to make progress. They wish. They feel. They intend. They hope. But there they stick fast! And why? Because they are fond of money.

Let us prove our own selves as we leave the passage. Let us see how it concerns our own souls. Are we honest and sincere in our professed desire to be true Christians? Have we given up all our idols? Is there no secret sin that we are silently clinging to and refusing to give up? Is there no thing or person that we are privately loving more than Christ and our souls? These are questions that ought to be answered. The true explanation of the unsatisfactory state of many hearers of the gospel is spiritual idolatry. John might well say, *Guard yourselves from idols* (1 John 5:21).

Matthew 19:23-30

And Jesus said to His disciples, "Truly I say to you, it is hard for a rich man to enter the kingdom of heaven. Again I say to you, it is easier for a camel to go through the eye of a needle, than for a rich man to enter the kingdom of God." When the disciples heard this, they were very astonished and said, "Then who can be saved?" And looking at them Jesus said to them, "With people this is impossible, but with God all things are possible." Then Peter said to Him, "Behold, we have left everything and followed You; what then will there be for us?" And Jesus said to them, "Truly I say to you, that you who have followed Me, in

*the regeneration when the Son of Man will sit on His glorious
throne, you also shall sit upon twelve thrones, judging the twelve
tribes of Israel. And everyone who has left houses or brothers or
sisters or father or mother or children or farms for My name's
sake, will receive many times as much, and will inherit eternal life. But many who are first will be last; and the last, first."*
(Matthew 19:23-30)

The first thing that we learn in these verses is *the immense danger which
riches bring on the souls of those that possess them.* The Lord Jesus declares
that *"It is hard for a rich man to enter the kingdom of heaven."* He goes
even further. He uses a proverbial saying to strengthen His assertion:
*"It is easier for a camel to go through the eye of a needle, than for a rich
man to enter the kingdom of God."*

Few of our Lord's sayings sound more startling than this. Few run
more counter to the opinions and prejudices of mankind. Few are so
little believed. Yet this saying is true and worthy of all acceptance. Riches,
which all desire to obtain – riches, for which men labor and toil and
become gray before their time – riches are a most perilous possession.
They often inflict great injury on the soul. They lead men into many
temptations. They engross men's thoughts and affections. They bind
heavy burdens on the heart and make the way to heaven even more
difficult than it naturally is.

Let us beware of the love of money. It is possible to use it well and
do good with it. But for each one who makes a right use of money,
there are thousands who make a wrong use of it and do harm both
to themselves and others. Let the worldly man, if he will, make an
idol of money and count him happiest who has most of it. But let the
Christian, who professes to have *treasure in heaven*, set his face like a
flint against the spirit of the world in this matter. Let him not worship
gold. He is not the best man in God's eyes who has most money, but
he who has most grace.

Let us pray daily for rich men's souls. They are not to be envied. They
are deeply to be pitied. They carry heavy weights in the Christian race.
They are of all men the least likely to *run in such a way that [they] may*

win (1 Corinthians 9:24). Their prosperity in this world is often their destruction in the world to come. Well may the litany of the Church of England contain the words, "In all time of our wealth, good Lord, deliver us."

The second thing that we learn in this passage is *the almighty power of God's grace in the soul.* The disciples were amazed when they heard our Lord's language about rich men. It was language so subversive to all their notions about the advantages of wealth that they cried out with surprise, *"Then who can be saved?"* They drew from our Lord a gracious answer: *"With people this is impossible, but with God all things are possible."*

The Holy Spirit can incline even the richest of men to seek treasure in heaven. He can dispose even kings to cast their crowns at the feet of Jesus and count all things but loss for the sake of the kingdom of God. Proof upon proof of this is given to us in the Bible. Abraham was very rich, yet he was the father of the faithful. Moses might have been a prince or king in Egypt, but he forsook all his brilliant prospects for the sake of Him who is invisible. Job was the wealthiest man in the east, yet he was a chosen servant of God. David, Jehoshaphat, Josiah, and Hezekiah were all wealthy monarchs, but they loved God's favor more than their earthly greatness. They all show us that nothing is *too difficult for the Lord*, and that faith can grow even in the most unlikely soil.

Let us hold fast this doctrine and never let it go. No man's place or circumstances shut him out from the kingdom of God. Let us never despair of anyone's salvation. No doubt rich people require special grace and are exposed to special temptations. But the Lord God of Abraham and Moses and Job and David has not changed. He who saved them in spite of their riches can save others also. When He works, who shall hinder it? (Isaiah 43:13).

The last thing that we learn in these verses is *the immense encouragement the gospel offers to those who give up everything for Christ's sake.* We are told that Peter asked our Lord what he and the other apostles, who had forsaken their little *all* for His sake, would receive in return. He obtained a most gracious reply. A full recompense shall be made to all who make sacrifices for Christ's sake – they *will receive many times as much, and will inherit eternal life.*

There is something very cheering in this promise. Few in the present day, except converts among the heathen, are ever required to forsake homes, relations, and lands on account of their religion. Yet there are few true Christians who have not much to go through, in one way or another, if they are really faithful to their Lord. The offense of the cross has not yet ceased. Laughter, ridicule, mockery, and family persecution are often the portion of an English believer. The favor of the world is often forfeited, and places and situations are often imperiled by a conscientious adherence to the demands of the gospel of Christ. All who are exposed to trials of this kind may take comfort in the promise of these verses. Jesus foresaw their need and intended these words to be their consolation.

We may rest assured that no man shall ever be a real loser by following Christ. The believer may seem to suffer loss for a time, when he first begins the life of a decided Christian. He may be much cast down by the afflictions that are brought upon him on account of his religion. But let him rest assured that he will never find himself a loser in the long run. Christ can raise up friends for us who shall more than compensate for those we lose. Christ can open hearts and homes to us far more warm and hospitable than those that are closed against us. Above all, Christ can give us peace of conscience, inward joy, bright hopes, and happy feelings which shall far outweigh every pleasant earthly thing that we have cast away for His sake. He has pledged His royal word that it shall be so. None ever found that word to fail. Let us trust it and not be afraid.

Matthew Chapter 20

Matthew 20:1-16

"For the kingdom of heaven is like a landowner who went out early in the morning to hire laborers for his vineyard. When he had agreed with the laborers for a denarius for the day, he sent them into his vineyard. And he went out about the third hour and saw others standing idle in the market place; and to those he said, 'You also go into the vineyard, and whatever is right I will give you.' And so they went. Again he went out about the sixth and the ninth hour, and did the same thing. And about the eleventh hour he went out and found others standing around; and he said to them, 'Why have you been standing here idle all day long?' They said to him, 'Because no one hired us.' He said to them, 'You go into the vineyard too.' When evening came, the owner of the vineyard said to his foreman, 'Call the laborers and pay them their wages, beginning with the last group to the first.' When those hired about the eleventh hour came, each one received a denarius. When those hired first came, they thought that they would receive more; but each of them also received each a denarius. When they received it, they grumbled at the landowner, saying, 'These last men have worked only one hour, and you have made them equal to us who have borne the burden and the scorching heat of the day.' But he answered and said to one of them, 'Friend, I am doing you no wrong; did you not agree with me for a denarius? Take what is yours and go, but I wish to give to this last man the same as to you. Is it not lawful for me to do what I wish with what is my own? Or is your eye envious because

I am generous?' So the last shall be first, and the first last."
(Matthew 20:1-16)

THERE ARE UNDENIABLE DIFFICULTIES in the parable contained in these verses. The key to the right explanation of them must be sought in the passage which concludes the previous chapter. There we find the apostle Peter asking our Lord a remarkable question: *"Behold, we have left everything and followed You; what then will there be for us?"* There we find Jesus giving a remarkable answer. He makes a special promise to Peter and his fellow disciples: *"You also shall sit upon twelve thrones, judging the twelve tribes of Israel."* He makes a general promise to all who suffer loss for His sake: *"[They] will receive many times as much, and will inherit eternal life."*

Now we must bear in mind that Peter was a Jew. Like most Jews, he had probably been brought up in much ignorance as to God's purposes regarding the salvation of the Gentiles. In fact, we know from Acts that it required a vision from heaven to take that ignorance away (Acts 10:28). Furthermore, we must bear in mind that Peter and his fellow disciples were weak in faith and knowledge. They were probably apt to attach a great importance to their own sacrifices for Christ's sake and be inclined to self-righteousness and self-conceit. Both these points our Lord knew well.

In expounding this parable, we need not inquire closely into the meaning of the *denarius*, the *market place*, the *foreman*, or the *hour*. Such inquiries often darken counsel by words without knowledge. Well says Calovius, "The theology of parables is not argumentative." The hint of Chrysostom deserves notice. He says, "It is not right to search curiously, and word by word, into all things in a parable, but when we have learned the object for which it was composed, to reap this, and not to busy ourselves about anything further." Two main lessons appear to stand out on the face of the parable and to embrace the general scope of its meaning. Let us content ourselves with these two.

We learn, in the first place, that *in the calling of nations to the professed knowledge of Himself, God exercises free, sovereign, and unconditional grace.* He calls the families of the earth into the visible church at His own time and in His own way.

We see this truth wonderfully brought out in the history of God's dealings with the world. We see the children of Israel called and chosen to be God's people in the very beginning of "the day." We see some of the Gentiles called at a later period by the preaching of the apostles. We see others being called in the present age by the labors of missionaries. We see others, like the millions of Chinese and Hindus, still *standing idle because no one hired* them. And why is all this? We cannot tell. We only know that God loves to hide pride from churches and to take away all occasion of boasting. He will never allow the older branches of His church to look contemptuously on the younger. His gospel holds out pardon and peace with God through Christ to the heathen of our own times as fully as it did to Paul. The converted inhabitants of New Zealand shall be as fully admitted to heaven as the holiest patriarch who died thirty-five hundred years ago. The old wall between Jews and Gentiles is removed. There is nothing to prevent the believing heathen from being a fellow heir and partaker of the same hope with the believing Israelite. The Gentiles converted at *the eleventh hour* of the world shall be as really and truly heirs of glory as the Jews. They shall sit down with Abraham, Isaac, and Jacob in the kingdom of heaven while many of the children of the kingdom are forever cast out. *The last shall be first.*

We learn, in the second place, that in *the saving of individuals, as well as in the calling of nations,* God acts as a sovereign and gives no account of His matters. He has mercy on whom He will have mercy, and that too at His own time (Romans 9:15).

This is a truth which we see illustrated on every side in the church of Christ as a matter of experience. We see one man called to repentance and faith in the beginning of his days, like Timothy, and laboring in the Lord's vineyard for forty or fifty years. We see another man called at *about the eleventh hour,* like the thief on the cross, and plucked like a brand out of the fire – one day a hard, impenitent sinner, and the next day in paradise. And yet the whole tenor of the gospel leads us to believe that both these men are equally forgiven before God. Both are equally washed in Christ's blood and clothed in Christ's righteousness. Both are equally justified, both accepted, and both will be found at Christ's right hand in the last day.

There can be no doubt that this doctrine sounds strange to the ignorant and inexperienced Christian. It confounds the pride of human nature. It leaves the self-righteous no room to boast. It is a leveling, humbling doctrine, and gives occasion to many a murmur. But it is impossible to reject it, unless we reject the whole Bible. _True faith in Christ, though it be but a day old, justifies a man before God as completely as the faith of him who has followed Christ for fifty years._ The righteousness in which Timothy will stand at the day of judgment is the same as that of the penitent thief. Both will be saved by grace alone. Both will owe all to Christ. We may not like this, but it is the doctrine of this parable, and not of this parable only, but of the whole New Testament. Happy is he who can receive the doctrine with humility! Well says Bishop Hall, "If some have cause to magnify God's bounty, none have cause to complain."

Before we leave this parable, let us arm our minds with some necessary cautions. It is a portion of Scripture that is frequently perverted and misapplied. Men have often drawn from it not milk but poison.

Let us beware of supposing from anything in this parable that salvation is in the slightest degree to be obtained by works. To suppose this is to overthrow the whole teaching of the Bible. Whatever a believer receives in the next world is a matter of grace and not of debt. God is never a debtor to us in any sense whatsoever. When we have done all, we are unprofitable servants (Luke 17:10).

Let us beware of supposing from this parable that the distinction between Jews and Gentiles is entirely done away with by the gospel. To suppose this is to contradict many plain prophecies, both of the Old Testament and the New. In the matter of justification, there is no distinction between the believing Jew and the Greek. Yet Israel is still a special people and not numbered among the nations. God has many purposes concerning the Jews which are yet to be fulfilled.

Let us beware of supposing from this parable that all saved souls will have the same degree of glory. To suppose this is to contradict many plain texts of Scripture. The title of all believers no doubt is the same: the righteousness of Christ. But all will not have the same place in heaven. *Each will receive his own reward according to his own labor* (1 Corinthians 3:8).

Finally, let us beware of supposing from this parable that it is safe for anyone to put off repentance until the end of his days. To suppose this is a most dangerous delusion. The longer men refuse to obey Christ's voice, the less likely they are to be saved. *Behold, now is "the acceptable time," behold, now is "the day of salvation"* (2 Corinthians 6:2). Few are ever saved on their deathbeds. One thief on the cross was saved, so that none should despair; but only one, so that none should presume. A false confidence in those words, *the eleventh hour*, has ruined thousands of souls.

Matthew 20:17-23

As Jesus was about to go up to Jerusalem, He took the twelve disciples aside by themselves, and on the way He said to them, "Behold, we are going up to Jerusalem; and the Son of Man will be delivered to the chief priests and scribes, and they will condemn Him to death, and will hand Him over to the Gentiles to mock and scourge and crucify Him, and on the third day He will be raised up." Then the mother of the sons of Zebedee came to Jesus with her sons, bowing down and making a request of Him. And He said to her, "What do you wish?" She said to Him, "Command that in Your kingdom these two sons of mine may sit one on Your right and one on Your left." But Jesus answered, "You do not know what you are asking. Are you able to drink the cup that I am about to drink?" They said to Him, "We are able." He said to them, "My cup you shall drink; but to sit on My right and on My left, this is not Mine to give, but it is for those for whom it has been prepared by My Father." (Matthew 20:17-23)

The first thing we should notice in these verses is *the clear announcement which the Lord Jesus Christ makes of His own approaching death.*

For the third time we find Him telling His disciples the astounding truth that He, their wonder-working Master, must soon suffer and die.

The Lord Jesus knew from the beginning all that was before Him. The treachery of Judas Iscariot – the fierce persecution of the chief priests and scribes – the unjust judgment – the delivery to Pontius Pilate – the mocking, the scourging, the crown of thorns, the cross, the hanging between two malefactors, the nails, and the spear – all, all were spread before His mind like a picture.

How great an aggravation of suffering foreknowledge is, as those know well who have lived in the prospect of some fearful surgical operation. Yet none of these things moved our Lord. He says, *I was not disobedient nor did I turn back. I gave my back to those who strike Me, and My cheeks to those who pluck out the beard; I did not cover My face from humiliation and spitting* (Isaiah 50:5-6). He saw Calvary in the distance all His life, and yet walked calmly up to it without turning to the right hand or to the left. Surely there never was sorrow like unto His sorrow, or love like His love.

The Lord Jesus was a voluntary sufferer. When He died on the cross, it was not because He had not power to prevent it. He suffered intentionally, deliberately, and of His own free will (John 10:18). He knew that without the shedding of His blood there could be no remission of man's sin. He knew that He was the Lamb of God who must die to take away the sin of the world. He knew that His death was the appointed sacrifice which must be offered up to make reconciliation for iniquity. Knowing all this, He went willingly to the cross. His heart was set on finishing the mighty work He came into the world to do. He was well aware that all hinged on His own death, and that without that death, His miracles and preaching would have done comparatively nothing for the world. No wonder that He three times pressed on the attention of His disciples that He *must* die. Blessed and happy are they who know the real meaning and importance of the sufferings of Christ!

The next thing that we should notice in these verses is *the mixture of ignorance and faith that may be found even in true-hearted Christians.* We see the mother of James and John coming to our Lord with her two sons and proposing on their behalf a strange petition. She asks that they *"may sit one on Your right and one on Your left"* in His kingdom. She seems to have forgotten all He had just been saying about His suffering. Her eager mind can think of nothing but His glory. His plain warnings about the crucifixion appear to have been thrown away on her sons. Their thoughts were full of nothing but His throne and the day of His power. There was much of *faith* in their request, but there was much more of *infirmity*. There was something to be commended in that they could see in Jesus of Nazareth a coming king. But there was also much to blame in that they did not remember that He was to be crucified before He could reign. Truly the flesh lusts against the spirit in all God's children, and Luther well remarks, "The flesh ever seeks to be glorified before it is crucified."

There are many Christians who are very much like this woman and her sons. They see in part, and know in part, the things of God. They have faith enough to follow Christ. They have knowledge enough to hate sin and come out from the world. And yet there are many truths of Christianity of which they are deplorably ignorant. They talk ignorantly, they act ignorantly, and they commit many sad mistakes. Their acquaintance with the Bible is very scanty. Their insight into their own hearts is very small. But we must learn from these verses to deal gently with such people, because the Lord has received them. We must not set them down as graceless and godless because of their ignorance. We must remember that true faith may lie at the bottom of their hearts, though there is much rubbish at the top. We must reflect that the sons of Zebedee, whose knowledge was at one time so imperfect, became at a later period pillars of the church of Christ. Just so a believer may begin his course in much darkness, and yet prove finally a man mighty in the Scriptures and a worthy follower of James and John.

The last thing that we should notice in these verses is *the solemn reproof which our Lord gives to the ignorant request of the mother of Zebedee's children and her two sons.* He says to them, *"You do not know what you are asking."* They had asked to share in their Master's *reward,* but they had not considered that they must first be partakers in their Master's *sufferings* (1 Peter 4:13). They had forgotten that those who would stand with Christ in glory must drink of His cup of suffering and be baptized with His baptism. They did not see that those who carry the *cross*, and those alone, shall receive the *crown*. Well might our Lord say, *"You do not know what you are asking."*

But do we never commit the same mistake that the sons of Zebedee committed? Do we never fall into their error and make thoughtless, inconsiderate requests? Do we not often say things in prayer without counting the cost, and ask for things to be granted to us without reflecting on how much our supplications involve? These are heart-searching questions. It may well be feared that many of us cannot give them a satisfactory answer.

We ask that our souls may be saved and go to heaven when we die. It is a good request indeed. But are we prepared to take up the cross and follow Christ? Are we willing to give up the world for His sake? Are we ready to put off the old man and put on the new, to fight, to labor, and to run so as to obtain? Are we ready to withstand a taunting world and endure hardships for Christ's sake? What shall we say? If we are not so ready, our Lord might say to us also, *"You do not know what you are asking."*

We ask that God would make us holy. It is a good request indeed. But are we prepared to be sanctified by any process that God in His wisdom may call on us to pass through? Are we ready to be purified by affliction, weaned from the world by bereavements, drawn nearer to God by losses, sicknesses, and sorrow? Alas! these are hard questions. But if we are not, our Lord might well say to us, *"You do not know what you are asking."*

Let us leave these verses with a solemn resolution to consider well what we are about when we draw near to God in prayer. Let us beware of thoughtless, inconsiderate, and rash petitions. Well has Solomon said, *Do not be hasty in word or impulsive in thought to bring up a matter in the presence of God* (Ecclesiastes 5:2).

Matthew 20:24-28

And hearing this, the ten became indignant with the two brothers. But Jesus called them to Himself and said, "You know that the rulers of the Gentiles lord it over them, and their great men exercise authority over them. It is not this way among you, but whoever wishes to become great among you shall be your servant, and whoever wishes to be first among you shall be your slave; just as the Son of Man did not come to be served, but to serve, and to give His life a ransom for many." (Matthew 20:24-28)

These verses are few in number, but they contain lessons of great importance to all professing Christians. Let us see what they are.

In the first place, we learn that *there may be pride, jealousy, and love of pre-eminence even among true disciples of Christ.* What says the Scripture? *And hearing this* (what James and John had asked), *the ten became indignant with the two brothers.*

Pride is one of the oldest and most mischievous of sins. By it the angels fell, for *they did not keep their own domain* (Jude v. 6). Through pride Adam and Eve were seduced into eating the forbidden fruit. They were not content with their lot and thought they would *be like God.* From pride the saints of God receive their greatest injuries after their conversion. Well says Hooker, "Pride is a vice, which cleaves so fast unto the heart of men, that if we were to strip ourselves off all faults, one by one, we should undoubtedly find it the very last and hardest to put off." It is a quaint but true saying of Bishop Hall, that "pride is the inmost coat, which we take off last, and which we put on first."

In the second place, we learn that *a life of self-denying kindness to others is the true secret of greatness in the kingdom of Christ.* What says the Scripture? *"Whoever wishes to become great among you shall be your servant, and whoever wishes to be first among you shall be your slave."*

The standard of the world and the standard of the Lord Jesus are indeed widely different. They are more than different. They are flatly contradictory one to the other. Among the children of this world, he is thought the greatest man who has most land, most money, most

EXPOSITORY THOUGHTS ON THE GOSPEL OF MATTHEW

servants, most rank, and most earthly power. Among the children of
God, he is reckoned the greatest who does most to promote the spiritual
and temporal happiness of his fellow men. True greatness consists not
in receiving, but in giving – not in selfish absorption of good things,
but in imparting good to others – not in being served, but in serving
– not in sitting still and being ministered to, but in going about and
ministering to others.

The angels of God see far more beauty in the work of the missionary than in the work of the Australian digger for gold. They take far
more interest in the labors of men like Howard and Judson than in the
victories of generals, the political speeches of statesmen, or the council chambers of kings. Let us remember these things. Let us beware of
seeking false greatness. Let as aim at that which alone is true. We may
be sure there is profound wisdom in that saying of our Lord's: *"It is
more blessed to give than to receive"* (Acts 20:35).

In the third place, we learn that *the Lord Jesus Christ is intended
to be the example of all true Christians.* What says the Scripture? We
ought to serve one another *"just as the Son of Man did not come to be
served, but to serve."*

The Lord God has mercifully provided His people with everything
necessary for their sanctification. He has given those who follow after
holiness the clearest of precepts, the best of motives, and the most
encouraging of promises. But this is not all. He has furthermore supplied them with the most perfect pattern and example, even the life
of His own Son. By that life He bids us model our own. In the steps
of that life He bids us walk (1 Peter 2:21). It is the model after which
we must strive to mold our tempers, our words, and our works in this
evil world. "Would my Master have spoken in this manner? Would my
Master have behaved in this way?" These are the questions by which we
ought daily to test ourselves.

How humbling this truth is! What searchings of heart it ought to
raise within us! What a loud call it is to *lay aside every encumbrance
and the sin which so easily entangles us.* What manner of people ought
they to be who profess to copy Christ! What poor, unprofitable religion
is that which makes a man content with talking and empty profession

while his life is unholy and unclean! Alas! those who know nothing of Christ as an example will find at last that He knows nothing of them as His saved people. *The one who says he abides in Him ought himself to walk in the same manner as He walked* (1 John 2:6).

Finally, let us learn from these verses that *Christ's death was an atonement for sin*. What says the Scripture? The Son of Man came *to give His life a ransom for many*.

This is the mightiest truth in the Bible. Let us take care that we grasp it firmly and never let it go. Our Lord Jesus Christ did not die merely as a martyr or as a splendid example of self-sacrifice and self-denial. Those who can see no more than that in His death fall infinitely short of the truth. They lose sight of the very foundation-stone of Christianity and miss the whole comfort of the gospel. *Christ died as a sacrifice for man's sin*. He died to make reconciliation for man's iniquity. He died to purge our sins by the offering of Himself. He died to redeem us from the curse which we all deserved, and to make satisfaction to the justice of God which must otherwise have condemned us. Never let us forget this!

We are all by nature debtors. We owe to our holy Maker ten thousand talents and are not able to pay. We cannot atone for our own transgressions, for we are weak and frail and only adding to our debts every day. But, blessed be God! What we could not do, Christ came into the world to do for us. What we could not pay, He undertook to pay for us. To pay it He died for us upon the cross. He *offered Himself without blemish to God* (Hebrews 9:14). *Christ also died for sins once for all, the just for the unjust, so that He might bring us to God* (1 Peter 3:18). Once more, never let us forget this!

Let us not leave these verses without asking ourselves, Where is our humility? What is our idea of true greatness? What is our example? What is our hope? Life, eternal life, depends on the answer we give to these questions. Happy is that man who is truly humble, strives to do good in his day, walks in the steps of Jesus, and rests all his hopes on the ransom paid for him by Christ's blood. Such a man is a true Christian!

Matthew 20:29-34

As they were leaving Jericho, a large crowd followed Him. And two blind men sitting by the road, hearing that Jesus was passing by, cried out, "Lord, have mercy on us, Son of David!" The crowd sternly told them to be quiet, but they cried out all the more, "Lord, Son of David, have mercy on us!" And Jesus stopped and called them, and said, "What do you want Me to do for you?" They said to Him, "Lord, we want our eyes to be opened." Moved with compassion, Jesus touched their eyes; and immediately they regained their sight and followed Him. (Matthew 20:29-34)

In these verses we have a touching picture of an event in our Lord's history. He heals two blind men sitting by the wayside near Jericho. The circumstances of the event contain several deeply interesting lessons which all professing Christians would do well to remember.

For one thing, let us mark *what strong faith may sometimes be found where it might least have been expected.* Blind as these two men were, they believed that Jesus was able to help them. They never saw any of our Lord's miracles. They knew Him only by hearsay and not face to face. And yet, as soon as they heard that He was passing by, they *cried out, "Lord, have mercy on us, Son of David!"*

Such faith may well put us to shame. With all our books of evidence, and lives of saints, and libraries of divinity, how few know anything of simple, childlike confidence in Christ's mercy and Christ's power. And even among those who are believers, the degree of faith is often strangely disproportionate to the privileges enjoyed. Many an unlearned man, who can only read his New Testament with difficulty, possesses the spirit of unhesitating trust in Christ's advocacy, while deeply knowledgeable theologians are harassed by questionings and doubts. They who, humanly speaking, ought to be first, are often last, and the last first.

For another thing, let us mark *what wisdom there is in using every opportunity for getting good for our souls.* These blind men sat *by the road.* Had they not done so, they might never have been healed. Jesus never returned to Jericho, so they might never have met with Him again.

Let us see, in this simple fact, the importance of diligence in church attendance. Let us never neglect the house of God, never forsake the assembling of ourselves with God's people, never omit the reading of our Bibles, and never let drop the practice of private prayer. These things, no doubt, will not save us without the grace of the Holy Spirit. Thousands make use of them and remain dead in trespasses and sins. But it is just in the use of these things that souls are converted and saved. They are *the ways in which Jesus walks.* It is those who sit *by the road* who are likely to be healed. Do we know the diseases of our souls? Do we feel any desire to see the Great Physician? If we do, we must not wait in idleness, saying, "If I am to be saved, I shall be saved." We must arise and go to the road where Jesus walks. Who can tell but He will soon pass by for the last time? Let us sit daily *by the road.*

For another thing, let us mark *the value of pains and perseverance in seeking Christ.* These blind men were rebuked by the multitude that accompanied our Lord. Men told them to be quiet. But they were not to be silenced in this way. They felt their need of help. They cared nothing for the check which they received. *They cried out all the more, "Lord, Son of David, have mercy on us!"*

We have in this part of their conduct a most important example. We are not to be deterred by opposition or discouraged by difficulties when we begin to seek the salvation of our souls. We must *at all times . . . pray and not . . . lose heart* (Luke 18:1). We must remember the parable of the importunate widow and of the friend who came to borrow bread at midnight. Like them we must press our petitions at the throne of grace and say, *"I will not let you go unless you bless me"* (Genesis 32:26). Friends, relatives, and neighbors may say unkind things and reprove our earnestness. We may meet with coldness and lack of sympathy where we might have looked for help. But let none of these things move us. If we feel our diseases and want to find Jesus, the great Physician, and if we know our sins and desire to have them pardoned, then let us press on. *The kingdom of heaven suffers violence, and violent men take it by force* (Matthew 11:12).

Finally, let us mark *how gracious the Lord Jesus is to those who seek Him.* Jesus stopped and called the blind men. He kindly asked them what it was that they desired. He heard their petition and did what they requested. He, *moved with compassion, touched their eyes; and immediately they regained their sight and followed Him.*

We see here an illustration of that old truth which we can never know too well – the mercifulness of Christ's heart towards the sons of men. The Lord Jesus is not only a mighty Savior, but also merciful, kind, and gracious to a degree that our minds cannot conceive. Well might the apostle Paul say, that *the love of Christ . . . surpasses knowledge* (Ephesians 3:19). Like him, let us pray that we may *know* more of that love. We need it when we first begin our Christian course as poor, trembling penitents and babes in grace. We need it afterwards as we travel along the narrow way, often erring, often stumbling, and often cast down. We shall need it in the evening of our days when we go down the valley of the shadow of death. Let us then grasp the love of Christ firmly and keep it daily before our minds. We shall never know, until we wake up in the next world, how much we are indebted to it.

Matthew Chapter 21

Matthew 21:1-11

When they had approached Jerusalem and had come to Bethphage, at the Mount of Olives, then Jesus sent two disciples, saying to them, "Go into the village opposite you, and immediately you will find a donkey tied there and a colt with her; untie them and bring them to Me. If anyone says anything to you, you shall say, 'The Lord has need of them,' and immediately he will send them." This took place to fulfill what was spoken through the prophet: "Say to the daughter of Zion, 'Behold your King is coming to you, gentle, and mounted on a donkey, even on a colt, the foal of a beast of burden.'" The disciples went and did just as Jesus had instructed them, and brought the donkey and the colt, and laid their coats on them; and Him sat on the coats. Most of the crowd spread their coats in the road, and others were cutting branches from the trees and spreading them in the road. The crowds going ahead of Him, and those who followed, were shouting, "Hosanna to the Son of David; Blessed is He who comes in the name of the Lord; Hosanna in the highest!" When He had entered Jerusalem, all the city was stirred, saying, "Who is this?" And the crowds were saying, "This is the prophet Jesus, from Nazareth in Galilee." (Matthew 21:1-11)

THESE VERSES CONTAIN A VERY REMARKABLE PASSAGE in our Lord Jesus Christ's life. They describe His public entry into Jerusalem when He came there for the last time before He was crucified.

There is something peculiarly striking in this incident in our Lord's history. The narrative reads like the account of some royal conqueror's return to his own city. *Most of the crowd* accompanies Him in a kind of triumphal procession. Loud cries and expressions of praise are heard around Him. *All the city was stirred.* The whole transaction is singularly at variance with the past tenor of our Lord's life. It is curiously unlike the ways of Him who did not *"quarrel, nor cry out; nor will anyone hear His voice in the streets"* – who withdrew Himself from the multitude on other occasions – and said to those He healed, *"See that you say nothing to anyone"* (Mark 1:44). And yet the whole transaction admits of explanation. The reasons for this public entry are not hard to find out. Let us see what they were.

The plain truth is that our Lord knew well that the time of His earthly ministry was drawing to a close. He knew that the hour was approaching when He must finish the mighty work He came to do, by dying for our sins upon the cross. He knew that His last journey had been accomplished and that there remained nothing now in His earthly ministry but to be offered as a sacrifice on Calvary. Knowing all this, He no longer, as in time past, sought secrecy. Knowing all this, He thought it good to enter the place where He was to be delivered to death with peculiar solemnity and publicity. It was not fitting that the Lamb of God should come to be slain on Calvary privately and silently. Before the great sacrifice for the sins of the world was offered up, it was right that every eye should be fixed on the victim. It was suitable that the crowning act of our Lord's life should be done with as much notoriety as possible. Therefore it was that He made this public entry. Therefore it was that He attracted to Himself the eyes of the wondering multitude. Therefore it was that all Jerusalem was moved. The atoning blood of the Lamb of God was about to be shed. The deed was not to be *done in a corner* (Acts 26:26).

It is good to remember these things. The real meaning of our Lord's conduct at this period of His history is not sufficiently considered by many readers of this passage. It remains for us to consider the practical lessons which these verses appear to point out.

In the first place, let us notice in these verses *an example of our Lord Jesus Christ's perfect knowledge.* He sends His two disciples into a village. He tells them that they will there find the donkey on which He was to ride. He provides them with an answer to the inquiry of those to whom the donkey belonged. He tells them that on giving that answer the donkey will be sent. And all happens exactly as He foretells.

There is nothing hidden from the Lord's eyes. There are no secrets with Him. Alone or in company, by night or by day, in private or in public, He is acquainted with all our ways. He who saw Nathanael under the fig tree is unchanged. Go where we will, and retire from the world as we may, we are never out of sight of Christ.

This is a thought that ought to exercise a restraining and sanctifying effect on our souls. We all know the influence which the presence of the rulers of this world has upon their subjects. Nature itself teaches us to put a check on our tongues, our demeanor, and our behavior when we are under the eye of a king. The sense of our Lord Jesus Christ's perfect knowledge of all our ways ought to have the same effect upon our hearts. Let us do nothing we would not like Christ to see and say nothing we would not like Christ to hear. Let us seek to live and move and have our being under a continual recollection of Christ's presence. Let us behave as we would have done had we walked beside Him in the company of James and John by the Sea of Galilee. This is the way to be trained for heaven. In heaven, *we shall always be with the Lord* (1 Thessalonians 4:17).

In the second place, let us notice in these verses *an example of the manner in which prophecies concerning our Lord's first coming were fulfilled.* We are told that His public entry fulfilled the words of Zechariah: *"'Your King is coming to you, gentle, and mounted on a donkey.'"*

It appears that this prediction was *literally and exactly fulfilled.* The words which the prophet spoke by the Holy Spirit received no figurative accomplishment. As he said it, so it came to pass. As he foretold it, so it was done. Five hundred and fifty years had passed away since the prediction was made – and then, when the appointed time arrived, the long-promised Messiah did literally ride into Zion on a donkey. No doubt the vast majority of the inhabitants of Jerusalem saw nothing in the circumstance. The veil was upon their hearts. But we are not left in doubt as to the fulfillment of the prophecy. We are told plainly, *This took place to fulfill what was spoken through the prophet.*

From the fulfillment of God's Word in time past, we are surely intended to gather something as to the manner of its fulfillment in time to come. We have a right to expect that prophecies respecting the second advent of Christ will be as literally fulfilled as those respecting His first advent. He came to this earth literally in person the first time. He will come to this earth literally in person the second time. He came in humiliation once literally to suffer. He will come again in glory literally to reign. Every prediction respecting things accompanying His first advent was literally accomplished. It will be just the same when He returns. All that is foretold about the restoration of the Jews – the judgments on the ungodly, the unbelief of the world, the gathering of the elect – shall be made good to the letter. Let us not forget this. In the study of unfulfilled prophecy, a fixed principle of interpretation is of the first importance.

Finally, let us notice in these verses *a striking example of the worthlessness of man's favor.* Of all the multitudes who crowded around our Lord as He entered Jerusalem, none stood by Him when He was delivered into the hands of wicked men. Many cried, *"Hosanna!"* who four days after cried, *"Away with Him, crucify Him!"*

But this is a faithful picture of human nature. This is a proof of the utter folly of thinking more of the praise of man than the praise of God. Nothing is so fickle and uncertain as popularity. It is here today and gone tomorrow. It is a sandy foundation and sure to fail those who build upon it. Let us not care for it. Let us seek the favor of Him who *is the same yesterday and today and forever* (Hebrews 13:8). Christ never changes. Those whom He loves, He loves to the end. His favor endures forever.

Matthew 21:12-22

And Jesus entered the temple and drove out all those who were buying and selling in the temple, and overturned the tables of the money changers and the seats of those who were selling doves.

And He said to them, "It is written, 'My house shall be called a house of prayer'; but you are making it a robbers' den." And the blind and the lame came to Him in the temple, and He healed them. But when the chief priests and scribes saw the wonderful things that He had done, and the children were shouting in the temple, "Hosanna to the Son of David," they became indignant and said to Him, "Do You hear what these children are saying?" And Jesus said to them, "Yes; have you never read, 'Out of the mouth of infants and nursing babies You have prepared praise for Yourself'?" And He left them and went out of the city to Bethany, and spent the night there. Now in the morning, when He was returning to the city, He became hungry. Seeing a lone fig tree by the road, He came to it and found nothing on it except leaves only; and He said to it, "No longer shall there ever be any fruit from you." And at once the fig tree withered. Seeing this, the disciples were amazed and asked, "How did the fig tree wither all at once?" And Jesus answered and said to them, "Truly I say to you, if you have faith and do not doubt, you will not only do what was done to the fig tree, but even if you say to this mountain, 'Be taken up and cast into the sea,' it will happen. And all things you ask in prayer, believing, you will receive." (Matthew 21:12-22)

We have in these verses an account of two remarkable events in our Lord's history. In both, there was something eminently figurative and typical. Each was an emblem of spiritual things. Beneath the surface of each of these lie lessons of solemn instruction.

The first event that demands our attention is *our Lord's visit to the temple.* He found His Father's house in a state which too truly shadowed forth the general condition of the whole Jewish church – everything out of order and out of course. He found the courts of that holy building disgracefully profaned by worldly transactions. Trading, buying, and selling were actually going on within its walls. There stood dealers ready to supply the Jew who came from distant countries with any sacrifice he wanted. There sat the money changer ready to change his foreign money for the current coin of the land. Bulls, sheep, goats, and pigeons were there exposed for sale as if the place had been a market. The jingling of money might there be heard as if these holy courts had been a bank or an exchange.

Such were the scenes that met our Lord's eyes. He saw it all with holy indignation. *He drove out all those who were buying and selling.* He *overturned the tables of the money changers.* Resistance there was none, for men knew that He was right. Objection there was none, for all felt that He was only reforming a notorious abuse which had been basely permitted for the sake of gain. Well might He sound in the ears of the astonished traders as they fled from the temple: *"It is written, 'My house shall be called a house of prayer'; but you are making it a robbers' den."*

Let us see in our Lord's conduct on this occasion a striking example of what He will do when He comes again the second time. He will purify His visible church as He purified the temple. He will cleanse it from everything that defiles and works iniquity, and cast every worldly professor out of its pale. He will allow no worshiper of money or lover of gain to have a place in that glorious temple which He will finally exhibit before the world. May we all strive to live in the daily expectation of that coming! May we judge ourselves that we be not condemned and cast out in that searching and sifting day! We should often study those words of Malachi: *"Who can endure the day of His coming? And who can stand when He appears? For He is like a refiner's fire and like fullers' soap"* (Malachi 3:2).

The second event that demands our attention in these verses is *our Lord's curse upon the fruitless fig tree.* We are told that being hungry He came to a fig tree in the way and *found nothing on it except leaves only; and He said to it, "No longer shall there ever be any fruit from you."* And at once the fig tree withered. This is an incident almost without parallel in all our Lord's ministry. It is almost the only occasion on which we find Him making one of His creatures suffer in order to teach a spiritual truth. There was a heart-searching lesson in that withered fig tree. It preaches a sermon we shall all do well to hear.

That fig tree, full of leaves but barren of fruit, was a striking emblem of the Jewish church when our Lord was upon earth. The Jewish church had everything to make an outward show. It had the temple, the priesthood, the daily service, the yearly feasts, the Old Testament Scriptures, the rituals of the Levites, and the morning and evening sacrifices. But beneath these goodly *leaves*, the Jewish church was utterly destitute of *fruit*. It had no grace, no faith, no love, no humility, no spirituality, no real holiness, and no willingness to receive its Messiah (John 1:11). And hence, like the fig tree, the Jewish church was soon to wither away. It was to be stripped of all its outward ornaments and its members scattered over the face of the earth. Jerusalem was to be destroyed. The temple was to be burned. The daily sacrifice was to be taken away. The tree was to wither away to the very ground. And so it came to pass. Never was there a type so literally fulfilled. In every wandering Jew we see a branch of the fig tree that was crushed.

But we may not stop here. We may find even more instruction in the event we are now considering. These things were written for our sake as well as for the Jews'.

Is not every fruitless branch of Christ's visible church in a dreadful danger of becoming a withered fig tree? Beyond doubt it is. High ecclesiastical profession without holiness among the people – much confidence in councils, bishops, liturgies, and ceremonies while repentance and faith have been neglected – have ruined many a visible church in time past and may yet ruin many more. Where are the once famous churches of Ephesus and Sardis and Carthage and Hippo? They are all gone. They had leaves but no fruit. Our Lord's curse came upon them. They became withered fig trees. The decree went forth, *"Chop down the tree"* (Daniel 4:23). Let us remember this. Let us beware of church pride. Let us not be high-minded, but fear (Romans 2:20).

Finally, is not every fruitless professor of Christianity in dreadful danger of becoming a withered fig tree? There can be no doubt of it. So long as a man is content with the "leaves" of religion – with a name to live while he is dead, and a form of godliness without the power – his soul is in great peril. So long as he is satisfied with going to church or chapel and receiving the Lord's Supper and being called a Christian, while his heart is not changed and his sins not forsaken – he is daily provoking God to cut him off without remedy. Fruit – the fruit of the Spirit – is the only sure proof that we are savingly united to Christ and on the way to heaven. May this sink down into our hearts and never be forgotten!

Matthew 21:23-32

God's Wisdom
+
Open arms to Sinners
willing to Repent

When He entered the temple, the chief priests and the elders of the people came to Him while He was teaching, and said, "By what authority are You doing these things, and who gave You this authority?" Jesus said to them, "I will also ask you one thing, which if you tell Me, I will also tell you by what authority I do these things. The baptism of John was from what source, from heaven or from men?" And they began reasoning among themselves, saying, "If we say, 'From heaven,' He will say to us, 'Then why did you not believe him?' But if we say, 'From men,' we fear the people; for they all regard John as a prophet." And answering Jesus, they said, "We do not know." He also said to them, "Neither will I tell you by what authority I do these things. But what do you think? A man had two sons, and he came to the first and said, 'Son, go work today in the vineyard.' And he answered, 'I will not'; but afterward he regretted it and went. The man came to the second and said the same thing; and he answered, 'I will, sir'; but he did not go. Which of the two did the will of his father?" They said, "The first." Jesus said to them, "Truly I say to you that the tax collectors and prostitutes will get into the kingdom of God before you. For John came to you in the way of righteousness and you did not believe him; but the tax collectors and prostitutes did believe him; and you, seeing this, did not even feel remorse afterward so as to believe him." (Matthew 21:23-32)

These verses contain a conversation between our Lord Jesus Christ and the chief priests and elders of the people. Those bitter enemies of all righteousness saw the sensation which the public entry into Jerusalem and the cleansing of the temple had produced. At once, they came around our Lord like bees and endeavored to find occasion for an accusation against Him.

Let us observe, in the first place, *how ready the enemies of truth are to question the authority of all who do more good than themselves.* The chief priests have not a word to say about our Lord's teaching. They make no charge against the lives or conduct of Himself or His followers. The point on which they fasten is His commission – *"By what authority are You doing these things, and who gave You this authority?"*

The same charge has often been made against the servants of God when they have striven to check the progress of ecclesiastical corruption. It is the old weapon by which the children of this world have often labored to stop the progress of revivals and reformations. It is the weapon which was often brandished in the face of the Reformers, the Puritans, and the Methodists of the last century. It is the poisoned arrow which is often shot at city missionaries and lay-agents in the present day. Too many care nothing for the manifest blessing of God on man's work so long as he is not sent forth by their own sect or party. It matters nothing to them that some humble laborer in God's harvest can point to numerous conversions of souls through his instrumentality. They still cry, *"By what authority are You doing these things?"*

His success is nothing – they demand His commission. His cures are nothing – they require His diploma. Let us neither be surprised nor moved when we hear such things. It is the old charge which was brought against Christ Himself. *There is nothing new under the sun* (Ecclesiastes 1:9).

Let us observe, in the second place, *the consummate wisdom with which our Lord replied to the question put to Him.* His enemies had asked Him for His authority for doing what He did. They doubtless intended to make His answer a handle for accusing Him. He knew the drift of their inquiry and said, *"I will also ask you one thing, which if you tell Me, I will also tell you by what authority I do these things. The baptism of John was from what source, from heaven or from men?"*

We must distinctly understand that in this answer of our Lord's there was no evasion. To suppose this is a great mistake. The counter question which He asked was in reality an answer to His enemies' question. He knew they dared not deny that John the Baptist was a man sent from God. He knew that, this being granted, He needed only to remind them of John's testimony to Himself. Had not John declared Him to be *the Lamb of God who takes away the sin of the world*? Had not John pronounced Him to be the mighty One who was to *baptize with the Holy Spirit*? In short, our Lord's question was a home-thrust to the conscience of His enemies. If they once conceded the divine authority of John the Baptist's mission, they must also concede the divinity of His own. If they acknowledged that John came from heaven, they must acknowledge that Jesus Himself was the Christ.

Let us pray that in this difficult world we may be supplied with the same kind of wisdom which was here displayed by our Lord. No doubt we ought to act on the injunction of Peter: *always being ready to make a defense to everyone who asks you to give an account for the hope that is in you, yet with gentleness and reverence* (1 Peter 3:15). We ought to shrink from no inquiry into the principles of our holy religion and to be ready at any time to defend and explain our practice. But for all this, we must never forget that *wisdom has the advantage of giving success*, and that we should strive to speak wisely in defense of a good cause. The words of Solomon deserve consideration: *Do not answer a fool according to his folly, or you will also be like him* (Proverbs 26:4).

In the last place, let us observe in these verses *what immense encouragement our Lord holds out to those who repent*. We see this strikingly brought out in the parable of the two sons. Both were told to go and work in their father's vineyard. One son, like the profligate publicans, for some time flatly refused obedience, but afterwards repented and went. The other, like the formal Pharisees, pretended willingness to go, but in reality went not. "Which of the two," says our Lord, "did the will of his father?" Even His enemies were obliged to reply, "The first."

Let it be a settled principle in our Christianity that the God and Father of our Lord Jesus Christ is infinitely willing to receive penitent sinners. It matters nothing what a man has been in time past. Does he repent and come to Christ? Then old things are passed away and all things are become new. It matters nothing how high and self-confident a man's profession of religion may be. Does he really give up his sins? If not, his profession is abominable in God's sight, and he himself is still under the curse. Let us take courage ourselves if we have been great sinners hitherto. Only let us repent and believe in Christ, and there is hope. Let us encourage others to repent. Let us hold the door wide open to the very chief of sinners. Never will that word fail: *If we confess our sins, He is faithful and righteous to forgive us our sins and to cleanse us from all unrighteousness* (1 John 1:9).

Matthew 21:33-46

"Listen to another parable: There was a landowner who planted a vineyard and put a wall around it and dug a wine press in it, and built a tower, and rented it out to vine-growers and went on a journey. When the harvest time approached, he sent his slaves to the vine-growers to receive his produce. The vine-growers took his slaves and beat one, and killed another, and stoned a third. Again he sent other group of slaves larger than the first; and they did the same thing to them. But afterward he sent his son to them, saying, 'They will respect my son.' But when the vine-growers saw the son, they said among themselves, 'This is the heir; come, let us kill him and seize his inheritance.' They took him, and threw him out of the vineyard and killed him. Therefore when the owner of the vineyard comes, what will he do to those vine-growers?" They said to Him, "He will bring those wretches to a wretched end, and will rent out the vineyard to other vine-growers who will pay him the proceeds at the proper seasons." Jesus said to them, "Did you never read in the Scriptures, 'The stone which the builders rejected, This became the chief corner stone; This came about from the Lord, and it is marvelous in our eyes'? Therefore I say to you, the kingdom of God will be taken from you and given to a people, producing the fruit of it. And he who falls on this stone will be broken to pieces; but on whomever it falls, it will scatter him like dust." When the chief priests and the Pharisees heard His parables, they understood that He

was speaking about them. When they sought to seize Him, they feared the people, because they considered Him to be a prophet. (Matthew 21:33-46)

The parable contained in these verses was spoken with special reference to the Jews. They are the vine-growers here described. Their sins are set before us here as in a picture. Of this there can be no doubt. It is written *that He was speaking about them.*

But we must not flatter ourselves that this parable contains nothing for the Gentiles. There are lessons laid down for us as well as for the Jews. Let us see what they are.

We see, in the first place, *what distinguishing privileges God is pleased to bestow on some nations.*

He chose Israel to be a peculiar people to Himself. He separated them from the other nations of the earth and bestowed on them countless blessings. He gave them revelations of Himself while all the rest of the earth was in darkness. He gave them the law, and the covenants, and the oracles of God, while all the rest of the world was let alone. In short, God dealt with the Jews as a man deals with a piece of land which he fences out and cultivates, while all the fields around are left untilled and as waste. The vineyard of the Lord was the house of Israel (Isaiah 5:7).

And have we no privileges? Beyond doubt we have many. We have the Bible and liberty for everyone to read it. We have the gospel and permission for everyone to hear it. We have spiritual mercies in abundance, of which five hundred millions of our fellow men know nothing at all. How thankful we ought to be! The poorest man in our country may say every morning, "There are five hundred million immortal souls worse off than I am. Who am I that I should differ? Bless the Lord, O my soul."

We see, in the next place, *what a bad use nations sometimes make of their privileges.*

When the Lord separated the Jews from other people, He had a right to expect that they would serve Him and obey His laws. When a man has taken pains with a vineyard, he has a right to expect fruit. But Israel rendered not a due return for all God's mercies. They mingled with the heathen and learned their ways. They hardened themselves in sin and unbelief. They turned aside after idols. They kept not God's ordinances. They despised God's temple. They refused to listen to His prophets. They abused those whom He sent to call them to repentance. And finally, they brought their wickedness to a height by killing the Son of God Himself, even Christ the Lord.

And what are we doing ourselves with our privileges? Truly that is a serious question and one that ought to make us think. It may well be feared that we are not, as a nation, living up to our light or walking worthy of our many mercies. Must we not confess with shame that millions among us seem utterly without God in the world? Must we not acknowledge that in many a town and in many a village Christ seems hardly to have any disciple and the Bible seems hardly to be believed? It is vain to shut our eyes to these facts. The fruit that the Lord receives from His vineyard in Great Britain, compared with what it ought to be, is disgracefully small. It may well be doubted whether we are not as provoking to Him as the Jews.

We see, in the next place, *what a dreadful reckoning God sometimes has with nations and churches which make a bad use of their privileges.*

A time came when the patience of God towards the Jews had an end. Forty years after our Lord's death, the cup of their iniquity was finally full, and they received a heavy chastisement for their many sins. Their holy city, Jerusalem, was destroyed. Their temple was burned. They themselves were scattered over the face of the earth. *"The kingdom of God [was] taken away from you and given to a people, producing the fruit of it."*

And will the same thing ever happen to us? Will the judgments of God ever come down on our nation because of her unfruitfulness under so many mercies? Who can tell? We may well cry with the prophet, "Lord God, *You alone know.*" We only know that judgments have come on many a church and nation in the last eighteen hundred years. The kingdom of God has been taken from the African churches. The Muhammadan power has overwhelmed most of the churches of the East. At all events it becomes all believers to intercede much on behalf of our country. *Nothing offends God so much as neglect of privileges. Much has been given to us, and much will be required.*

We see, in the last place, *the power of conscience even in wicked men.*

The chief priests and elders at last discovered that our Lord's parable was specially meant for themselves. The point of its closing words was too sharp to be escaped. *They understood that He was speaking about them.*

There are many hearers of the gospel in every congregation who are exactly in the condition of these unhappy men. They know that what they hear Sunday after Sunday is all true. They know that they are wrong themselves and that every sermon condemns them. But they have neither will nor courage to acknowledge this. They are too proud and too fond of the world to confess their past mistakes and to take up the cross and follow Christ. Let us all beware of this dreadful state of mind. The last day will prove that there was more going on in the consciences of hearers than was at all known to preachers. Thousands and ten thousands will be found, like the chief priests, to have been convicted by their own conscience and yet to have died unconverted.

Matthew Chapter 22

Matthew 22:1-14

Jesus spoke to them again in parables, saying, "The kingdom of heaven may be compared to a king who gave a wedding feast for his son. And he sent out his slaves to call those who had been invited to the wedding feast, and they were unwilling to come. Again he sent out other slaves saying, 'Tell those who have been invited, "Behold, I have prepared my dinner; my oxen and my fattened livestock are butchered and everything is ready; come to the wedding feast."' But they paid no attention and went their way, one to his own farm, another to his business, and the rest seized his slaves and mistreated them and killed them. But the king was enraged, and he sent his armies and destroyed those murderers and set their city on fire. Then he said to his slaves, 'The wedding is ready, but those who were invited were not worthy. Go therefore to the main highways, and as many as you find there, invite to the wedding feast.' Those slaves went out into the streets and gathered together all they found, both evil and good; and the wedding hall was filled with dinner guests. But when the king came in to look over the dinner guests, he saw a man there who was not dressed in wedding clothes, and he said to him, 'Friend, how did you come in here without wedding clothes?' And the man was speechless. Then the king said to the servants, 'Bind him hand and foot, and throw him into the outer darkness; in that place there will be weeping and gnashing of teeth.' For many are called, but few are chosen." (Matthew 22:1-14)

THE PARABLE RELATED IN THESE VERSES is one of very wide significance. In its first application it unquestionably points to the Jews. But we may not confine it to them. It contains heart-searching lessons for all among whom the gospel is preached. It is a spiritual picture which speaks to us this day, if we have an ear to hear. The remark of Olshausen is wise and true: "Parables are like many-sided precious stones, cut so as to cast luster in more than one direction."

Let us observe, in the first place, that *the salvation of the gospel is compared to a marriage feast.* The Lord Jesus tells us that a certain king *gave a wedding feast for his son.*

There is in the gospel a complete provision for all the needs of man's soul. There is a supply of everything that can be required to relieve spiritual hunger and spiritual thirst. Pardon, peace with God, lively hope in this world, and glory in the world to come are set before us in rich abundance. It is *a feast of fat things.* All this provision is owing to the love of the Son of God, Jesus Christ our Lord. He offers to take us into union with Himself, to restore us to the family of God as dear children, to clothe us with His own righteousness, to give us a place in His kingdom, and to present us faultless before His Father's throne at the last day. The gospel, in short, is an offer of food to the hungry, joy to the mourner, a home to the outcast, and a loving friend to the lost. It is glad tidings. God offers, through His dear Son, to be at peace with sinful man. Let us not forget this – *In this is love, not that we loved God, but that He loved us and sent His Son to be the propitiation for our sins* (1 John 4:10).

Let us observe, in the second place, that *the invitations of the gospel are wide, full, broad, and unlimited.* The Lord Jesus tells us in the parable that the king's servants said to those who were bidden, *"Everything is ready; come to the wedding feast."*

There is nothing lacking on God's part for the salvation of sinners' souls. No one will ever be able to say at last that it was God's fault if he is not saved. The Father is ready to love and receive. The Son is ready to pardon and cleanse guilt away. The Spirit is ready to sanctify and renew. Angels are ready to rejoice over the returning sinner. Grace is ready to assist him. The Bible is ready to instruct him. Heaven is ready to be his everlasting home. One thing only is needful, and that is, the sinner must be ready and willing himself. Let this also never be forgotten. Let us not quibble and split hairs upon this point. God will be found clear of the blood of all lost souls. The gospel always speaks of sinners as responsible and accountable beings. The gospel places an open door before all mankind. No one is excluded from the range of its offers. Though *efficient* only to believers, those offers are *sufficient* for all the world. Though few enter the strait gate, all are invited to come in.

Let us observe, in the third place, that *the salvation of the gospel is rejected by many to whom it is offered.* The Lord Jesus tells us that those whom the king's servants invited to the wedding *paid no attention and went their way.*

There are thousands of hearers of the gospel who derive from it no benefit whatsoever. They listen to it Sunday after Sunday, and year after year, and do not believe it to the saving of the soul. They feel no special need of the gospel. They see no special beauty in it. They do not perhaps hate it, or oppose it, or scoff at it, but they do not receive it into their hearts. They like other things far better. Their money, their lands, their business, or their pleasures are all far more interesting subjects to them than their souls. It is a dreadful state of mind to be in but awfully common. Let us search our own hearts and take heed that it is not our own. Open sin may kill its thousands, but indifference and neglect of the gospel kill their tens of thousands. Multitudes will find themselves in hell not so much because they openly broke the Ten Commandments, as because they made light of the gospel. Christ died for them on the cross, but they neglected Him.

Let us observe, in the last place, that *all false professors of religion will be detected, exposed, and eternally condemned at the last day.* The Lord Jesus tells us that when the wedding was at last furnished with guests, the king came in to see them and *saw a man there who was not dressed in wedding clothes.* He asked him how he came in there without such, and he received no reply. He then commanded the servants to *bind him hand and foot, and throw him into the outer darkness.*

There will always be some false professors in the church of Christ as long as the world stands. In this parable, as Quesnel says, "One single castaway represents all the rest." It is impossible to read the hearts of men. Deceivers and hypocrites will never be entirely excluded from the ranks of those who call themselves Christians. So long as a man professes subjection to the gospel and lives an outwardly correct life, we dare not say positively that he is not clothed in the righteousness of Christ.

But there will be no deception at the last day. The unerring eye of God will discern who are His own people and who are not. Nothing but true faith shall abide the fire of His judgment. All spurious Christianity shall be weighed in the balance and found lacking. None but true believers shall sit down at the marriage supper of the Lamb. It shall avail the hypocrite nothing that he has been a loud talker about religion and had the reputation of being an eminent Christian among men. His triumphing shall be but for a moment. He shall be stripped of all his borrowed plumage and stand naked and shivering before the bar of God, speechless, self-condemned, hopeless, and helpless. He shall be cast into outer darkness with shame, and shall reap according to what he has sown. Well may our Lord say, *"There will be weeping and gnashing of teeth."*

Let us learn wisdom from the solemn pictures of this parable and give diligence to make our calling and election sure. We ourselves are among those to whom the word is spoken, *"Everything is ready; come to the wedding feast."* Let us see that we refuse not Him who speaks. Let us not sleep as others do, but watch and be sober. Time hastens on. The King will soon come in to see the guests. Have we or have we not put on the wedding clothes? Have we put on Christ? That is the grand question that arises out of this parable. May we never rest until we can give a satisfactory answer! May those heart-searching words daily ring in our ears: *"Many are called, but few are chosen."*

Matthew 22:15-22

Then the Pharisees went and plotted together how they might trap Him in what He said. And they sent their disciples to Him, along with the Herodians, saying, "Teacher, we know that You are truthful and teach the way of God in truth, and defer to no one; for You are not partial to any. Tell us then, what do You think? Is it lawful to give a poll-tax to Caesar, or not?" But Jesus perceived their malice, and said, "Why are you testing Me, you hypocrites? Show Me the coin used for the poll-tax." And they brought Him a denarius. And He said to them, "Whose likeness and inscription is this?" They said to Him, "Caesar's." Then He said to them, "Then render to Caesar the things that are Caesar's; and to God the things that are God's." And hearing this, they were amazed, and leaving Him, they went away. (Matthew 22:15-22)

We see in this passage the first of a series of subtle attacks which were made on our Lord during the last days of His earthly ministry. His deadly foes, the Pharisees, saw the influence He was obtaining, both by His miracles and His preaching. They were determined by some means to silence Him or put Him to death. They therefore endeavored to *trap Him in what He said.* They sent forth *their disciples to Him, along with the Herodians*, to test Him with a hard question. They wished to entice Him into saying something which might serve as a handle for an accusation against Him. Their scheme, we are told in these verses, entirely failed. They took nothing by their movement and retreated in confusion.

The first thing which demands our attention in these verses is *the flattering language with which our Lord was accosted by His enemies.* "*Teacher,*" they said, "*we know that You are truthful and teach the way of God in truth, and defer to no one; for You are not partial to any.*" How well these Pharisees and Herodians talked! What smooth and honeyed words were these! They thought, no doubt, that by good words and fair speeches they would throw our Lord off His guard. It might truly be said of them, *His speech was smoother than butter, but his heart was war; his words were softer than oil, yet they were drawn swords* (Psalm 55:21).

It becomes all professing Christians to be much on their guard against flattery. We mistake greatly if we suppose that persecution and hard usage are the only weapons in Satan's armory. That crafty foe has other engines for doing us mischief, which he knows well how to work. He knows how to poison souls by the world's seductive kindness when he cannot frighten them by the fiery dart and the sword. Let us not be ignorant of his devices. By peace he destroys many.

We are only too apt to forget this truth. We overlook the many examples God has given us in Scripture for our learning. What brought about the ruin of Samson? Not the armies of the Philistines, but the pretended love of a Philistine woman. What led to Solomon's backsliding? Not the strength of outward enemies, but the blandishment of his numerous wives. What was the cause of King Hezekiah's greatest mistake? Not the sword of Sennacherib or the threats of Rabshakeh, but the flattery of the Babylonian ambassadors. Let us remember these things and be on our guard. Peace often ruins nations more than war. Sweet things occasion far more sicknesses than bitter. The sun makes the traveler cast off his protective garments far sooner than the north wind. Let us beware of the flatterer. Satan is never so dangerous as when he appears as an angel of light. The world is never so dangerous to the Christian as when it smiles. When Judas betrayed his Lord, it was with a kiss. The believer who is proof against the world's frown does well, but he who is proof against its flattery does better.

The second thing that demands our attention in these verses is *the marvelous wisdom of the reply which our Lord made to His enemies.* The Pharisees and Herodians asked whether it was lawful to give tribute to Caesar or not. They doubtless thought that they had put out a question which our Lord could not answer without giving them an advantage. Had He simply replied that it was *lawful* to pay tribute, they would have denounced Him to the people as one who dishonored the privileges of Israel and considered the children of Abraham no longer free, but subjects to a foreign power. Had He, on the other hand, replied that it was *not lawful* to pay tribute, they would have denounced Him to the Romans as a mover of sedition and a rebel against Caesar who refused to pay His taxes. But our Lord's conduct completely baffled them. He demanded to see the tribute money. He asks them whose head is on that coin. They reply, *"Caesar's."* They acknowledge that Caesar has some authority over them by using money bearing his image and superscription, since he that coins the current money is ruler of the land where that money is current. And at once they receive an irresistibly conclusive answer to their question: *"Then render to Caesar the things that are Caesar's; and to God the things that are God's."*

The principle laid down in these well-known words is one of deep importance. There is one obedience owing by every Christian to the civil government under which he lives, in all matters which are temporal and not purely spiritual. He may not approve of every requirement of that civil government. But he must submit to the laws of the commonwealth so long as those laws are unrepealed. He must *render to Caesar the things that are Caesar's.*

There is another obedience which the Christian owes to the God of the Bible in all matters which are purely spiritual. No temporal loss, no civil disability, and no displeasure of the powers that be must ever tempt him to do things which the Scripture plainly forbids. His position may be very trying. He may have to suffer much for his conscience's sake. But he must never fly in the face of unmistakable requirements of Scripture. If Caesar coins a new gospel, he is not to be obeyed. We must give *to God the things that are God's.*

The subject unquestionably is one of great difficulty and delicacy. It is certain that the church must not swallow up the state. It is no less certain that the state must not swallow up the church. On no point, perhaps, have conscientious men been so much tried. On no point have good men disagreed so much as in solving the problem of where the things of Caesar end and the things of God begin. The civil power, on the one hand, has often encroached terribly on the rights of conscience – as the English Puritans found to their cost in the unhappy time of the Stuarts. The spiritual power, on the other hand, has often pushed its claims to an extravagant extent so as to take Caesar's scepter out of his hands as it did when the Church of Rome trampled on our own English King John. In order to have a right judgment in all questions of this kind, every true Christian should constantly pray for wisdom from above. The man whose eye is single, and who daily seeks for grace and practical common sense, will never be allowed greatly to err.

Matthew 22:23-33

On that day some Sadducees (who say there is no resurrection) came to Jesus and questioned Him, asking, "Teacher, Moses said, 'If a man dies having no children, his brother as next of kin shall marry his wife, and raise up children for his brother.' Now there were seven brothers with us; and the first married and died, and having no children left his wife to his brother; so also the second, and the third, down to the seventh. Last of all, the woman died. In the resurrection, therefore, whose wife of the seven will she be? For they all had married her." But Jesus answered and said to them, "You are mistaken, not understanding the Scriptures nor the power of God. For in the resurrection they neither marry nor are given in marriage, but are like angels in heaven. But regarding the resurrection of the dead, have you not read what was spoken to you by God: 'I am the God of Abraham, and the God of Isaac, and the God of Jacob'? He is not the God of the dead but of the living." When the crowds heard this, they were astonished at His teaching. (Matthew 22:23-33)

This passage describes a conversation between our Lord Jesus Christ and the Sadducees. These unhappy men, who said that there was no resurrection, attempted, like the Pharisees and Herodians, to perplex our Lord with hard questions. Like them, they hoped to *trap Him in what He said* and to injure His reputation among the people. Like them, they were completely baffled.

Let us observe, in the first place, that *absurd skeptical objections to Bible truths are not new.* The Sadducees wished to show the absurdity of the doctrine of the resurrection and the life to come. They therefore came to our Lord with a story which was probably invented for the occasion. They told Him that a certain woman had married seven brothers in succession who had all died and left no children. They then asked *whose wife* this woman would be in the next world, when all rose again. The object of the question was plain and transparent. They meant, in reality, to bring the whole doctrine of a resurrection into contempt. They

248

meant to insinuate that there must needs be confusion and strife and unseemly disorder if, after death, men and women were to live again.

It must never surprise us if we meet with similar objections against the doctrines of Scripture, and especially against those doctrines which concern another world. There never will be a lack of "unreasonable men" who will "intrude" into things unseen and make imaginary difficulties their excuse for unbelief. "Supposed cases" are one of the favorite strongholds in which an unbelieving mind loves to entrench itself. Such a mind will often set up a shadow of its own imagining and fight with it as if it was a truth. Such a mind will often refuse to look at the overwhelming mass of plain evidence by which Christianity is supported, and will fasten down on some one single difficulty which it fancies is unanswerable.

The talk and arguments of people of this character should never shake our faith for a moment. For one thing, we should remember that there must needs be deep and dark things in a religion which comes from God, and that a child may put out questions which the greatest philosopher cannot answer. For another thing, we should remember that there are countless truths in the Bible which are clear and unmistakable. Let us first attend them, believe them, and obey them. In so doing, we need not doubt that many a thing now unintelligible to us will yet be made plain. In so doing, we may be sure that what we know not now we shall know hereafter.

Let us observe, in the second place, *what a remarkable text our Lord brings forward in proof of the reality of a life to come.* He places before the Sadducees the words which God spoke to Moses in the bush: *"I am the God of your father, the God of Abraham, the God of Isaac, and the God of Jacob"* (Exodus 3:6). He adds the comment, God *"is not the God of the dead but of the living."* At the time when Moses heard these words, Abraham, Isaac, and Jacob had been dead and buried many years. Two centuries had passed away since Jacob, the last of the three, was carried to his tomb. And yet God spoke of them as being still His people, and of Himself as being still their God. He said not, "I *was* their God," but *"I am."*

Perhaps we are often tempted to doubt the truth of a resurrection and a life to come. But, unhappily, *it is easy to hold truths theoretically and yet not realize them practically.* There are few of us who would not find it good to meditate on the mighty truth which our Lord here unfolds and to give it a prominent place in our thoughts. Let us settle it in our minds that the dead are in one sense still alive. From our eyes they have passed away, and their place knows them no more. But in the eyes of God they live, and they will one day come forth from their graves to receive an everlasting sentence. There is no such thing as annihilation. The idea is a miserable delusion. The sun, moon, and stars, the solid mountains, and the deep sea will one day come to nothing. But the weakest babe of the poorest man shall live forevermore in another world. May we never forget this! Happy is he who can say from his heart the words of the Nicene Creed: "We look for the resurrection of the dead, and the life of the world to come."

Let us observe, in the last place, *the account which our Lord gives of the state of men and women after the resurrection.* He silences the fancied objections of the Sadducees by showing that they entirely mistook the true character of the resurrection state. They took it for granted that it must needs be a gross, carnal existence, like that of mankind upon earth. Our Lord tells them that in the next world we will have a real material body, and yet a body of very different constitution and different necessities from that which we have now. He speaks only of the saved, be it remembered. He omits all mention of the lost. He says, *"In the resurrection they neither marry nor are given in marriage, but are like angels in heaven."*

We know but little of the life to come in heaven. Perhaps our clearest ideas of it are drawn from considering what it will not be rather than what it will be. It is a state in which we shall hunger no more, nor thirst anymore. Sickness, pain, and disease will not be known. Wasting, old age, and death will have no place. Marriages, births, and a constant succession of inhabitants will be no more needed. They who are once admitted into heaven shall dwell there forevermore. And, to pass from negatives to positives, one thing we are told plainly – we shall be *like angels.* Like them, we shall serve God perfectly, unhesitatingly, and unweariedly. Like them, we shall ever be in God's presence. Like them, we shall ever delight to do His will. Like them, we shall give all glory to the Lamb. These are deep things. But they are all true.

Are we ready for this life? Would we enjoy it if admitted to take part in it? Is the company of God and the service of God pleasant to us now? Is the occupation of angels one in which we would delight? These are solemn questions. Our hearts must be heavenly on earth, while we live, if we hope to go to heaven when we rise again in another world (Colossians 3:1-4).

Matthew 22:34-46

But when the Pharisees heard that Jesus had silenced the Sadducees, they gathered themselves together. One of them, a lawyer, asked Him a question, testing Him, "Teacher, which is the great commandment in the Law?" And He said to him, "'You shall love the LORD your God with all your heart, and with all your soul, and with all your mind.' This is the great and foremost commandment. The second is like it, 'You shall love your neighbor as yourself.' On these two commandments depend the whole Law and the Prophets." Now while the Pharisees were gathered together, Jesus asked them a question: "What do you think about the Christ, whose son is He?" They said to Him, "The son of David." He said to them, "Then how does David in the Spirit call Him 'Lord,' saying, 'The LORD said to my LORD, "Sit at My right hand, until I put Your beneath Your feet"'? If David then calls Him 'Lord, how is He his Son?" No one was able to answer Him a word, nor did anyone dare from that day on to ask Him another question. (Matthew 22:34-46)

In the beginning of this passage we find our Lord replying to the question of a certain lawyer who asked him which was *the great commandment in the law.* That question was asked in no friendly spirit. But we have reason to be thankful that it was asked at all. It drew from our

Lord an answer full of precious instruction. Thus we see how good may come out of evil.

Let us mark *what an admirable summary these verses contain of our duty towards God and our neighbor.* Jesus says, *"You shall love the* Lord *your God with all your heart, and with all your soul, and with all your mind."* He says again, *"You shall love your neighbor as yourself."* And He adds, *"On these two commandments depend the whole Law and the Prophets."*

How simple are these two rules and yet how comprehensive! How soon the words are repeated and yet how much they contain! How humbling and condemning they are! How much they prove our daily need of mercy and the precious blood of atonement! Happy would it be for the world if these rules were more known and more practiced!

Love is the grand secret of true obedience to God. When we feel towards Him as children feel towards a dear father, we shall delight to do His will. We shall not find His commandments grievous or work for Him like slaves under fear of the lash. We shall take pleasure in trying to keep His laws and mourn when we transgress them. *None work so well as those who work out of love.* The fear of punishment or the desire of reward are principles of far less power. They do the will of God best who do it from the heart. Do we desire to train children right? Let us teach them to love God.

Love is the grand secret of right behavior towards our fellow men. He who loves his neighbor will scorn to do him any willful injury either in person, property, or character. But he will not rest there. He will desire in every way to do him good. He will strive to promote his comfort and happiness in every way. He will endeavor to lighten his sorrows and increase his joys. When a man loves us, we feel confidence in him. We know that he will never intentionally do us harm, and that in every time of need he will be our friend. Do we desire to teach children to behave aright towards others? Let us teach them to love everybody as themselves, and do to others as they would have others do to them.

But how shall we obtain this love towards God? It is no natural feeling. We are born in sin and, as sinners, are afraid of God. How then can we love Him? We can never really love Him until we are at peace with Him through Christ. When we feel our sins forgiven and ourselves reconciled to our holy Maker, then, and not until then, we shall love Him and have the spirit of adoption. Faith in Christ is the true spring of love to God. They love most who feel most forgiven. *We love, because He first loved us* (1 John 4:19).

And how shall we obtain this love towards our neighbor? This is also no natural feeling. We are born selfish, hateful, and hating one another (Titus 3:3). We shall never love our fellow man aright until our hearts are changed by the Holy Spirit. We must be born again. We must put off the old man and put on the new, and receive the mind that was in Christ Jesus. Then, and not until then, our cold hearts will know true godlike love towards all. *The fruit of the Spirit is love* (Galatians 5:22).

Let these things sink down into our hearts. There is much vague talk in these latter days about love and charity. Men profess to admire them and desire to see them increased and yet hate the principles which alone can produce them. Let us stand fast in the old paths. We cannot have fruits and flowers without roots. We cannot have love for God and man without faith in Christ and without regeneration. The way to spread true love in the world is to teach the atonement of Christ and the work of the Holy Spirit.

The concluding portion of the passage contains a question put to the Pharisees by our Lord. After answering with perfect wisdom the inquiries of His adversaries, He at last asks them, *"What do you think about the Christ, whose son is He?"* They reply at once, *"The son of David."* He then asks them to explain why David in the book of Psalms calls Him Lord (Psalm 110:1). *"If David then calls him 'Lord,' how is He his son?"* At once His enemies were put to silence. *No one was able to answer Him a word.* The scribes and Pharisees no doubt were familiar with the psalm He quoted, but they could not explain its application. It could only be explained by conceding the pre-existence and divinity of the Messiah. This the Pharisees would not concede. Their only idea of Messiah was that He was to be a man like one of themselves. Their ignorance of the Scriptures, of which they pretended to know more than others, and their low, carnal view of the true nature of Christ were thus exposed at one and the same time. Well may Matthew say, by the Holy Spirit, *nor did anyone dare from that day on to ask Him another question.*

Let us not leave these verses without making a practical use of our Lord's solemn question, *"What do you think about the Christ?"* What do we think of His person and His offices? What do we think of His life, and what of His death for us on the cross? What do we think of His resurrection, ascension, and intercession at the right hand of God? Have we tasted that He is gracious? Have we laid hold on Him by faith? Have we found by experience that He is precious to our souls? Can we truly say He is my Redeemer, my Savior, my Shepherd, and my Friend?

These are serious questions. May we never rest until we can give a satisfactory answer to them. It will not profit us to read about Christ if we are not joined to Him by living faith. Once more, then, let us test our religion by this question: What do we think of Christ?

Matthew Chapter 23

Matthew 23:1-12

Then Jesus spoke to the crowds and to His disciples, saying: "The scribes and the Pharisees have seated themselves in the chair of Moses; therefore all that they tell you, do and observe, but do not do according to their deeds; for they say things and do not do them. They tie up heavy burdens and lay them on men's shoulders, but they themselves are unwilling to move them with so much as a finger. But they do all their deeds to be noticed by men; for they broaden their phylacteries and lengthen the tassels of their garments. They love the place of honor at banquets and the chief seats in the synagogues, and respectful greetings in the market places, and being called Rabbi by men. But do not be called Rabbi; for One is your Teacher, and you are all brothers. Do not call anyone on earth your father; for One is your Father, He who is in heaven. Do not be called leaders; for One is your Leader, that is, Christ. But the greatest among you shall be your servant. Whoever exalts himself shall be humbled, and whoever humbles himself shall be exalted." (Matthew 23:1-12)

WE ARE NOW BEGINNING A CHAPTER WHICH IN ONE RESPECT IS THE MOST REMARKABLE in the four Gospels. It contains the last words the Lord Jesus ever spoke within the walls of the temple. Those last words consist of a withering exposure of the scribes and Pharisees and a sharp rebuke of their doctrines and practices. Knowing full well that His time on earth was drawing to a close, our Lord no longer keeps back His opinion of the leading teachers of the Jews. Knowing that He would soon leave His followers alone, like sheep among wolves, He warns them plainly against the false shepherds by whom they were surrounded.

The whole chapter is a signal example of boldness and faithfulness in denouncing error. It is a striking proof that *it is possible for the most loving heart to use the language of stern reproof.* Above all it is a dreadful evidence of the guilt of unfaithful teachers. So long as the world stands, this chapter ought to be a warning and a beacon to all ministers of religion. No sins are so sinful as theirs in the sight of Christ.

In the twelve verses which begin the chapter, we see first *the duty of distinguishing between the office of a false teacher and his example.* *"The scribes and the Pharisees have seated themselves in the chair of Moses."* Rightly or wrongly, they occupied the position of the chief public teachers of religion among the Jews. However unworthily they filled the place of authority, their office entitled them to respect. But while their office was respected, their bad lives were not to be copied. And although their teaching was to be adhered to, so long as it was scriptural, it was not to be observed when it contradicted the Word of God. To use the words of Brentius, "They were to be heard when they taught what Moses taught," but no longer. That such was our Lord's meaning is evident from the whole tenor of the chapter we are reading. False doctrine is there denounced as well as false practice.

The duty here placed before us is one of great importance. There is a constant tendency in the human mind to run into extremes. If we do not regard the office of the minister with *idolatrous veneration,* we are apt to treat it with *improper contempt.* Against both these extremes we have need to be on our guard. However much we may disapprove of a minister's practice or dissent from his teaching, we must never forget to respect his office. We must show that we can honor the commission, whatever we may think of the officer that holds it. The example of Paul on a certain occasion is worthy of notice: *"I was not aware, brethren, that he was high priest; for it is written, 'You shall not speak evil of a ruler of your people'"* (Acts 23:5).

We see secondly in these verses, that *inconsistency, ostentation, and love of pre-eminence among professors of religion are specially displeasing to Christ.* As to inconsistency, it is remarkable that the very first thing

our Lord says of the Pharisees is that *they say things and do not do them.*
They required from others what they did not practice themselves. As to
ostentation, our Lord declares that they did all their works *to be noticed
by men.* They had their phylacteries, or strips of parchment, with texts
written on them, which many Jews wore on their clothes, made of an
excessive size. They had the *tassels* or fringes of their garments, which
Moses instructed the Israelites to wear as a remembrance of God,
made of an extravagant width (Numbers 15:38). And all this was done
to attract notice and to make people think how holy they were. As to
love of pre-eminence, our Lord tells us that the Pharisees loved to have
the chief seats given them in public places and to have flattering titles
addressed to them. All these things our Lord holds up to reprobation.
Against all He would have us watch and pray. They are soul-ruining
sins. *How can you believe, when you receive glory from one another?*
(John 5:44). Happy would it have been for the church of Christ if this
passage had been more deeply pondered and the spirit of it more implic-
itly obeyed. The Pharisees are not the only people who have imposed
austerities on others, and affected a sanctity of apparel, and loved the
praise of man. The annals of church history show that only too many
Christians have walked closely in their steps. May we remember this
and be wise! It is perfectly possible for a baptized Englishman to be in
spirit a thorough Pharisee.

We see in the third place, from these verses, that *Christians must
never give to any man the titles and honors which are due to God alone
and to His Christ.* We are not to *call anyone on earth our Father.*

The rule here laid down must be interpreted with proper scriptural
qualification. We are not forbidden to esteem ministers very highly
in love for their work's sake (1 Thessalonians 5:13). Even Paul, one
of the humblest saints, called Titus his *true child in a common faith,*
and says to the Corinthians, *I became your father through the gospel*
(1 Corinthians 4:15). But still we must be very careful that we do not
insensibly give to ministers a place and an honor which do not belong to
them. We must never allow them to come between ourselves and Christ.
The very best are not infallible. They are not priests who can atone for
us. They are not mediators who can undertake to manage our soul's

affairs with God. They are men of like passions as ourselves, needing the same cleansing blood and the same renewing Spirit, set apart to a high and holy calling, but still after all, only men. Let us never forget these things. Such cautions are always useful. *Human nature would always rather lean on a visible minister than an invisible Christ.*

We see in the last place, that *there is no grace which should distinguish the Christian so much as humility.* He that would be great in the eyes of Christ must aim at a totally different mark from that of the Pharisees. His aim must be not so much to *rule* as to *serve* the church. Well says Baxter, "Church greatness consists in being greatly serviceable." The desire of the Pharisees was to receive honor and to be called *leaders.* The desire of the Christian must be to do good and to give himself and all that he has to the service of others. Truly this is a high standard, but a lower one must never content us. The example of our blessed Lord, the direct command of the apostolic Epistles, both alike require us to be clothed with humility (1 Peter 5:5). Let us seek that blessed grace day by day. No grace is so beautiful, however much despised by the world. No grace is such an evidence of saving faith and true conversion to God. No grace is so often commended by our Lord. Of all His sayings, hardly any is so often repeated as that which concludes the passage we have now read: *"Whoever humbles himself shall be exalted."*

Matthew 23:13-33

"But woe to you, scribes and Pharisees, hypocrites, because you shut off the kingdom of heaven from people; for you do not enter in yourselves, nor do you allow those who are entering to go in. Woe to you, scribes and Pharisees, hypocrites, because you devour widows' houses, and for a pretense you make long prayers; therefore you will receive greater condemnation. Woe to you, scribes and Pharisees, hypocrites, because you travel around on sea and land to make one proselyte; and when he becomes one, you make him twice as much a son of hell as your-selves. Woe to you, blind guides, who say, 'Whoever swears by

the temple, that is nothing; but whoever swears by the gold of the temple is obligated.' You fools and blind men! Which is more important, the gold or the temple that sanctified the gold? And, 'Whoever swears by the altar, that is nothing, but whoever swears by the offering on it, he is obligated.' You blind men, which is more important, the offering, or the altar that sanctifies the offering? Therefore, whoever swears by the altar, swears both by the altar and by everything on it. And whoever swears by the temple, swears both by the temple and by Him who dwells within it. And whoever swears by heaven, swears both by the throne of God and by Him who sits upon it. Woe to you, scribes and Pharisees, hypocrites! For you tithe mint and dill and cummin, and have neglected the weightier provisions of the law: justice and mercy and faithfulness; but these are the things you should have done without neglecting the others. You blind guides, who strain out a gnat and swallow a camel! Woe to you, scribes and Pharisees, hypocrites! For you clean the outside of the cup and of the dish, but inside they are full of robbery and self-indulgence. You blind Pharisee, first clean the inside of the cup and of the dish, so that the outside of it may become clean also. Woe to you, scribes and Pharisees, hypocrites! For you are like whitewashed tombs which on the outside appear beautiful, but inside they are full of dead men's bones and all uncleanness. So you, too, outwardly appear righteous to men, but inwardly you are full of hypocrisy and lawlessness. Woe to you, scribes and Pharisees, hypocrites! For you build the tombs of the prophets and adorn the monuments of the righteous, and say, 'If we had been living in the days of our fathers, we would not have been partners with them in shedding the blood of the prophets.' So you testify against yourselves, that you are sons of those who murdered the prophets. Fill up, then, the measure of the guilt of your fathers. You serpents, you brood of vipers, how can you escape the sentence of hell?"
(Matthew 23:13-33)

We have in these verses the charges of our Lord against the Jewish teachers ranged under eight heads. Standing in the midst of the temple, with a listening crowd around Him, He publicly denounces the main errors of the scribes and Pharisees in unsparing terms. Eight times He uses the solemn expression *Woe to you.* Seven times He calls them *hypocrites.* Twice He speaks of them as *blind guides,* once as *fools and blind,* and once as *you serpents, you brood of vipers.* Let us mark that language well. It teaches a solemn lesson. It shows how utterly abominable the spirit of the scribes and Pharisees is in God's sight, in whatever form it may be found.

Let us glance briefly at the eight charges which our Lord brings forward, and then seek to draw from the whole passage some general instruction.

The first *woe* in the list is directed against the systematic opposition of the scribes and Pharisees to the progress of the gospel. They *shut off the kingdom of heaven.* They would neither go in themselves nor allow others to go in. They rejected the warning voice of John the Baptist. They refused to acknowledge Jesus when He appeared among them as the Messiah. They tried to keep back Jewish inquirers. They would not believe the gospel themselves, and they did all in their power to prevent others from believing it. This was a great sin.

The second *woe* in the list is directed against the covetousness and self-aggrandizing spirit of the scribes and Pharisees. They *devour widows' houses, and for a pretense they make long prayers.* They imposed on the credulity of weak and unprotected women by an affectation of great devoutness until they were regarded as their spiritual directors. They scrupled not to abuse the influence thus unrighteously obtained to their own temporal advantage, and in a word to make money by their religion. This again was a great sin.

The third *woe* in the list is directed against the zeal of the scribes and Pharisees for making adherents. They *travel around on sea and land to make one proselyte.* They labored incessantly to make men join their party and adopt their opinions. They did this from no desire to benefit men's souls in the least, or to bring them to God. They only did it to swell the ranks of their sect and to increase the number of their adherents and their own importance. Their religious zeal arose from sectarianism and not from the love of God. This also was a great sin.

The fourth *woe* in the list is directed against the doctrines of the scribes and Pharisees about oaths. They drew subtle distinctions between one kind of oath and another. They taught the jesuitical tenet that some oaths were binding on men while others were not. They attached greater importance to oaths sworn *by the gold* offered to the temple than to oaths sworn *by the temple* itself. By so doing they brought the third commandment into contempt, and by making men overrate the value of alms and oblations, they advanced their own interests. This again was a great sin.

The fifth *woe* in the list is directed against the practice of the scribes and Pharisees to exalt trifles in religion above serious things, to put the last things first and the first last. They made great ado about tithing mint and other garden herbs as if they could not be too strict in their obedience to God's law. And yet at the same time they neglected great, plain duties such as justice, charity, and honesty. This again was a great sin.

The sixth and seventh "woes" in the list possess too much in common to be divided. They are directed against a general characteristic of the religion of the Scribes. *They set outward decency above inward sanctification and purity of heart.* They made it a religious duty to cleanse the *outside* of their cups and dishes, but neglected their own inward man. They were like whitened sepulchers, clean and beautiful externally, but internally full of all corruption. They outwardly appeared righteous to men, but inwardly were full of hypocrisy and iniquity. This also was a great sin.

The last *woe* in the list is directed against the affected veneration of the scribes and Pharisees for the memory of dead saints. They built *the tombs of the prophets* and adorned *the monuments of the righteous.* And yet their own lives proved that they were of one mind with *those who murdered the prophets.* Their own conduct was a daily evidence that *they liked dead saints better than living ones.* The very men who pretended to honor dead prophets could see no beauty in a living Christ. This also was a great sin.

Such is the sad picture which our Lord gives of Jewish teachers. Let us turn from the contemplation of it with sorrow and humiliation. It is a fearful exhibition of the morbid anatomy of human nature. It is a picture which unhappily has been reproduced over and over again in the history of the church of Christ. There is not a point in the character of the scribes and Pharisees in which it might not be easily shown that people calling themselves Christians have often walked in their steps.

Let us learn from the whole passage *how deplorable was the condition of the Jewish nation* when our Lord was upon earth. When such were the teachers, what must have been the miserable darkness of those who were taught by them! Truly the iniquity of Israel had come to the full. It was high time indeed for the Sun of Righteousness to arise and the gospel to be preached.

Let us learn from the whole passage *how abominable is hypocrisy in the sight of God.* These scribes and Pharisees are not charged with being thieves or murderers, but with being hypocrites to the very core. Whatever we are in our religion, let us resolve never to wear a cloak. Let us by all means worship God *in spirit and truth.*

Let us learn from the whole passage how awfully dangerous is the position of *an unfaithful minister.* It is bad enough to be blind ourselves. It is a thousand times worse to be a blind guide. Of all men, none is so culpably wicked as an unconverted minister, and none will be judged so severely. It is a solemn saying about such a one: "He resembles an unskillful pilot – he does not perish alone."

Finally, let us beware of supposing from this passage that the safest course in religion is to make no profession at all. This is to run into a dangerous extreme. It does not follow that there is no such thing as true profession because some men are hypocrites. It does not follow that all money is bad because there are many counterfeit coins. Let not hypocrisy prevent our confessing Christ or move us from our steadfastness if we have confessed Him. Let us press on, looking unto Jesus, and resting on Him, praying daily to be kept from error, and saying with David, *May my heart be blameless in Your statutes* (Psalm 119:80).

Matthew 23:34-39

"Therefore, behold, I am sending you prophets and wise men and scribes; some of them you will kill and crucify, and some of them you will scourge in your synagogues, and persecute from city to city, so that upon you may fall the guilt of all the righteous blood shed on earth, from the blood of righteous Abel to the blood of Zechariah, the son of Berechiah, whom you murdered between the temple and the altar. Truly I say to you, all these things will come upon this generation. Jerusalem, Jerusalem, who kills the prophets and stones those who are sent to her! How often I wanted to gather your children together, the way a hen gathers her chicks under her wings, and you were unwilling. Behold, your house is being left to you desolate! For I say to you, from now on you will not see Me until you say, 'Blessed is He who comes in the name of the LORD!'" (Matthew 23:34-39)

These verses form the conclusion of our Lord Jesus Christ's address on the subject of the scribes and Pharisees. They are the last words which He ever spoke as a public teacher in the hearing of the people. The characteristic tenderness and compassion of our Lord shine forth in a striking manner at the close of His ministry. Though He left His enemies in unbelief, He shows that He loved and pitied them to the end.

We learn, in the first place from these verses, that *God often takes great pains with ungodly men.* He sent the Jews *prophets and wise men and scribes.* He gave them repeated warnings. He sent them message after message. He did not allow them to go on sinning without rebuke. They could never say that they were not told when they did wrong.

This is the way in which God generally deals with the unconverted. He does not cut them off in their sins without a call to repentance. He knocks at the door of their hearts by sicknesses and afflictions. He assails their consciences by sermons or by the advice of friends. He summons them to consider their ways by opening the grave under their eyes and taking away from them their idols. They often know not what it all means. They are often blind and deaf to all His gracious messages. But they will see His hand at last, though perhaps too late. They will find that *Indeed God speaks once, or twice, yet no one notices it* (Job 33:14). They will discover that they too, like the Jews, had prophets and wise men and scribes sent to them. There was a voice in every providence saying, *"Turn back, turn back from your evil ways! Why then will you die?"* (Ezekiel 33:11).

We learn, in the second place from these verses, that *God takes notice of the treatment which His messengers and ministers receive and will one day reckon for it.* The Jews, as a nation, had often given the servants of God most shameful usage. They had often dealt with them as enemies because they told them the truth. Some they had persecuted, and some they had scourged, and some they had even killed. They thought perhaps that no account would be required of their conduct. But our Lord tells them they were mistaken. There was an eye that saw all their doings. There was a hand that registered all the innocent blood they shed in books of everlasting remembrance. The dying words of Zachariah, who was *murdered between the temple and the altar,* would be found after 850 years not to have fallen to the ground. He said as he died, *"May the* LORD *see and avenge!"* (2 Chronicles 24:22).

Yet a few years and there would be such an inquisition for blood at Jerusalem as the world had never seen. The holy city would be destroyed. The nation which had murdered so many prophets would itself be wasted by famine, pestilence, and the sword. And even those who escaped would be scattered to the four winds and become like Cain the murderer, fugitives and vagabonds upon earth. We all know how literally these sayings were fulfilled. Well might our Lord say, *"All these things will come upon this generation."*

It is good for us all to mark this lesson well. We are too apt to think that "bygones are bygones," and that things which to us are past and done and old will never be raked up again. But we forget that with God *one day is like a thousand years,* and that the events of a thousand years ago are as fresh in His sight as the events of this very hour. God "requires that which is past," and above all, God will require an account of the treatment of His saints. The blood of the primitive Christians shed by the Roman Emperors – the blood of the Vallenses and Albigenses, and the sufferers at the massacre of Bartholomew – the blood of the martyrs who were burned at the time of the Reformation, and of those who have been put to death by the Inquisition – all, all will yet be accounted for. It is an old saying, that "the millstones of God's justice grind slowly, but they grind very fine." The world will yet see that *there is a God who judges on earth* (Psalm 58:11).

Let those who persecute God's people in the present day take heed to what they are doing. Let them know that all who injure, or ridicule, or mock, or slander others on account of their religion commit a great sin. Let them know that Christ takes notice of everyone who persecutes his neighbor because he is better than himself, or because he prays, reads his Bible, and thinks about his soul. He lives who said, *He who touches you, touches the apple of His eye* (Zechariah 2:8). The judgment day will prove that the King of Kings will reckon with all who insult His servants.

We learn, in the last place from these verses, that *those who are lost forever are lost through their own fault.*

The words of our Lord Jesus Christ are very remarkable. He says, "*I wanted to gather your children together, and you were unwilling.*"

There is something peculiarly deserving of notice in this expression. It throws light on a mysterious subject and one which is often darkened by human explanations. It shows that *Christ has feelings of pity and mercy for many who are not saved, and that the grand secret of man's ruin is his lack of will.* Impotent as man is by nature – unable to think a good thought of himself – without power to turn himself to faith and calling upon God, he still appears to have a mighty ability to ruin his own soul. Powerless as he is to do good, he is still powerful to do evil. We say rightly that a man can do nothing of himself, but we must always remember that the seat of impotence is his will. A will to repent and believe, no man can give himself, but a will to reject Christ and have his own way, every man possesses by nature, and if not saved at last, that will shall prove to have been his destruction. "*You are unwilling to come to Me,*" says Christ, "*that you may have life*" (John 5:40).

Let us leave the subject with the comfortable reflection that with Christ nothing is impossible. The hardest heart can be made willing in the day of His power. Beyond doubt, grace is irresistible. But never let us forget that the Bible speaks of man as a responsible being, and that it says of some, *"You . . . are always resisting the Holy Spirit"* (Acts 7:51). Let us understand that the ruin of those who are lost is not because Christ was not willing to save them – nor because they wanted to be saved, but could not – but because they would not come to Christ. Let the ground we take up be always that of the passage we are now considering. Christ wants to gather men, but they choose not to be gathered; Christ wants to save men, but they choose not to be saved. Let it be a settled principle in our religion that men's salvation, if they are truly saved, is wholly of God, and that man's ruin, if he is lost, is wholly of himself. The evil that is in us is all our own. The good, if we have any, is all of God. The saved in the next world will give God all the glory. The lost in the next world will find that *they have destroyed themselves* (Hosea 13:9).

Matthew Chapter 24

Matthew 24:1-14

Jesus came out from the temple and was going away when His disciples came up to point out the temple buildings to Him. And He said to them, "Do you not see all these things? Truly I say to you, not one stone here will be left upon another, which will not be torn down." As He was sitting on the Mount of Olives, the disciples came to Him privately, saying, "Tell us, when will these things happen, and what will be the sign of Your coming, and of the end of the age?" And Jesus answered and said to them, "See to it that no one misleads you. For many will come in My name, saying, 'I am the Christ,' and will mislead many. You will be hearing of wars and rumors of wars. See that you are not fright-ened, for those things must take place, but that is not yet the end. For nation will rise against nation, and kingdom against kingdom, and in various places there will be famines and earth-quakes. But all these things are merely the beginning of birth pangs. Then they will deliver you to tribulation, and will kill you, and you will be hated by all nations because of My name. At that time many will fall away and will betray one another and hate one another. Many false prophets will arise and will mislead many. Because lawlessness is increased, most people's love will grow cold. But the one who endures to the end, he will be saved. This gospel of the kingdom shall be preached in the whole world as a testimony to all the nations, and then the end will come." (Matthew 24:1-14)

THESE VERSES BEGIN A CHAPTER FULL OF PROPHECY – prophecy of which a large portion is unfulfilled – prophecy which ought to be deeply interesting to all true Christians. It is a subject to which the Holy Spirit says we *do well to pay attention* (2 Peter 1:19).

All portions of Scripture like this ought to be approached with deep humility and earnest prayer for the teaching of the Spirit. On no point have good men so entirely disagreed as on the interpretation of prophecy. On no point have the *prejudices* of one class, the *dogmatism* of a second, and the *extravagance* of a third done so much to rob the church of truths which God intended to be a blessing. Well says Olshausen, "What does not man see, or fail to see, when it serves to establish his own favorite opinions?"

To understand the drift of the whole chapter, we must carefully keep in view the question which gave rise to our Lord's discourse. On leaving the temple for the last time, the disciples, with the natural feeling of Jews, had called their Master's attention to the splendid buildings of which it was composed. To their surprise and amazement, He tells them that the whole was about to be destroyed. These words appear to have sunk deeply into the minds of the disciples. They came to Him, as He sat upon the Mount of Olives, and asked Him with evident anxiety, *"Tell us, when will these things happen, and what will be the sign of Your coming, and of the end of the age?"* In these words we see the clue to the subject of the prophecy now before us. It embraces three points: one, the destruction of Jerusalem; two, the second personal advent of Christ; and three, the end of the world. These three points are undoubtedly in some parts of the chapter so entwined together that it is difficult to separate and disentangle them. But all these points appear distinctly in the chapter, and without them it cannot be fairly explained.

The first fourteen verses of the prophecy are taken up with general lessons of wide range and application. They seem to apply with equal force to the close of both Jewish and Christian dispensations, the one event being strikingly typical of the other. They certainly demand special notice from us on whom the latter ends of the world have come. Let us now see what those lessons are.

The first general lesson before us is *a warning against deception.* The very first words of the discourse are, *"See to it that no one misleads you."*

A more needful warning than this cannot be conceived. Satan knows well the value of prophecy and has ever labored to bring the subject into contempt. How many false christs and false prophets arose before the destruction of Jerusalem the works of Josephus abundantly prove. In how many ways the eyes of man are continually blinded in the present day as to things to come it might easily be shown. Irvingism and Mormonism have been only too successfully used as arguments for rejecting the whole doctrine of the second advent of Christ. Let us watch and be on our guard.

Let no man deceive us as to the leading *facts* of unfulfilled prophecy, by telling us they are impossible, or as to the *manner* in which they will be brought to pass, by telling us it is improbable and contrary to past experience. Let no man deceive us as to the *time* when unfulfilled prophecies will be accomplished, either by fixing dates on the one hand, or bidding us wait for the conversion of the world on the other. On all these points let the plain meaning of Scripture be our only guide, and not the traditional interpretations of men. Let us not be ashamed to say that we expect a literal fulfillment of unfulfilled prophecy. Let us frankly allow that there are many things we do not understand, but still hold our ground tenaciously, believe much, wait long, and not doubt that all will one day be made clear. Above all, let us remember that the first coming of Messiah to *suffer* was the most improbable event that could have been conceived, and let us not doubt that as He literally came in person to suffer, so He will literally come again in person to *reign.*

The second grand lesson before us is *a warning against over-optimistic and extravagant expectations as to things which are to happen before the end comes.* It is a warning as deeply important as the preceding one. Happy would it have been for the church if it had not been so much neglected.

We are not to expect a reign of universal peace, happiness, and prosperity before the end comes. If we do, we shall be greatly deceived. Our Lord bids us look for wars, famines, pestilence, and persecution. It is vain to expect peace until the Prince of Peace returns. Then, and not until then, the swords shall be beaten into plowshares, and nations will learn war no more. Then, and not until then, the earth shall bring forth her increase (Isaiah 2:4; Psalm 68:6).

We are not to expect a time of universal purity of doctrine and practice in the church of Christ before the end comes. If we do, we shall be greatly mistaken. Our Lord bids us look for the rising of false prophets, the increase of lawlessness, and the growing cold of most people's love. The truth will never be received by all professing Christians and holiness be the rule among men until the Lord returns and Satan is bound. Then, and not until then, there will be a glorious church without spot or blemish (Ephesians 5:27).

We are not to expect that all the world will be converted before the end comes. If we do, we shall be greatly mistaken. *"The gospel of the kingdom shall be preached in the whole world as a testimony to all the nations,"* but we must not think that we shall see it universally believed. It will *take a people*, wherever it is faithfully preached, as witnesses to Christ, but the full gathering of the nations shall never take place until Christ comes. Then, and not until then, shall the earth be full of the knowledge of the Lord, as the waters cover the sea (Acts 15:14; Habakkuk 2:14).

Let us lay these things to heart and remember them well. They are eminent truths for the present times. Let us learn to be moderate in our expectations from any existing machinery in the church of Christ, and we shall be spared much disappointment. Let us make haste to spread the gospel in the world, for the time is short, not long. The night comes when no man can work. Troublous times are ahead. Heresies and persecutions may soon weaken and distract the churches. A fierce war of principles may soon convulse the nations. The doors now open to do good may soon be shut forever. Our eyes may yet see the sun of Christianity go down like the sun of Judaism in clouds and storms. Above all, let us long for our Lord's return. Oh! for a heart to pray daily, "Come, Lord Jesus!"

Matthew 24:15-28

"Therefore when you see the abomination of desolation which was spoken of through Daniel the prophet, standing in the holy place (let the reader understand), then those who are in Judea must flee to the mountains. Whoever is on the housetop must not go down to the things out that are in his house. Whoever is in the field must not turn back to get his cloak. But woe to those who are pregnant and to those who are nursing babies in those days! But pray that your flight will not be in winter, or on a Sabbath. For then there will be a great tribulation, such as has not occurred since the beginning of the world until now, nor ever will. Unless those days had been cut short, no life would have been saved; but for the sake of the elect those days will be cut short. Then if anyone says to you, 'Behold, here is the Christ,' or 'There He is,' do not believe him. For false christs and false prophets will rise and will show great signs and wonders, so as to mislead, if possible, even the elect. Behold, I have told you in advance. So if they say to you, 'Behold, He is in the wilderness,' do not go out, or, 'Behold, He is in the inner rooms,' do not believe them. For just as the lightning comes from the east and flashes even to the west, so will the coming of the Son of Man be. Wherever the corpse is, there the vultures will gather." (Matthew 24:15-28)

One main subject of this part of our Lord's prophecy is the taking of Jerusalem by the Romans. That great event took place about forty years after the words we have now read were spoken. A full account of it is to be found in the writings of the historian Josephus. Those writings are the best comment on our Lord's words. They are a striking proof of the accuracy of every jot and tittle of His predictions. The horrors and miseries which the Jews endured throughout the siege of their city exceed anything on record. It was truly a time of *tribulation, such as has not occurred since the beginning of the world.* It surprises some to find so much importance attached to the taking of Jerusalem. They would rather regard the whole chapter as unfulfilled.

271

Such people forget that Jerusalem and the temple were the heart of the old Jewish dispensation. When they were destroyed, the old Mosaic system came to an end. The daily sacrifice, the yearly feasts, the altar, the holy of holies, and the priesthood were all essential parts of revealed religion until Christ came, but no longer. When He died upon the cross, their work was done. They were dead, and it only remained that they should be buried. But it was not fitting that this thing should be done quietly. The ending of a dispensation given with so much solemnity at Mount Sinai might well be expected to be marked with peculiar solemnity. The destruction of the holy temple, where so many old saints had seen "shadows of good things to come," might well be expected to form a subject of prophecy. And so it was. The Lord Jesus specially predicts the desolation of *the holy place*. The Great High Priest describes the end of the dispensation which had been a schoolmaster to bring men to Himself.

But we must not suppose that this part of our Lord's prophecy is exhausted by the first taking of Jerusalem. It is more than probable that our Lord's words have a further and deeper application still. It is more than probable that they apply to a *second siege of Jerusalem*, which is yet to take place, when Israel has returned to their own land and to a *second tribulation* on the inhabitants thereof, which shall only be stopped by the advent of our Lord Jesus Christ. Such a view of this passage may sound startling to some. But those who doubt its correctness would do well to study the last chapter of the prophet Zechariah and the last chapter of Daniel. These two chapters contain solemn things. They throw great light on the verses we are now reading and their connection with the verses which immediately follow.

It now remains for us to consider the lessons which this passage contains for our own personal edification. These lessons are plain and unmistakable. In them at least there is no darkness at all.

For one thing, we see that *flight from danger may sometimes be the positive duty of a Christian*. Our Lord Himself commanded His people under certain circumstances that they *must flee*.

The servant of Christ undoubtedly is not to be a coward. He is to confess his Master before men. He is to be willing to die, if needful, for the truth. But the servant of Christ is not required to run into danger unless it comes in the line of duty. He is not to be ashamed to use reasonable means to provide for his personal safety when no good is to be done by dying at his post. There is deep wisdom in this lesson. The true martyrs are not always those who court death and are in a hurry to be beheaded or burned. There are times when it shows more grace to be quiet, and wait, and pray, and watch for opportunities than to defy our adversaries and rush into the battle. May we have wisdom to know how to act in time of persecution! It is possible to be rash as well as to be a coward, and to stop our own usefulness by being over hot as well as by being over cold.

We see, for another thing, that *in delivering this prophecy, our Lord makes special mention of the Sabbath. "Pray,"* He says, *"that your flight will not be on a Sabbath."*

This is a fact that deserves special notice. We live in times when the obligation of the Sabbath upon Christians is frequently denied by good men. They tell us that it is no more binding on us than the ceremonial law. It is difficult to see how such a view can be reconciled with our Lord's words on this solemn occasion. He seems intentionally to mention the Sabbath when He is foretelling the final destruction of the temple and the Mosaic ceremonies, as if to mark the day with honor. He seems to hint that although His people would be absolved from the yoke of sacrifices and ordinances, there would yet remain the keeping of a Sabbath for them (Hebrews 4:9). The friends of a holy Sunday ought carefully to remember this text. It is one which will bear much weight.

We see for another thing that *God's elect are always special objects of God's care.* Twice in this passage our Lord mentions them. *"But for the sake of the elect those days will be cut short."* It will not be possible to deceive *the elect.*

Those whom God has chosen for salvation by Christ are those whom God specially loves in this world. They are the jewels among mankind. He cares more for them than for kings on their thrones, if kings are not converted. He hears their prayers. He orders all the events of nations and the issues of wars for their good and their sanctification. He keeps them by His Spirit. He allows neither man nor devil to pluck them out of His hand. Whatever tribulation comes on the world, God's elect are safe. May we never rest until we know that we are of this blessed number! There breathes not the man or woman who can prove that he is not one. The promises of the gospel are open to all. May we give diligence to make our calling and election sure! God's elect are a people who cry unto Him night and day. When Paul saw the faith, hope, and love of the Thessalonians, then he knew *His choice of [them]* (1 Thessalonians 1:4; Luke 18:7).

Finally, we see from these verses that *whenever the second advent of Christ takes place, it will be a very sudden event.* It will be *as the lightning comes from the east and flashes even to the west.*

This is a practical truth that we should ever keep before our minds. That our Lord Jesus will come again in person to this world we know from Scripture. That He will come in a time of great tribulation we also know. But the precise period, the year, the month, the day, and the hour are all hidden things. We only know that it will be a very sudden event. Our plain duty then is to live always prepared for His return. Let us walk by faith and not by sight. Let us believe in Christ, serve Christ, follow Christ, and love Christ. If we are living this way, then whenever Christ may return we shall be ready to meet Him.

Matthew 24:29-35

"But immediately after the tribulation of those days the sun will be darkened, and the moon will not give its light, and the stars will fall from the sky, and the powers of the heavens will be shaken. And then the sign of the Son of Man will appear in the sky, and then all the tribes of the earth will mourn, and they will see the Son of Man coming on the clouds of the sky with power and great glory. And He will send forth His angels with a great trumpet and they will gather together His elect from the four winds, from one end of the sky to the other. Now learn the parable from the fig tree: when its branch has already become tender and puts forth its leaves, you know that summer is near; so, you

too, when you see all these things, recognize that He is near, right at the door. Truly I say to you, this generation will not pass away until all these things take place. Heaven and earth will pass away, but My words will not pass away." (Matthew 24:29-35)

In this part of our Lord's prophecy, He describes His own second coming to judge the world. This, at all events, seems the natural meaning of the passage. To take any lower view appears to be a violent straining of Scripture language. If the solemn words here used mean nothing more than the coming of the Roman armies to Jerusalem, we may explain away anything in the Bible. The event here described is one of far greater moment than the march of any earthly army. It is nothing less than the closing act of this dispensation, the second personal advent of Jesus Christ.

These verses teach us, in the first place, that *when the Lord Jesus returns to this world, He shall come with peculiar glory and majesty.* He shall come *on the clouds of the sky with power and great glory.* Before His presence the very sun, moon, and stars shall be darkened, and *the powers of the heavens will be shaken.*

The second personal coming of Christ shall be as different as possible from the first. He came the first time as a Man of Sorrows and acquainted with grief. He was born in a manger in Bethlehem in lowliness and humility. He took on Him the form of a servant and was despised and rejected of men. He was betrayed into the hands of wicked men, condemned by an unjust judgment, mocked, scourged, crowned with thorns, and at last crucified between two thieves. He shall come the second time as the King of all the earth with all royal majesty. The princes and great men of this world shall themselves stand before His throne to receive an eternal sentence. Before Him every mouth shall be stopped, and every knee shall bow, and every tongue shall confess that Jesus Christ is Lord. May we all remember this. Whatever ungodly men may do now, there will be no scoffing, no jesting at Christ, and no infidelity at the last day. The servants of Jesus may well wait patiently. Their Master shall one day be acknowledged King of Kings by all the world.

These verses teach us, in the second place, that *when Christ returns to this world, He will first take care of His believing people.* He shall *send forth His angels* and *gather together His elect.*

In the day of judgment true Christians shall be perfectly safe. Not a hair of their heads shall fall to the ground. Not one bone of Christ's mystical body shall be broken. There was an ark for Noah in the day of the flood. There was a Zoar for Lot when Sodom was destroyed. There shall be a hiding place for all believers in Jesus when the wrath of God at last bursts on this wicked world. Those mighty angels who rejoiced in heaven when each sinner repented shall gladly catch up the people of Christ to meet their Lord in the air. That day no doubt will be a dreadful day, but believers may look forward to it without fear.

In the day of judgment true Christians shall at last be gathered together. The saints of every age and every tongue shall be assembled out of every land. All shall be there, from righteous Abel down to the last soul that is converted to God, from the oldest patriarch down to the little infant that just breathed and died. Let us think what a happy gathering that will be when all the family of God are at last together. If it has been pleasant to meet one or two saints occasionally on earth, how much more pleasant will it be to meet a multitude that no man can number! Surely we may be content to carry the cross and put up with being apart for a few years. We travel on towards a day when we shall meet to part no more.

These verses teach us, in the third place, that *until Christ returns to this earth, the Jews will always remain a separate people.* Our Lord tells us, *"This generation will not pass away until all these things take place."*

The continued existence of the Jews as a distinct nation is undeniably a great miracle. It is one of those evidences of the truth of the Bible which the infidel can never overthrow. Without a land, without a king, without a government, scattered and dispersed over the world for eighteen hundred years, the Jews are never absorbed among the people of the countries where they live, like Frenchmen, Englishmen, and Germans, but they *dwell alone.* Nothing can account for this but the finger of God. The Jewish nation stands before the world as a crushing answer to infidelity and a living book of evidence that the Bible is true. But we ought not to regard the Jews only as witnesses of the truth of Scripture. We should see in them a continual pledge that the Lord Jesus is coming again one day. Like the sacrament of the Lord's Supper, they witness to the reality of the second advent as well as of the first. Let us remember this. Let us see in every wandering Jew a proof that the Bible is true and that Christ will one day return.

Finally, these verses teach us that *our Lord's predictions will certainly be fulfilled.* He says, *"Heaven and earth will pass away, but My words will not pass away."*

Our Lord knew well the natural unbelief of human nature. He knew that scoffers would arise in the last days, saying, *Where is the promise of His coming?* (2 Peter 3:4). He knew that when He came, faith would be rare on the earth. He foresaw how many would contemptuously reject the solemn predictions He had just been delivering as improbable, unlikely, and absurd. He warns us all against such skeptical thoughts with a caution of peculiar solemnity. He tells us that whatever man may say or think, His words shall be fulfilled in their season and shall not *pass away* unaccomplished. May we all lay to heart His warning. We live in an unbelieving age. Few believed the report of our Lord's first coming, and few believe the report of His second (Isaiah 53:1). Let us beware of this infection and believe to the saving of our souls. We are not reading cunningly devised fables but deep and momentous truths. May God give us a heart to believe them.

Matthew 24:36-51

"But of that day and hour no one knows, not even the angels of heaven, nor the Son, but the Father alone. For the coming of the Son of Man will be just like the days of Noah. For as in those days before the flood they were eating and drinking, marrying and giving in marriage, until the day that Noah entered the ark, and they did not understand until the flood came and took them all away; so will the coming of the Son of Man be. Then there will be two men in the field; one will be taken and one will be left. Two women will be grinding at the mill; one will be taken and one

will be left. Therefore be on the alert, for you do not know which day your Lord is coming. But be sure of this, that if the head of the house had known at what time of the night the thief was coming, he would have been on the alert and would not have allowed his house to be broken into. For this reason you also must be ready; for the Son of Man is coming at an hour when you do not think He will. Who then is the faithful and sensible slave whom his master put in charge of his household to give them their food at the proper time? Blessed is that slave whom his master finds so doing when he comes. Truly I say to you that he will put him in charge of all his possessions. But if that evil slave says in his heart, 'My master is not coming for a long time,' and begins to beat his fellow slaves and eat and drink with drunkards; the master of that slave will come on a day when he does not expect him and at an hour which he does not know, and will cut him in pieces and assign him a place with the hypocrites; in that place there will be weeping and gnashing of teeth." (Matthew 24:36-51)

There are verses in this passage which are often much misapplied. *The coming of the Son of Man* is often spoken of as being the same thing as death. The texts which describe the uncertainty of His coming are often used in epitaphs and thought suitable to the tomb. But there is really no solid ground for such an application of this passage. Death is one thing, and the coming of the Son of Man is quite another. The subject of these verses is not death but the second advent of Jesus Christ. Let us remember this. *It is a serious thing to wrest Scripture out of its true meaning.*

The first thing that demands our attention in these verses is *the dreadful account that they give of the state of the world when the Lord Jesus comes again.*

The world will not be converted when Christ returns. It will be found in the same condition that it was in the day of the flood. When the flood came, men were found *eating and drinking, marrying and giving in marriage,* absorbed in their worldly pursuits, and utterly heedless of Noah's repeated warnings. They saw no likelihood of a flood. They would not believe there was any danger. But at last the flood came suddenly and *took them all away.* All who were not with Noah in the ark were drowned. They were all swept away to their last account, unpardoned, unconverted, and unprepared to meet God. And our Lord says, *"So will the coming of the Son of Man be."*

Let us mark this text and store it up in our minds. There are many strange opinions current on this subject, even among good men. Let us not flatter ourselves that the heathen will all be converted and the earth filled with the knowledge of God before the Lord comes. Let us not dream that the end of all things cannot be at hand because there is still much wickedness both in the church and in the world. Such views receive a flat contradiction in the passage now before us. The days of Noah are the true type of the days when Christ shall return. Millions of professing Christians will be found thoughtless, unbelieving, godless, Christless, worldly, and unfit to meet their judge. Let us take heed that we are not found among them.

The second thing that demands our attention is *the dreadful separation that will take place when the Lord Jesus comes again.* We read twice over that *one will be taken and one will be left.*

The godly and the ungodly, at present, are all mingled together. In the congregation and in the place of worship –in the city and in the field – the children of God and the children of the world are all side by side. But it shall not be so always. In the day of our Lord's return there shall at last be a complete division. In a moment, in the twinkling of an eye, at the last trumpet, each party shall be separated from the other forevermore. Wives shall be separated from husbands, parents from children, brothers from sisters, masters from servants, preachers from hearers. There shall be no time for parting words or a change of mind when the Lord appears. All shall be taken as they are and reap according as they have sown. Believers shall be caught up to glory, honor, and eternal life. Unbelievers shall be left behind to shame and everlasting contempt. Blessed and happy are they who are of one heart in following Christ! Their union alone shall never be broken. It shall last forevermore. Who can describe the happiness of those who are taken when the Lord returns? Who can imagine the misery of those who are left behind? May we think on these things and consider our ways.

The last thing that demands our attention in these verses is the *practical duty of watchfulness in the prospect of Christ's second coming.* *"Be on the alert,"* says our Lord, *"for you do not know which day your Lord is coming. Be ready; for the Son of Man is coming at an hour when you do not think He will."*

This is a point which our blessed Master frequently presses upon our notice. We hardly ever find Him dwelling on the second advent without adding an injunction to *be on the alert.* He knows the sleepiness of our nature. He knows how soon we forget the most solemn subjects in religion. He knows how unceasingly Satan labors to obscure the glorious doctrine of His coming again. He arms us with heart-searching exhortations to keep awake if we desire not to be ruined forevermore. May we all have an ear to hear them.

True Christians ought to live like watchmen. The day of the Lord so comes as a thief in the night. They should strive to be always on their guard. They should behave like the sentinel of an army in an enemy's land.

They should resolve by God's grace not to sleep at their post. That text of Paul deserves many a thought: *So then let us not sleep as others do, but let us be alert and sober* (1 Thessalonians 5:6).

True Christians ought to live like good servants whose master is not at home. They should strive to be always ready for their master's return. They should never give way to the feeling, "My Lord is delaying His coming." They should seek to keep their hearts in such a frame that whenever Christ appears, they may at once give Him a warm and loving reception. There is a vast depth in that saying, *"Blessed is that slave whom his master finds so doing when he comes."* We may well doubt whether we are true believers in Jesus if we are not ready at any time to have our faith changed into sight.

Let us close the chapter with solemn feelings. The things we have just been reading call loudly for great searchings of heart. Let us seek to make sure that we are in Christ and have an ark of safety when the day of wrath breaks on the world. Let us strive to live that we may be pronounced "blessed" at the last and not cast off forevermore. Not least, let us dismiss from our minds the common idea that unfulfilled prophecy is a speculative and not a practical thing. If the things we have been considering are not practical, there is no such thing as practical religion at all. Well might John say, *Everyone who has this hope fixed on Him purifies himself, just as He is pure* (1 John 3:3).

Matthew Chapter 25

Matthew 25:1-13

"Then the kingdom of heaven will be comparable to ten virgins, who took their lamps and went out to meet the bridegroom. Five of them were foolish, and five were prudent. For when the foolish took their lamps, they took no oil with them, but the prudent took oil in flasks along with their lamps. Now while the bridegroom was delaying, they all got drowsy and began to sleep. But at midnight there was a shout, 'Behold, the bridegroom! Come out to meet him.' Then all those virgins rose and trimmed their lamps. The foolish said to the prudent, 'Give us some of your oil, for our lamps are going out.' But the prudent answered, 'No, there will not be enough for us and you too; go instead to the dealers and buy some for yourselves.' And while they were going away to make the purchase, the bridegroom came, and those who were ready went in with him to the wedding feast; and the door was shut. Later the other virgins also came, saying, 'Lord, lord, open up for us.' But he answered, 'Truly I say to you, I do not know you.' Be on the alert then, for you do not know the day nor the hour." (Matthew 25:1-13)

THE CHAPTER WE HAVE NOW BEGUN IS A CONTINUATION of our Lord's prophetical discourse on the Mount of Olives. The time to which it all refers is plain and unmistakable. From first to last, there is a continual reference to the second advent of Christ and the end of the world. The whole chapter contains three great divisions. In the first, our Lord uses His own second coming as an argument for watchfulness and heart-religion. This He does by the parable of the ten virgins. In the second, He uses His own second coming as an argument for diligence and faithfulness. This He does by the parable of the talents. In the third, He winds up all by a description of the great day of judgment, a passage which for majesty and beauty stands unequaled in the New Testament.

The parable of the ten virgins, which we have now read, contains lessons peculiarly solemn and awakening. Let us see what they are.

We see for one thing, that *the second coming of Christ will find His church a mixed body, containing evil as well as good.*

The professing church is compared to *ten virgins, who took their lamps and went out to meet the bridegroom.* All of them had lamps, but only five had oil in their vessels to feed the flame. All of them professed to have one object in view, but five only were truly wise, and the rest were foolish. The visible church of Christ is in just the same condition. All its members are baptized in the name of Christ, but not all really hear His voice and follow Him. All are called Christians and profess to be of the Christian religion, but not all have the grace of the Spirit in their hearts and really are what they profess to be. Our own eyes tell us that it is so now. The Lord Jesus tells us that it will be so when He comes again.

Let us mark well this description. It is a humbling picture. After all our preachings and prayings – after all our visiting and teaching – after all our missionary exertions abroad and attendance of church at home, many will be found at last *dead in their trespasses and sins!* The wickedness and unbelief of human nature is a subject about which we all have much to learn.

We see, for another thing, that *Christ's second coming, whenever it may be, will take men by surprise.*

This is a truth which is set before us in the parable in a very striking manner. At midnight, when the virgins were slumbering and sleeping, there was a cry, *"Behold, the bridegroom! Come out to meet him."* It will be just the same when Jesus returns to the world. He will find the vast majority of mankind utterly unbelieving and unprepared. He will find the bulk of His believing people in a sleepy and lazy state of soul. Business will be going on in town and country just as it does now. Politics, trades, farming, buying, selling, and pleasure-seeking will be taking up men's attention just as they do now. Rich men will still be faring sumptuously, and poor men murmuring and complaining. Churches will still be full of divisions and wrangling about trifles, and theological controversies will be still raging. Ministers will still be calling men to repent, and congregations still putting off the day of decision. In the midst of all this, the Lord Jesus Himself shall suddenly appear. In an hour when no man thinks, the startled world shall be summoned to break off all its employments and to stand before its lawful King. There is something unspeakably dreadful in the idea. But thus it is written and thus it shall be. Well might a dying minister say, "We are none of us more than half-awake."

We see, in the next place, that *when the Lord comes again, many will find out the value of saving religion too late.*

The parable tells us that when the bridegroom came, the foolish virgins said unto the prudent, *"Give us some of your oil, for our lamps are going out."* It tells us further that as the prudent had no oil to spare, the foolish went to buy some for themselves. It tells us finally that they came when the door was shut and asked in vain for admission. *"Lord, lord,"* they cried, *"open up for us."* All these expressions are striking emblems of things to come. Let us take heed that we do not find them true by experience, to our own eternal ruin.

We may settle it in our minds that there will be an entire change of opinion one day as to the necessity of decided Christianity. At present, we must all be aware that the vast majority of professing Christians care nothing at all about it. They have no sense of sin. They have no love towards Christ. They know nothing of being born again. Repentance, faith, grace, and holiness are mere words and names to them. They are subjects which they either dislike or about which they feel no concern. But all this state of things shall one day come to an end. Knowledge, conviction, the value of the soul, and the need of a Savior shall all burst on men's minds one day like a flash of lightning. But alas! it will be too late. It will be too late to be buying oil when the Lord returns. The mistakes that are not found out until that day are irretrievable.

Are we ever mocked and persecuted and thought foolish because of our religion? Let us bear it patiently and pray for those who persecute us. They know not what they are doing. They will certainly alter their minds one day. We may yet hear them confessing that we were wise and they were foolish. The whole world shall one day acknowledge that the saints of God made a wise choice.

We see lastly, in this parable, that *when Christ returns, true Christians shall receive a rich reward for all they have suffered for their Master's sake.* We are told that when the bridegroom came, *those who were ready went in with him to the wedding feast; and the door was shut.*

True Christians shall alone be found ready at the second advent. Washed in the blood of atonement, clothed in Christ's righteousness, and renewed by the Spirit, they shall meet their Lord with boldness and sit down at the marriage supper of the Lamb to go out no more. Surely this is a blessed prospect.

They shall be with their Lord – with Him who loved them and gave Himself for them – with Him who bore with them and carried them through their earthly pilgrimage – with Him whom they loved truly and followed faithfully on earth, though with much weakness and many a tear. Surely this also is a blessed prospect.

The door shall be shut at last – shut on all pain and sorrow – shut on an ill-natured and wicked world – shut on a tempting devil – shut on all doubts and fears – shut, to be opened again no more. Surely, we may again say, this is a blessed prospect.

Let us remember these things. They will bear meditation. They are all true. The believer may have much tribulation, but he has before him abounding consolations. Heaviness may endure for a night, but joy comes in the morning. The day of Christ's return shall surely make amends for all.

Let us leave this parable with a settled determination never to be content with anything short of indwelling grace in our hearts. The lamp and the name of *Christian*, the profession and the ordinances of Christianity, are all well in their way, but they are not the one thing needful. Let us never rest until we know that we have the oil of the Spirit in our hearts.

Matthew 25:14-30

"For it is just like a man about to go on a journey, who called his
own slaves and entrusted his possessions to them. To one he gave
five talents, to another, two, and to another, one, each according to his own ability; and he went on his journey. Immediately
the one who had received the five talents went and traded with
them, and gained five more talents. In the same manner the one
who had received the two talents gained two more. But he who
received the one talent went away, and dug a hole in the ground
and hid his master's money. Now after a long time the master of
those slaves came and settled accounts with them. The one who
had received the five talents came up and brought five more talents, saying, 'Master, you entrusted five talents to me. See, I have
gained five more talents.' His master said to him, 'Well done,
good and faithful slave. You were faithful with a few things, I will
put you in charge of many things; enter into the joy of your master.' Also the one who had received the two talents came up and
said, 'Master, you entrusted two talents to me. See, I have gained
two more talents.' His master said to him, 'Well done, good and
faithful slave. You were faithful with a few things, I will put you
in charge of many things; enter into the joy of your master.' And
the one also who had received the one talent came up and said,
'Master, I knew you to be a hard man, reaping where you did not
sow and gathering where you scattered no seed. And I was afraid,
and went away and hid your talent in the ground. See, you have
what is yours.' But his master answered and said to him, 'You
wicked, lazy slave, you knew that I reap where I did not sow and
gather where I scattered no seed. Then you ought to have put my
money in the bank, and on my arrival I would have received my
money back with interest. Therefore take away the talent from
him, and give it to the one who has the ten talents. For to everyone who has, more shall be given, and he will have an abundance; but from the one who does not have, even what he does
have shall be taken away. Throw out the worthless slave into the

outer darkness; in that place there will be weeping and gnashing of teeth.'" (Matthew 25:14-30)

The parable of the talents which we have now read is near akin to that of the ten virgins. Both direct our minds to the same important event, the second advent of Jesus Christ. Both bring before us the same people, the members of the professing church of Christ. The virgins and the servants are one and the same people, but the same people regarded from a different point and viewed on different sides. The practical lesson of each parable is the main point of difference. Vigilance is the key note of the first parable, while diligence is that of the second. The story of the virgins calls on the church to *watch*; the story of the talents calls on the church to *work*.

We learn, in the first place from this parable, that *all professing Christians have received something from God.* We are all God's *slaves.* We all have *talents* entrusted to our charge.

The word *talents* is an expression that has been curiously turned aside from its original meaning. It is generally applied to none but people of remarkable ability or gifts. They are called "talented" people. Such a use of the expression is a mere modern invention. In the sense in which our Lord used the word in this parable, it applies to all baptized people without distinction. We all have talents in God's sight. We are all talented people.

Anything whereby we may glorify God is a talent. Our gifts, our influence, our money, our knowledge, our health, our strength, our time, our senses, our reason, our intellect, our memory, our affections, our privileges as members of Christ's church, our advantages as possessors of the Bible – all, all are talents. Whence came these things? What hand bestowed them? Why are we what we are? Why are we not the worms that crawl on the earth? There is only one answer to these questions. All that we have is a loan from God. We are God's stewards. We are God's debtors. Let this thought sink deeply into our hearts.

We learn in the second place, that *many make a bad use of the privileges and mercies they receive from God.* We are told in the parable of one who *dug a hole in the ground and hid his master's money.* That man represents a large class of mankind.

To hide our talent is to neglect opportunities of glorifying God when we have them. The Bible-despiser, the prayer-neglecter, and the Sabbath-breaker – the unbelieving, the sensual, and the earthly-minded – the trifler, the thoughtless, and the pleasure-seeker – the money-lover, the covetous, and the self-indulgent – all, all are alike burying their Lord's money in the ground. They have all light that they do not use. They might all be better than they are. But they are all daily robbing God. He has lent them much and they make Him no return. The words of Daniel to Belshazzar are strictly applicable to every unconverted person: *The God in whose hand are your life-breath and all your ways, you have not glorified* (Daniel 5:23).

We learn in the third place, that *all professing Christians must one day have a reckoning with God.* The parable tells us that *after a long time the master of those slaves came and settled accounts with them.*

There is a judgment before us all. Words have no meaning in the Bible if there is no judgment. It is mere trifling with Scripture to deny it. There is a judgment before us according to our works – certain, strict, and unavoidable. High or low, rich or poor, learned or unlearned, we shall all have to stand at the bar of God and receive our eternal sentence. There will be no escape. Concealment will be impossible. We and God must at last meet face to face. We shall have to render an account of every privilege that was granted to us and of every ray of light that we enjoyed. We shall find that we are dealt with as accountable and responsible creatures, and that to whomsoever much is given, of them much will be required. Let us remember this every day we live. Let us judge ourselves that we be not condemned of the Lord.

We learn, in the fourth place, that *true Christians will receive an abundant reward in the great day of reckoning.* The parable tells us that the servants who had used their master's money well were commended as *good and faithful* and told to *enter into the joy of their master.*

These words are full of comfort to all believers and may well fill us with wonder and surprise. The best of Christians is a poor frail creature and needs the blood of atonement every day that he lives. But the least and lowest of believers will find that he is counted among Christ's servants and that his labor has not been in vain in the Lord. He will discover to his amazement that his Master's eye saw more beauty in his efforts to please Him than he ever saw himself. He will find that every hour spent in Christ's service, and every word spoken on Christ's behalf, has been written in a book of remembrance. Let believers remember these things and take courage. The cross may be heavy now, but the glorious reward shall make amends for all. Well says Leighton, "Here some drops of joy enter into us, but there we shall enter into joy."

We learn in the last place, that *all unfruitful members of Christ's church will be condemned and cast away in the day of judgment*. The parable tells us that the servant who buried his master's money was condemned as *wicked, lazy,* and *worthless,* and was cast into *the outer darkness*. And our Lord adds the solemn words: *There will be weeping and gnashing of teeth*.

There will be no excuse for an unconverted Christian at the last day. The reasons with which he now pretends to satisfy himself will prove useless and vain. The judge of all the earth will be found to have done right. The ruin of the lost soul will be found to be his own fault. Those words of our Lord, *"you knew,"* are words that ought to ring loudly in many a man's ears and pierce him to the heart. Thousands are living today without Christ and without conversion and yet pretending that they cannot help it. And all this time they know in their own conscience that they are guilty. They are burying their talent. They are not doing what they can. Happy are they who find this out quickly. It will all come out at the last day.

Let us leave this parable with a solemn determination, by God's grace, *never to be content with a profession of Christianity without practice*. Let us not only talk about religion but also act. Let us not only feel the importance of religion but do something too. We are not told that the unprofitable servant was a murderer, or a thief, or even a waster of his master's money. But he *did nothing*, and this was his ruin. Let us beware of a do-nothing Christianity. Such Christianity does not come from the Spirit of God. "To do no harm," says Baxter, "is the praise of a stone, not of a man."

Matthew 25:31-46

"But when the Son of Man comes in His glory, and all the angels with Him, then He will sit on His glorious throne. All the nations will be gathered before Him; and He will separate them from one another, as the shepherd separates the sheep from the goats; and He will put the sheep on His right, and the goats on the left. Then the King will say to those on His right, 'Come, you who are blessed of My Father, inherit the kingdom prepared for you from the foundation of the world. For I was hungry, and you gave Me something to eat; I was thirsty, and you gave Me something to drink; I was a stranger, and you invited Me in; naked, and you clothed Me; I was sick, and you visited Me; I was in prison, and you came to Me.' Then the righteous will answer Him, 'Lord, when did we see You hungry, and feed You, or thirsty, and give You something to drink? And when did we see You a stranger, and invite You in, or naked, and clothe You? When did we see You sick, or in prison, and come to You?' The King will answer and say to them, 'Truly I say to you, to the extent that you did it to one of these brothers of Mine, even the least of them, you did it to Me.' Then He will also say to those on His left, 'Depart from Me, accursed ones, into the eternal fire which has been prepared for the devil and his angels; for I was hungry, and you gave Me nothing to eat; I was thirsty and you gave Me nothing to drink; I was a stranger, and you did not invite Me in; naked, and you did not clothe Me; sick, and in prison, and you did not visit Me.' Then they themselves also will answer, 'Lord, when did we see You hungry, or thirsty, or a stranger, or naked, or sick, or in prison, and did not take care of You?' Then He will answer them, 'Truly I say to you, to the extent that you did not do it to one of the least of these, you did not do it to Me.' These will go away into eternal punishment, but the righteous into eternal life."
(Matthew 25:31-46)

In these verses our Lord Jesus Christ describes the judgment day and some of its leading circumstances. There are few passages in the whole

Bible more solemn and heart-searching than this. May we read it with the deep and serious attention it deserves.

Let us mark, in the first place, *who will be the judge in the last day.* We read that it will be *the Son of Man*, Jesus Christ Himself.

That same Jesus who was born in a manger in Bethlehem and took upon Himself the form of a servant – who was despised and rejected of men and often had nowhere to lay His head – who was condemned by the princes of this world, beaten, scourged, and nailed to the cross – that same Jesus shall Himself judge the world when He comes in His glory. To Him the Father has committed all judgment (John 5:22). To Him at last every knee shall bow and every tongue confess that He is Lord (Philippians 2:10-11).

Let believers think of this and take comfort. He that sits upon the throne in that great and dreadful day will be their Savior, their Shepherd, their High Priest, their elder Brother, their Friend. When they see Him, they will have no cause to be alarmed.

Let unconverted people think of this and be afraid. Their judge will be that very Christ whose gospel they now despise and whose gracious invitations they refuse to hear. How great will be their confusion at last, if they go on in unbelief and die in their sins! To be condemned in the day of judgment by anyone would be dreadful. But to be condemned by Him who would have saved them will be dreadful indeed. Well may the psalmist say, *Do homage to the Son, that He not become angry* (Psalm 2:12).

Let us mark, in the second place, *who will be judged in the last day.* We read that *all the nations will be gathered before Him.*

All who have ever lived shall one day give account of themselves at the bar of Christ. All must obey the summons of the great King and come forward to receive their sentence. Those who would not come to worship Christ on earth will find they must come to His great judicial inquest when He returns to judge the world.

All who are judged will be divided into two great classes. There will no longer be any distinction between kings and subjects, or masters and servants, or dissenters and churchmen. There will be no mention of ranks and denominations, for the former things will have passed away.

Grace, or no grace, conversion or unconversion, faith or no faith, will be the only distinctions at the last day. All who are found in Christ will be placed among the sheep at His right hand. All who are not found in Christ will be placed among the goats at His left. Well says Sherlock, "Our separations will avail us nothing, unless we take care to be found in the number of Christ's sheep, when He comes to judgment."

Let us mark, in the third place, *in what manner the judgment will be conducted in the last day.* We read of several striking particulars on this point. Let us see what they are.

The last judgment will be a judgment *according to evidence.* The works of men are the witnesses which will be brought forward, and above all their works of charity. The question to be ascertained will not merely be what we said, but what we did – not merely what we professed, but what we practiced. Our works unquestionably will not justify us. We are justified by faith without the deeds of the law. But the truth of our faith will be tested by our lives. Faith which has not works is dead, being alone (James 2:20).

The last judgment will be a judgment that will bring *joy to all true believers.* They will hear those precious words, *"Come, you who are blessed of my Father, inherit the kingdom."* They will be owned and confessed by their Master before His Father and the holy angels. They shall find that the wages He gives to His faithful servants are nothing less than *the kingdom.* The least and lowest and poorest of the family of God shall have a crown of glory and be a king.

The last judgment will be a judgment that will bring confusion on all unconverted people. They will hear those dreadful words, *"Depart from Me, accursed ones, into the eternal fire."* They will be disowned by the Lord before the assembled world. They will find that as they would sow to the flesh, so of the flesh they must reap corruption. They would not hear Christ when He said, *"Come to Me, and I will give you rest,"* and now they must hear Him say, *"Depart into the eternal fire."* They would not carry His cross, and so they can have no place in His kingdom.

The last judgment will be a judgment that will strikingly bring out the characters both of the lost and the saved. Those on the right hand who are Christ's sheep will still be *clothed with humility.* They will marvel to hear any work of theirs brought forward and commended. Those on the left hand who are not Christ's will still be blind and self-righteous. They will not be sensible of any neglect of Christ. *"Lord,"* they say, *"when did we see You and not take care of You?"* Let this thought sink down into our hearts. Our characters on earth will prove an everlasting possession in the world to come. With the same heart that men die, with that heart they will rise again.

Let us mark, in the last place, *what will be the final results of the judgment day.* We are told this in words that ought never to be forgotten: the wicked *will go away into eternal punishment, but the righteous into eternal life.*

The state of things after the judgment is changeless and without end. The misery of the lost and the blessedness of the saved are both alike forever. Let no man deceive us on this point. It is clearly revealed in Scripture. The eternity of God and heaven and hell all stand on the same foundation. As surely as God is eternal, so surely is heaven an endless day without night, and hell an endless night without day.

Who shall describe *the blessedness of eternal life?* It surpasses the power of man to conceive. It can only be measured by contrast and comparison. An eternal rest, after warfare and conflict – the eternal company of saints, after buffeting with an evil world – an eternally glorious and painless body, after struggling with weakness and infirmity – an eternal sight of Jesus face to face, after only hearing and believing – all this is blessedness indeed. And yet the half of it remains untold.

Who shall describe *the misery of eternal punishment?* It is something utterly indescribable and inconceivable. The eternal pain of body – the eternal sting of an accusing conscience – the eternal society of none but the wicked, the devil and his angels – the eternal remembrance of opportunities neglected and Christ despised – the eternal prospect of a weary, hopeless future – all this is misery indeed. It is enough to make our ears tingle and our blood run cold. And yet this *picture* is nothing compared to the *reality.*

Let us close these verses with serious self-inquiry. Let us ask ourselves on which side of Christ we are likely to be at the last day. Shall we be on the right hand or shall we be on the left? Happy is he who never rests until he can give a satisfactory answer to this question.

Matthew Chapter 26

Matthew 26:1-13

When Jesus had finished all these words, He said to His disciples, "You know that after two days the Passover is coming, and the Son of Man is to be handed over for crucifixion." Then the chief priests and the elders of the people were gathered together in the court of the high priest, named Caiaphas; and they plotted together to seize Jesus by stealth and kill Him. But they were saying, "Not during the festival, otherwise a riot might occur among the people." Now when Jesus was in Bethany, at the home of Simon the leper, a woman came to Him with an alabaster vial of very costly perfume, and she poured it on His head as He reclined at the table. But the disciples were indignant when they saw this, and said, "Why this waste? For this perfume might have been sold for a high price and the money given to the poor." But Jesus, aware of this, said to them, "Why do you bother the woman? For she has done a good deed to Me. For you always have the poor with you; but you do not always have Me. For when she poured this perfume on My body, she did it to prepare me for burial. Truly I say to you, wherever this gospel is preached in the whole world, what this woman has done will be spoken of in memory of her." (Matthew 26:1-13)

WE NOW APPROACH THE CLOSING SCENE of our Lord Jesus Christ's earthly ministry. Hitherto we have read of His sayings and doings; we are now about to read of His sufferings and death. Hitherto we have seen Him as the great prophet; we are now about to see Him as the Great High Priest.

It is a portion of Scripture which ought to be read with peculiar reverence and attention. The place whereon we stand is holy ground. Here we see how the seed of the woman bruised the Serpent's head. Here we see the great sacrifice to which all the sacrifices of the Old Testament had long pointed. Here we see how the blood was shed which *cleanses us from all sin*, and the Lamb slain who *takes away the sin of the world*. We see in the death of Christ the great mystery revealed: how God can be just, and yet justify the ungodly. No wonder that all the four Gospels contain a full account of this wonderful event. On other points in our Lord's history we often find that when one evangelist speaks, the other three are silent. But when we come to the crucifixion, we find it minutely described by all four.

In these verses we have now read, let us first observe *how careful our Lord is to recall the attention of His disciples to His own death.* He said to them, *"You know that after two days the Passover is coming, and the Son of Man is to be handed over for crucifixion."*

The connection of these words with the preceding chapter is exceedingly striking. Our Lord had just been dwelling on His own second coming in power and glory at the end of the world. He had been describing the last judgment and all its dreadful accompaniments. He had been speaking of Himself as the judge before whose throne all nations would be gathered. And then at once, without pause or interval, He goes on to speak of His crucifixion. While the marvelous predictions of His final glory were yet ringing in the ears of His disciples, He tells them once again of His coming sufferings. He reminds them that He must die as a sin offering before He reigns as a king, and that He must make atonement on the cross before He takes the crown.

We can never attach too much importance to the atoning death of Christ. It is the leading fact in the Word of God on which the eyes of our soul ought to be ever fixed. Without the shedding of His blood, there is no remission of sin. It is the cardinal truth on which the whole system of Christianity hinges. Without it the gospel is an arch without a keystone, a fair building without a foundation, a solar system without a sun. Let us make much of our Lord's incarnation and example, His miracles and His parables, and His works and His words, but above all let us make much of His death. Let us delight in the hope of His second personal coming and millennial reign, but let us not think more even of these blessed truths than of the atonement on the cross. This, after all, is the master-truth of Scripture, that *Christ died for our sins.* To this let us daily return. On this let us daily feed our souls. Some, like the Greeks of old, may sneer at the doctrine and call it foolishness. But let us never be ashamed to say with Paul, *May it never be that I would boast, except in the cross of our Lord Jesus Christ* (Galatians 6:14).

Let us observe, in the second place in these verses, *what honor Christ loves to put on those who honor Him.* We are told that when He was *at the home of Simon the leper,* a certain woman came, while He sat at table, and poured a vial of costly perfume on His head. She did it, no doubt, out of reverence and affection. She had received soul-benefit from Him, and she thought no mark of honor too costly to be bestowed on Him in return. But this deed of hers called forth disapproval from some who saw it. They called it a *waste.* They said it might have been better to sell the ointment and give the money to the poor. At once our Lord rebuked these coldhearted faultfinders. He tells them that the woman has *done a good deed* and one that He accepts and approves. And He goes on to make a striking prediction: *"Wherever this gospel is preached in the whole world, what this woman has done will also be spoken of in memory of her."*

We see in this little incident how perfectly our Lord knew things to come and how easy it is for Him to confer honor. This prophecy of His about this woman is receiving a fulfillment every day before our eyes. Wherever the Gospel of Matthew is read, the deed that she did is known. The deeds and titles of many a king, emperor, and general are as completely forgotten as if written in the sand. But the grateful act of one humble Christian woman is recorded in 150 different languages and is known all over the globe. The praise of man is but for a few days. The praise of Christ endures forever. The pathway to lasting honor is to honor Christ.

Last, but not least, we see in this incident a blessed foretaste of things that will yet take place in the day of judgment. In that great day no honor done to Christ on earth shall be found to have been forgotten. The speeches of parliamentary orators, the exploits of warriors, the works of poets and painters shall not be mentioned in that day. But the least work that the weakest Christian woman has done for Christ or His members shall be found written in a book of everlasting remembrance. Not a single kind word or deed, not a cup of cold water, or a box of perfume shall be omitted from the record. Silver and gold she may have had none – rank, power, and influence she may not have possessed – but if she loved Christ and confessed Christ and worked for Christ, her memorial shall be found on high. She shall be commended before assembled worlds.

Do we know what it is to work for Christ? If we do, let us take courage and work on. What greater encouragement can we desire than we see here? We may be laughed at and ridiculed by the world. Our motives may be misunderstood. Our conduct may be misrepresented. Our sacrifices for Christ's sake may be called a *waste* – a waste of time, a waste of money, and a waste of strength. Let none of these things move us. The eye of Him who sat in Simon's house in Bethany is upon us. He notes all we do and is well-pleased. Let us be *steadfast, immovable, always abounding in the work of the Lord, knowing that [our] toil is not in vain in the Lord* (1 Corinthians 15:58).

Matthew 26:14-25

Then one of the twelve, named Judas Iscariot, went to the chief priests and said, "What are you willing to give me to betray Him to you?" And they weighed out thirty pieces of silver to him. From then on he began looking for a good opportunity to betray Jesus. Now on the first day of Unleavened Bread the disciples came to Jesus and asked, "Where do You want us to prepare for You to eat the Passover?" And He said, "Go into the city to a certain man, and say to him, 'The Teacher says, "My time is near; I am to keep the Passover at your house with My disciples."'"

The disciples did as Jesus had directed them; and they prepared the Passover. Now when evening came, Jesus was reclining at the table with the twelve disciples. As they were eating, He said, "Truly I say to you that one of you will betray Me." Being deeply grieved, they each one began to say to Him, "Surely not I, Lord?" And He answered, "He who dipped his hand with Me in the bowl is the one who will betray Me. The Son of Man is to go, just as it is written of Him; but woe to that man by whom the Son of Man is betrayed! It would have been good for that man if he had not been born." And Judas, who was betraying Him, said, "Surely it is not I, Rabbi?" Jesus said to him, "You have said it yourself." (Matthew 26:14-25)

We read in the beginning of this passage how our Lord Jesus Christ was betrayed into the hands of His deadly enemies. The priests and scribes, however anxious to put Him to death, were at a loss how to effect their purpose for fear of an uproar among the people. At this juncture, a fitting instrument for carrying out their designs offered himself to them in the person of Judas Iscariot. That false apostle undertook to deliver his Master into their hands for thirty pieces of silver.

There are few blacker pages in all history than the character and conduct of Judas Iscariot. There is no more dreadful evidence of the wickedness of man. A poet of our own has said that "sharper than a serpent's tooth is a thankless child." But what shall we say of a disciple who could betray his own Master – an apostle who could sell Christ? Surely this was not the least bitter part of the cup of suffering which our Lord drank.

Let us learn, in the first place from these verses, that *a man may enjoy great privileges and make a great religious profession, and yet his heart all the time may not be right before God.*

Judas Iscariot had the highest possible religious privileges. He was a chosen apostle and companion of Christ. He was an eyewitness of our Lord's miracles and a hearer of His sermons. He saw what Abraham and Moses never saw and heard what David and Isaiah never heard. He lived in the society of the eleven apostles. He was a fellow laborer with

Peter, James, and John. But for all this his heart was never changed. He clung to one darling sin.

Judas Iscariot made a reputable profession of religion. There was nothing but what was right, proper, and becoming in his outward conduct. Like the other apostles he appeared to believe and to give up all for Christ's sake. Like them he was sent forth to preach and work miracles. No one of the eleven appears to have suspected him of hypocrisy. When our Lord said, *"One of you will betray Me,"* no one said, "Is it Judas?" Yet all this time his heart was never changed.

We ought to observe these things. They are deeply humbling and instructive. Like Lot's wife, Judas is intended to be a beacon to the whole church. Let us often think about him and say, as we think, *Search me, O God, and know my heart; and see if there be any hurtful way in me.* Let us resolve, by God's grace, that we will never be content with anything short of sound and thorough heart conversion.

Let us learn, in the second place from these verses, that *the love of money is one of the greatest snares to a man's soul.* We cannot conceive a clearer proof of this than the case of Judas. That wretched question, *"What are you willing to give me?"* reveals the secret sin which was his ruin. He had given up much for Christ's sake, but he had not given up his covetousness.

The words of the apostle Paul should often ring in our ears: *The love of money is a root of all sorts of evil* (1 Timothy 6:10). The history of the church abounds in illustrations of this truth. For money Joseph was sold by his brethren. For money Samson was betrayed to the Philistines. For money Gehazi deceived Naaman and lied to Elisha. For money Ananias and Sapphira tried to deceive Peter. For money the Son of God was delivered into the hands of wicked men. Astonishing indeed does it seem that the cause of so much evil should be loved so well.

Let us all be on our guard against the love of money. The world is full of it in our days. The plague is abroad. Thousands who would abhor the idea of worshiping Juggernaut are not ashamed to make an idol of gold. We are all liable to the infection, from the least to the greatest. We may love money without having it, just as we may have money without loving it. It is an evil that works very deceitfully. It carries us captives before we are aware of our chains. Once we let it get the mastery, it will harden, paralyze, scorch, freeze, blight, and wither our souls. It overthrew an apostle of Christ. Let us take heed that it does not overthrow us. One leak may sink a ship. One unmortified sin may ruin a soul.

We ought frequently to call to mind the solemn words, *What will it profit a man if he gains the whole world and forfeits his soul? We have brought nothing into the world, so we cannot take anything out of it either.* Our daily prayer should be, *Give me neither poverty nor riches; feed me with the food that is my portion* (Proverbs 30:8). Our constant aim should be to be rich in grace. Those who will be rich in worldly possessions often find at last that they have made the worst of bargains. Like Esau, they have bartered an eternal portion for a little temporary gratification. Like Judas Iscariot, they have sold themselves to everlasting perdition.

Let us learn, in the last place from these verses, *the hopeless condition of all who die unconverted.* The words of our Lord on this subject are peculiarly solemn. He says of Judas, *"It would have been good for that man if he had not been born."* This saying allows for only one interpretation. It teaches plainly that it is better never to live at all than to live without faith and die without grace. To die in this state is to be ruined forevermore. It is a fall from which there is no rising. It is a loss which is utterly irretrievable. There is no change in hell. The gulf between hell and heaven is one that no man can pass. This saying could never have been used if there was any truth in the doctrine of universal salvation. If it really was true that all would sooner or later reach heaven, and hell would sooner or later be emptied of inhabitants, it never could be said that it would have been good for a man not to have been born. Hell itself would lose its terrors if it had an end. Hell itself would be endurable if after millions of ages there was a hope of freedom and of heaven. But universal salvation will find no foothold in Scripture. The teaching of the Word of God is plain and express on the subject. There is a worm that never dies, and a fire that is not quenched (Mark 9:44). *Unless one is born again*, he will wish one day he had never been born at all. "Better," says Burkitt, "have no being, than not have a being in Christ."

Let us grasp this truth firmly and not let it go. There are always people who dislike the reality and eternity of hell. We live in a day when a morbid charity induces many to exaggerate God's mercy at the expense of His justice, and when false teachers are daring to talk of a "love of God, lower even than hell." Let us resist such teaching with a holy jealousy and abide by the doctrine of Holy Scripture. Let us not be ashamed to walk in the old paths, and to believe that there is an eternal God, an eternal heaven, and an eternal hell. Once we depart from this belief, we admit the thin edge of the wedge of skepticism and may at last deny any doctrine of the gospel. We may rest assured that there is no firm standing ground between a belief in the eternity of hell and downright infidelity.

Matthew 26:26-35

While they were eating, Jesus took some bread, and after a blessing, He broke it and gave it to the disciples, and said, "Take, eat; this is My body." And when He had taken a cup and given thanks, He gave it to them, saying, "Drink from it, all of you; for this is My blood of the covenant, which is poured out for many for forgiveness of sins. But I say to you, I will not drink of this fruit of the vine from now on until that day when I drink it new with you in My Father's kingdom." After singing a hymn, they went out to the Mount of Olives. Then Jesus said to them, "You will all fall away because of Me this night, for it is written, 'I will strike down the Shepherd, and the sheep of the flock will be scattered.' But after I have been raised, I will go ahead of you to Galilee." But Peter said to Him, "Even though all may fall away because of You, I will never fall away." Jesus said to him, "Truly I say to you that this very night, before a rooster crows, you will deny Me three times." Peter said to Him, "Even if I have to die with You, I will not deny You." All the disciples said the same thing too. (Matthew 26:26-35)

These verses describe the appointment of the sacrament of the Lord's

Supper. Our Lord knew well the things that were before Him, and He graciously chose the last quiet evening that He could have before His crucifixion as an occasion for bestowing a parting gift on His church. How precious must this ordinance have afterwards appeared to His disciples when they remembered the events of that night. How mournful is the thought that no ordinance has led to such fierce controversy and been so grievously misunderstood as the ordinance of the Lord's Supper. It ought to have united the church, but our sins have made it a cause of division. The thing which should have been for our welfare has been too often made an occasion of falling.

The first thing that demands our notice in these verses is *the right meaning of our Lord's words, "This is My body, this is My blood."*

It is needless to say that this question has divided the visible church of Christ. It has caused volumes of controversial theology to be written. But we must not shrink from having decided opinions upon it just because theologians have disputed and differed. Unsoundness on this point has given rise to many deplorable superstitions.

The plain meaning of our Lord's words appears to be this: "This bread *represents* My body. This wine *represents* My blood." He did not mean that the bread He gave to His disciples was really and literally His body. He did not mean that the wine He gave to His disciples was really and literally His blood. Let us lay firm hold on this interpretation. It may be supported by several grave reasons.

The conduct of the disciples at the Lord's Supper forbids us to believe that the bread they received was Christ's body and the wine they received was Christ's blood. They were all Jews, taught from their infancy to believe that it was sinful to eat flesh with the blood (Deuteronomy 12:23-25). Yet there is nothing in the narrative to show that they were startled by our Lord's words. They evidently perceived no change in the bread and wine.

Our own senses in the present day forbid us to believe that there is any change in the bread and wine in the Lord's Supper. Our own taste tells us that they are really and literally what they appear to be. Things above our reason the Bible requires us to believe. But we are never bid to believe that which contradicts our senses.

The true doctrine about our Lord's human nature forbids us to believe that the bread in the Lord's Supper can be His body or the wine His blood. The natural body of Christ cannot be at one time in more places than one. If our Lord's body could sit at a table and at the same time be eaten by the disciples, it is perfectly clear that it was not a human body like our own. But this we must never allow for one moment. It is the glory of Christianity that our Redeemer is perfect man as well as perfect God.

Finally, the genius of the language in which our Lord spoke at the Lord's Supper makes it entirely unnecessary to interpret His words literally. The Bible is full of expressions of a similar kind to which no one thinks of giving anything but a figurative meaning. Our Lord speaks of Himself as the *door* and the *vine*, and we know that He is using emblems and figures when He so speaks. There is therefore no inconsistency in supposing that He used figurative language when He appointed the Lord's Supper; and we have the more right to say so when we remember the grave objections which stand in the way of a literal view of His words.

Let us lay up these things in our minds and not forget them. In a day of abounding heresy, it is good to be well armed. *Ignorant and confused views of the meaning of Scripture language are one great cause of religious error.*

The second thing which demands our notice in these verses is *the purpose and object for which the Lord's Supper was appointed.*

This is a subject again on which great darkness prevails. The ordinance of the Lord's Supper has been regarded as something mysterious and beyond understanding. Immense harm has been done to Christianity by the vague and high-flown language in which many writers have indulged in treating the sacrament. There is certainly nothing to warrant such language in the account of its original institution. The more simple our views of its purpose, the more scriptural they are likely to be.

The Lord's Supper is *not a sacrifice.* There is no oblation in it – no offering up of anything but our prayers, praises, and thanksgivings. From the day that Jesus died, no more offering for sin was needed. By one offering He perfected forever those who are sanctified (Hebrews 10:14). Priests, altars, and sacrifices all ceased to be necessary when the Lamb of God offered up Himself. Their office came to an end. Their work was done.

The Lord's Supper has *no power to automatically confer benefit on those who come to it, if they do not come to it with faith*. The mere formal act of eating the bread and drinking the wine is utterly unprofitable unless it is done with a right heart. It is eminently an ordinance for the living soul, not for the dead – for the converted, not for the unconverted.

The Lord's Supper was ordained for *a continual remembrance of the sacrifice of Christ's death* until He comes again. The benefits it confers are spiritual, not physical. Its effects must be looked for in our inward man. It was intended to remind us, by the visible and tangible emblems of bread and wine, that the offering of Christ's body and blood for us on the cross is the only atonement for sin and the life of a believer's soul. It was meant to help our poor weak faith to experience closer fellowship with our crucified Savior, and to assist us in spiritually feeding on Christ's body and blood. It is an ordinance for redeemed sinners and not for unfallen angels. By receiving it we publicly declare our sense of guilt and need of a Savior – our trust in Jesus, and our love to Him – our desire to live upon Him, and our hope to live with Him. Using it in this spirit, we shall find our repentance deepened, our faith increased, our hope brightened, and our love enlarged – our besetting sins weakened, and our graces strengthened. It will draw us nearer to Christ.

Let us bear these things in mind. They need to be remembered in these latter days. There is nothing in our religion which we are so ready to pervert and misunderstand as those parts which approach our senses. *Whatever we can touch with our hand and see with our eyes we are apt to exalt into an idol, or to expect good from it as a mere charm.* Let us especially beware of this tendency in the matter of the Lord's Supper. Above all, "Let us take heed," in the words of the Homily, "lest of the memory it be made a sacrifice."

The last thing which deserves a brief notice in this passage is the *character of the first of those who fellowshipped with Christ*. It is a point full of comfort and instruction.

The little company to which the bread and wine were first administered by our Lord was composed of the apostles whom He had chosen to accompany Him during His earthly ministry. They were poor and unlearned men who loved Christ but were weak alike in faith and knowledge. They knew but little of the full meaning of their Master's sayings and doings. They knew but little of the frailty of their own hearts. They thought they were ready to die with Jesus, and yet that very night they all forsook Him and fled. All this our Lord knew perfectly well. The state of their hearts was not hidden from Him. And yet He did not keep back from them the Lord's Supper.

There is something very instructive in this circumstance. It shows us plainly that we must not make great knowledge and great strength of grace an indispensable qualification for those in the church of Christ. A man may know but little and be no better than a child in spiritual strength, but he is not on that account to be excluded from the Lord's Table. Does he really feel his sins? Does he really love Christ? Does he really desire to serve Him? If this be so, we ought to encourage and receive him. Doubtless we must do all we can to exclude unworthy persons. No graceless person ought to come to the Lord's Supper. But we must take heed that we do not reject those whom Christ has not rejected. There is no wisdom in being more strict than our Lord and His apostles.

Let us leave the passage with serious self-inquiry as to our own conduct with respect to the Lord's Supper. Do we turn away from it when it is administered? If so, how can we justify our conduct? It will not do to say it is not a necessary ordinance. To say so is to pour contempt on Christ Himself and declare that we do not obey Him. It will not do to say that we feel unworthy to come to the Lord's Table. To say so is to declare that we are unfit to die and unprepared to meet God. These are solemn considerations. All those in the church should ponder them well.

Are we in the habit of coming to the Lord's Table? If so, in what frame of mind do we come? Do we draw near intelligently, humbly, and with faith? Do we understand what we are doing? Do we really feel our sinfulness and need of Christ? Do we really desire to live a Christian life as well as profess the Christian faith? Happy is that soul who can give a satisfactory answer to these questions. Let him go forward and persevere.

Matthew 26:36-46

Then Jesus came with them to a place called Gethsemane, and said to the disciples, "Sit here while I go over there and pray." And He took with Him Peter and the two sons of Zebedee, and began to be grieved and distressed. Then He said to them, "My soul is deeply grieved, to the point of death; remain here and keep watch with Me." And He went a little beyond them and fell on His face and prayed, saying, "My Father, if it is possible, let this cup pass from Me; yet not as I will, but as You will." And He came to the disciples and found them sleeping, and said to Peter, "So you men could not keep watch with Me for one hour? Keep watching and praying that you may not enter into temptation; the spirit is willing, but the flesh is weak." He went away again a second time and prayed, saying, "My Father, if this cannot pass away unless I drink it, Your will be done." Again He came and found them sleeping, for their eyes were heavy. And He left them again, and went away and prayed a third time, saying the same thing once more. Then He came to the disciples and said to them, "Are you still sleeping and resting? Behold, the hour is at hand and the Son of Man is being betrayed into the hands of sinners. Get up, let us be going; behold, the one who betrays Me is at hand." (Matthew 26:36-46)

The verses we have now read describe what is commonly called Christ's agony at Gethsemane. It is a passage which undoubtedly contains deep and mysterious things. We ought to read it with reverence and wonder, for there is much in it which we cannot fully comprehend.

Why do we find our Lord so *grieved and distressed* as He is here described? What are we to make of His words, *"My soul is deeply grieved, to the point death"*? Why do we see Him going apart from His disciples, and falling on His face, and crying to His Father with strong cries and thrice-repeated prayer? Why is the almighty Son of God, who had worked so many miracles, so grieved and distressed? Why is

Jesus, who came into the world to die, so like one ready to faint at the approach of death? Why is all this?

There is but one reasonable answer to these questions. The weight that pressed down our Lord's soul was not the fear of death and its pains. Thousands have endured the most agonizing sufferings of body and died without a groan, and so, no doubt, might our Lord. But the real weight that bowed down the heart of Jesus was *the weight of the sin* of the world, which seems to have now pressed down upon Him with peculiar force. It was the burden of our guilt imputed to Him which was now laid on Him as on the head of the scapegoat. No heart of man can conceive how great that burden must have been. It is known only to God. Well may the Greek Litany speak of the "unknown sufferings of Christ." The words of Scott on this subject are probably correct: "Christ at this time endured as much misery, of the same kind with that of condemned spirits, as could possibly consist with a pure conscience, perfect love of God and man, and an assured confidence of a glorious event."

But however mysterious this part of our Lord's history may seem to us, we must not fail to observe the precious lessons of practical instruction which it contains. Let us now see what those lessons are.

Let us learn, in the first place, that *prayer is the best practical remedy that we can use in time of trouble*. We see that Christ Himself prayed when His soul was sorrowful. All true Christians ought to do the same.

Trouble is a cup that all must drink in this world of sin. We are *born for trouble, as sparks fly upward* (Job 5:7). We cannot avoid it. Of all creatures, none is so vulnerable as man. Our bodies, our minds, our families, our business, and our friends are all so many doors through which trials will come in. The holiest saints can claim no exemption from it. Like their Master, they are often "men of sorrow."

But what is the first thing to be done in time of trouble? We must pray. Like Job, we must fall down and worship (Job 1:20). Like Hezekiah, we must spread our matters before the Lord (2 Kings 19:14). The first person we must turn to for help must be our God. We must tell all our sorrow to our Father in heaven. We must believe confidently that nothing is too trivial or minute to be laid before Him, so long as we do it with entire submission to His will. It is the mark of faith to keep nothing back from our best Friend. In so doing, we may be sure we shall have an answer. *"If it is possible,"* and the thing we ask is for God's glory, it shall be done. The thorn in the flesh shall either be removed, or grace to endure it will be given to us, as it was to Paul (2 Corinthians 12:9). May we all store up this lesson against the day of need. It is a true saying that "prayers are the leeches of care."

Let us learn, in the second place, that *entire submission of will to the will of God should be one of our chief aims in this world.* The words of our Lord are a beautiful example of the spirit that we should follow after in this matter. He says, *"Not as I will, but as You will."* He says again, *"Your will be done."*

A will unsanctified and uncontrolled is one great cause of unhappiness in life. It may be seen in little infants. It is born with us. We all like our own way. We wish and want many things and forget that we are entirely ignorant of what is for our good, and unfit to choose for ourselves. Happy is he who has learned to have no wishes and in every state to be content. It is a lesson which we are slow to learn, and like Paul, we must learn it not in the school of mortal man, but of Christ (Philippians 4:11).

Do we want to know whether we are born again and growing in grace? Let us see how it is with us in the matter of our wills. Can we bear disappointment? Can we put up patiently with unexpected trials and vexations? Can we see our pet plans and darling schemes crossed without murmuring and complaint? Can we sit still and suffer calmly as well as go up and down and work actively? These are the things that prove whether we have the mind of Christ. It ought never to be forgotten that warm feelings and joyful frames are not the truest evidences of grace. A mortified will is a far more valuable possession. Even our Lord Himself did not always rejoice; but He could always say, *"Your will be done."*

Let us learn, in the last place, that *there is great weakness even in true disciples of Christ, and that they have need to watch and pray against it.* We see Peter, James, and John – those three chosen apostles – sleeping when they ought to have been watching and praying. And we find our Lord addressing them in these solemn words: *"Keep watching and praying that you may not enter into temptation; the spirit is willing, but the flesh is weak."*

There is a double nature in all believers. Converted, renewed, and sanctified as they are, they still carry about with them a mass of indwelling corruption, a body of sin. Paul speaks of this when he says, *I find then the principle that evil is present in me, the one who wants to do good. For I joyfully concur with the law of God in the inner man, but I see a different law in the members of my body, waging war against the law of my mind* (Romans 7:21-23). The experience of all true Christians in every age confirms this. They find within themselves two contrary principles and a continual strife between the two. To these two principles our Lord alludes when He addresses His half-awakened disciples. He calls the one *flesh* and the other *spirit*. He says, *"The spirit is willing, but the flesh is weak."*

But does our Lord excuse this weakness of His disciples? Be it far from us to think so. Those who draw this conclusion mistake His meaning. He uses that very weakness as an argument for watchfulness and prayer. He teaches us that the very fact that we are encompassed with infirmity should stir us up continually to *keep watching and praying*.

If we know anything of true religion, let us never forget this lesson. If we desire to walk with God comfortably and not fall, like David or Peter, let us never forget to watch and pray. Let us live like men on enemy ground and be always on our guard. We cannot walk too carefully. We cannot be too jealous over our souls. The world is very ensnaring. The devil is very busy. Let our Lord's words ring in our ears daily like a trumpet. Our spirits may sometimes be very willing, but our flesh is always very weak. Then let us always watch and always pray.

Matthew 26:47-56

While He was still speaking, behold, Judas, one of the twelve, came up accompanied by a large crowd with swords and clubs, who came from the chief priests and elders of the people. Now he who was betraying Him gave them a sign, saying, "Whomever I kiss, He is the one; seize Him." Immediately Judas went to Jesus and said, "Hail, Rabbi!" and kissed Him. And Jesus said to him, "Friend, do what you have come for." Then they came and laid hands on Jesus and seized Him. And behold, one of those who were with Jesus reached and drew out his sword, and struck the slave of the high priest and cut off his ear. Then Jesus said to him, "Put your sword back into its place; for all those who take up the sword shall perish by the sword. Or do you think that I cannot appeal to My Father, and He will at once put at my disposal more than twelve legions of angels? How then will the Scriptures be fulfilled, which say that it must happen this way?" At that time Jesus said to the crowds, "Have you come out with swords and clubs to arrest Me as you would against a robber? Every day I used to sit in the temple teaching and you did not seize Me. But all this has taken place to fulfill the Scriptures of the prophets." Then all the disciples left Him and fled. (Matthew 26:47-56)

We see in these verses the cup of our Lord Jesus Christ's sufferings beginning to be filled. We see Him betrayed by one of His disciples, forsaken by the rest, and taken prisoner by His deadly enemies. Never surely was there sorrow like His sorrow! Never may we forget, as we read this part of the Bible, that *our sins were the cause of these sorrows!* Jesus was *delivered over for our transgressions* (Romans 4:25).

Let us notice, for one thing in these verses, *what gracious condescension marked our Lord's communion with His disciples.*

We have this point proved by a deeply touching circumstance at the moment of our Lord's betrayal. When Judas Iscariot undertook to guide the multitude to the place where his Master was, he gave them a sign by which they might distinguish Jesus in the dim moonlight from His disciples. He said, *"Whomever I kiss, He is the one."* And so, when he came to Jesus, he said, *"Hail, Rabbi!" and kissed Him.* That simple fact reveals the affectionate terms on which the disciples associated with our Lord. It is a universal custom in Eastern countries, when friend meets friend, to salute one another with a kiss (Exodus 18:7; 1 Samuel 20:41). It would seem, therefore, that when Judas kissed our Lord, he only did that which all the apostles were accustomed to doing when they met their Master after an absence.

Let us draw comfort from this little circumstance for our own souls. Our Lord Jesus Christ is a most gracious and condescending Savior. He is not an austere man, repelling sinners and keeping them at a distance. He is not a being so different from us in nature that we must regard Him with awe rather than affection. He would have us rather regard Him as an elder brother and a beloved friend. His heart in heaven is still the same that it was upon earth. He is ever meek, merciful, and condescending to men of low estate. Let us trust Him and not be afraid.

Let us notice, for another thing, how *our Lord condemns those who think to use carnal weapons in defense of Him and His cause.* He reproves one of His disciples for striking a servant of the high priest. He bids him *"put your sword back into its place."* And he adds a solemn declaration of perpetual significance: *"All those who take up the sword shall perish by the sword."*

The sword has a lawful office of its own. It may be used righteously in the defense of nations against oppression. It may become positively necessary to use it to prevent confusion, plunder, and pillage upon earth. But the sword is not to be used in the propagation and maintenance of the gospel. Christianity is not to be enforced by bloodshed and belief in it extorted by force. Happy would it have been for the church if this sentence had been more frequently remembered! There are few countries in Christendom where the mistake has not been made of attempting to change men's religious opinions by compulsion, penalties, imprisonment, and death. And with what effect? The pages of history supply an answer. No wars have been so bloody as those which have arisen out of the collision of religious opinions. Often, mournfully often, the very men who have been most forward to promote those wars have themselves been slain. May we never forget this! The weapons of the Christian warfare are not carnal but spiritual (2 Corinthians10:4).

Let us notice, for another thing, how *our Lord submitted to be made a prisoner of His own free will.* He was not taken captive because He could not escape. It would have been easy for Him to scatter His enemies to the winds if He had thought fit. *"Do you think,"* He says to a disciple, *"that I cannot appeal to My Father, and He will at once put at My disposal more than twelve legions of angels? How then will the Scriptures be fulfilled, which say that it must happen this way?"*

We see in those words the secret of His voluntary submission to His foes. He came on purpose to fulfill the types and promises of Old Testament Scriptures, and by fulfilling them to provide salvation for the world. He came intentionally to be the true Lamb of God, the Passover Lamb. He came to be the scapegoat on whom the iniquities of the people were to be laid. His heart was set on accomplishing this great work. It could not be done without the "hiding" of His power for a time. To do it He became a willing sufferer. He was taken, tried, condemned, and crucified entirely of His own free will.

Let us observe this. There is much encouragement in it. The willing sufferer will surely be a willing Savior. The almighty Son of God, who allowed men to bind Him and lead Him away captive, when He might have prevented them with a word, must surely be full of readiness to save the souls that flee to Him. Once more, then, let us learn to trust Him and not be afraid.

Let us notice, in the last place, *how little Christians know the weakness of their own hearts until they are tried.* We have a mournful illustration of this in the conduct of our Lord's apostles. The verses we have read conclude with the words, *Then all the disciples left Him and fled.* They forgot their confident assertions made a few hours before. They forgot that they had declared their willingness to die with their Master. They forgot everything but the danger that stared them in the face. The fear of death overcame them. They *left Him and fled.*

How many professing Christians have done the same? How many, under the influence of excited feelings, have promised that they would never be ashamed of Christ? They have come away from the communion table, or the striking sermon, or the Christian meeting full of zeal and love, and ready to say to all who caution them against backsliding, "Is your servant a dog that he should do this thing?" And yet in a few days these feelings have cooled down and passed away. A trial has come and they have fallen before it. They have forsaken Christ.

Let us learn from the passage lessons of humiliation and self-abasement.

Let us resolve by God's grace to cultivate a spirit of lowliness and self-distrust. Let us settle it in our minds that there is nothing so bad that the best of us may not do it, unless we watch, pray, and are held up by the grace of God. And let it be one of our daily prayers, *Uphold me that I may be safe* (Psalm 119:117).

Matthew 26:57-68

Those who had seized Jesus led Him away to Caiaphas, the high priest, where the scribes and the elders were gathered together. But Peter was following Him at a distance as far as the court-yard of the high priest, and entered in, and sat down with the officers to see the outcome. Now the chief priests and the whole Council kept trying to obtain false testimony against Jesus, so that they might put Him to death. They did not find any, even though many false witnesses came forward. But later on two came forward, and said, "This man stated, 'I am able to destroy the temple of God and to rebuild it in three days.'" The high priest stood up and said to Him, "Do You not answer? What is it that these men are testifying against You?" But Jesus kept silent. And the high priest said to Him, "I adjure You by the living God, that You tell us whether You are the Christ, the Son of God." Jesus said to him, "You have said it yourself; nevertheless I tell you, hereafter you will see the Son of Man sitting at the right hand of Power, and coming on the clouds of heaven." Then the high priest tore his robes and said, "He has blasphemed! What further need do we have of witnesses? Behold, you have now heard the blas-phemy; what do you think?" They answered, "He deserves death!" Then they spat in His face and beat Him with their fists; and oth-ers slapped Him, and said, "Prophesy to us, You Christ; who is the one who hit You?" (Matthew 26:57-68)

We read in these verses how our Lord Jesus Christ was brought before Caiaphas the high priest, and solemnly pronounced guilty. It was fitting that it should be so. The great day of atonement had come. The wondrous type of the scapegoat was about to be completely fulfilled. It was only suitable that the Jewish high priest should do his part and declare sin to be upon the head of the victim before he was led forth to be crucified. May we ponder these things and understand them. There was a deep meaning in every step of our Lord's passion.

Let us observe in these verses that *the chief priests were the principal agents in bringing about our Lord's death*. It was not so much the Jewish people, we must remember, who pushed forward this wicked deed, as it was Caiaphas and his companions, the chief priests.

This is an instructive fact and deserves notice. It is a clear proof that high ecclesiastical office exempts no man from gross errors in doctrine and tremendous sins in practice. The Jewish priests could trace their pedigree to Aaron and were his lineal successors. Their office was one of peculiar sanctity and entailed peculiar responsibilities. And yet these very men were the murderers of Christ!

Let us beware of regarding any minister of religion as infallible. His orders, however regularly conferred, are no guarantee that he may not lead us astray and even ruin our souls. The teaching and conduct of all ministers must be tried by the Word of God. They are to be followed so long as they follow the Bible, but no longer. The maxim laid down in Isaiah must be our guide: *To the law and the testimony! If they do not speak according to this word, it is because they have no dawn* (Isaiah 8:20).

Let us observe, in the second place, *how fully our Lord declared to the Jewish council His own Messiahship and His future coming in glory*.

The unconverted Jew can never tell us at the present day that his forefathers were left in ignorance that Jesus was the Messiah. Our Lord's answer to the solemn adjuration of the high priest is a sufficient reply. He tells the council plainly that He is *the Christ, the Son of God*. He goes on to warn them that though He had not yet appeared in glory, as they expected Messiah would have done, a day would come when He would do so. *"Hereafter you will see the Son of Man sitting at the right hand of power, and coming on the clouds of heaven."* They would yet see that very Jesus of Nazareth, whom they had arraigned at their bar, appear in all majesty as King of Kings (Revelation 1:7).

It is a striking fact which we should not fail to notice, that almost the last word spoken by our Lord to the Jews was a warning prediction about His own second advent. He tells them plainly that they would yet see Him in His glory. No doubt He referred to the seventh chapter of Daniel in the language that He used. But He spoke to deaf ears. Unbelief, prejudice, and self-righteousness covered them like a thick cloud. Never was there such an instance of spiritual blindness. Well may the Church of England litany contain the prayer, "From all blindness – and from hardness of heart, good Lord deliver us."

Let us observe, in the last place, *how much our Lord endured before the council, from false witness and mockery.*

Falsehood and ridicule are old and favorite weapons of the devil. *He is a liar and the father of lies* (John 8:44). All through our Lord's earthly ministry we see these weapons continually employed against Him. He was called a glutton, a wine-bibber, and a friend of publicans and sinners. He was held up to contempt as a Samaritan. The closing scene of His life was only in keeping with all the past tenor of it. Satan stirred up His enemies to add insult to injury. No sooner was He pronounced guilty than every sort of mean indignity was heaped upon Him. *They spat in His face and beat Him with their fists; and others slapped Him.* They said mockingly, *"Prophesy to us, You Christ; who is the one who hit You?"*

How astonishing and strange it all sounds! How astonishing that the holy Son of God should have voluntarily submitted to such indignities to redeem such miserable sinners as we are! How wonderful, not least, that every tittle of these insults was foretold seven hundred years before they were inflicted! Seven hundred years before, Isaiah had written down the words, *I did not cover my face from humiliation and spitting* (Isaiah 50:6).

Let us draw from the passage one practical conclusion. Let it never surprise us if we have to endure mockery, and ridicule, and false reports because we belong to Christ. The disciple is not greater than his Master, nor the servant than his Lord. If lies and insults were heaped upon our Savior, we need not wonder if the same weapons are constantly used against His people. It is one of Satan's great devices to blacken the characters of godly men and bring them into contempt. The lives of Luther, Cranmer, Calvin, and Wesley supply abundant examples of this. If we are ever called upon to suffer in this way, let us bear it patiently. We drink the same cup that was drunk by our beloved Lord. But there is one great difference. At the worst, we only drink a few bitter drops. He drank the cup to the very dregs.

Matthew 26:69-75

Now Peter was sitting outside in the courtyard, and a servant-girl came to him and said, "You too were with Jesus the Galilean." But he denied it before them all, saying, "I do not know what you are talking about." When he had gone out to the gateway, another servant-girl saw him and said to those who were there, "This man was with Jesus of Nazareth." And again he denied it with an oath, "I do not know the man." A little later the bystanders came up and said to Peter, "Surely you too are one of them; for even the way you talk gives you away." Then he began to curse and swear, "I do not know the man!" And immediately a rooster crowed. And Peter remembered the word which Jesus had said, "Before a rooster crows, you will deny Me three times." And he went out and wept bitterly. (Matthew 26:69-75)

These verses relate a remarkable and deeply instructive event – the apostle Peter's denial of Christ. It is one of those events which indirectly prove the truth of the Bible. If the gospel had been a mere invention of man, we would never have been told that one of its principal preachers was once so weak and erring as to deny his Master.

The first thing that demands our notice is *the full nature of the sin of which Peter was guilty.*

It was a great sin. We see a man who had followed Christ for three years and been forward in professing faith and love towards Him – a man who had received boundless mercies and loving-kindness and been treated by Christ as a familiar friend – we see this man denying three times that he knows Jesus! This was bad. It was sin committed under circumstances of great aggravation. Peter had been warned plainly of his danger and had heard the warning. He had just been receiving the bread and wine at our Lord's hand and declaring loudly that though he died with Him he would not deny Him! This also was bad. It was a sin committed under apparently small provocation. Two weak women make the remark that he was with Jesus. Those who stood by say, *"Surely you too are one of them."* No threat seems to have been used. No violence seems to have been done. But it was enough to overthrow Peter's faith. He denies before all. He denies with an oath. He curses and swears. Truly it is a humbling picture!

Let us mark this history and store it up in our minds. It teaches us plainly that the best of saints are only men, and men encompassed with many infirmities. A man may be converted to God, have faith and hope and love towards Christ, and yet be overtaken in a fault and have dreadful falls. It shows us the necessity of humility. So long as we are in the body we are in danger. The flesh is weak, and the devil is active. We must never think, "I cannot fall." It points out to us the duty of charity towards erring saints. We must not set down men as graceless reprobates because they occasionally stumble and err. We must remember Peter and *restore such a one in a spirit of gentleness* (Galatians 6:1).

The second thing that demands our notice is *the series of steps by which Peter was led to deny his Lord.*

These steps are mercifully recorded for our learning. The Spirit of God has taken care to have them written down for the perpetual benefit of the church of Christ. Let us trace them out one by one.

The first step to Peter's fall was self-confidence. He said, *"Even though all may fall away because of You, I will never fall away."* The second step was indolence. His Master told him to watch and pray. Instead of doing so, he slept. The third step was cowardly compromising. Instead of keeping close to his Master, he first forsook Him and then *followed Him at a distance.* The last step was needless venturing into evil company. He went into the priest's palace and *sat down with the officers,* like one of themselves. And then came the final fall, the cursing, the swearing, and the threefold denial. Startling as it appears, his heart had been preparing for it. It was the fruit of seeds which he himself had sown. He ate the fruit of his own ways.

Let us remember this part of Peter's history. It is deeply instructive to all who profess and call themselves Christians. Great illnesses seldom attack the body without a previous train of warning symptoms. Great falls seldom happen to a saint without a previous course of secret backsliding. The church and the world are sometimes shocked by the sudden misconduct of some great professor of religion. Believers are discouraged and stumbled by it. The enemies of God rejoice and blaspheme. But if the truth could be known, the explanation of such cases would generally be found to have been *private departure from God*. Men fall in private long before they fall in public. The tree falls with a great crash, but the secret decay which accounts for it is often not discovered until it is down on the ground.

The last thing that demands our notice is *the sorrow which Peter's sin brought upon him*. We read at the end of the chapter, *He went out and wept bitterly*.

These words deserve more attention than they generally receive. Thousands have read the history of Peter's sin who have thought little of Peter's tears and Peter's repentance. May we have an eye to see and a heart to understand.

We see in Peter's tears *the close connection between unhappiness and departure from God*. It is a merciful arrangement of God that in one sense holiness shall always be its own reward. A heavy heart, and an uneasy conscience, a clouded hope, and an abundant crop of doubts, will always be the consequences of backsliding and inconsistency. The words of Solomon describe the experience of many an inconsistent child of God: *The backslider in heart will have his fill of his own ways* (Proverbs 14:14). Let it be a settled principle in our religion that if we love inward peace, we must walk closely with God.

We see in Peter's bitter tears the grand mark of difference between the hypocrite and the true believer. When the hypocrite is overtaken by sin, he generally falls to rise no more. He has no principle of life within him to raise him up. When the child of God is overtaken, he rises again by true repentance, and by the grace of God amends his life. Let no man flatter himself that he may sin with impunity, because David committed adultery and because Peter denied his Lord. No doubt these holy men sinned greatly. But they did not continue in their sin. They repented greatly. They mourned over their falls. They loathed and abhorred their own wickedness. Well would it be for many if they would imitate them in their repentance as well as in their sins. Too many are acquainted with their fall but not with their recovery. Like David and Peter, they have sinned, but they have not, like David and Peter, repented.

The whole passage is full of lessons that ought never to be forgotten. Do we profess to have a hope in Christ? Let us mark the weakness of a believer and the steps that lead to a fall. Have we unhappily backslidden and left our first love? Let us remember that the Savior of Peter still lives. There is mercy for us as well as for him. But we must repent and seek that mercy if we would find it. Let us turn unto God and He will turn to us. His compassions fail not (Lamentations 3:22).

Matthew Chapter 27

Matthew 27:1-10

Now when morning came, all the chief priests and the elders of the people conferred together against Jesus to put Him to death; and they bound Him, and led Him away and delivered Him to Pilate the governor. Then when Judas, who had betrayed Him, saw that He had been condemned, he felt remorse and returned the thirty pieces of silver to the chief priests and elders, saying, "I have sinned by betraying innocent blood." But they said, "What is that to us? See to that yourself!" And he threw the pieces of silver into the temple sanctuary and departed; and he went away and hanged himself. The chief priests took the pieces of silver and said, "It is not lawful to put them into the temple treasury, since it is the price of blood." And they conferred together and with the money bought the Potter's Field as a burial place for strangers. For this reason that field has been called the Field of Blood to this day. Then that which was spoken through Jeremiah the prophet was fulfilled: "And they took the thirty pieces of silver, the price of one whose price had been by the sons of Israel; and they gave them for the Potter's Field, as the Lord directed me." (Matthew 27:1-10)

THE OPENING OF THIS CHAPTER describes the delivery of our Lord Jesus Christ into the hands of the Gentiles. The chief priests and elders of the Jews led Him away to Pontius Pilate, the Roman governor. We may see in this incident the finger of God. It was ordered by His providence that Gentiles as well as Jews should be involved in the murder of Christ. It was ordered by His providence that the priests should publicly confess that the "scepter had departed from Judah." They were unable to put anyone to death without going to the Romans. The words of Jacob were therefore fulfilled. The Messiah, *Shiloh*, had indeed come (Genesis 49:10).

The subject that principally occupies the verses we have read is the bad end of the false apostle Judas Iscariot. It is a subject full of instruction. Let us mark well what it contains.

We see in the end of Judas a plain proof of our Lord's innocence of every charge laid against Him.

If there was any living witness who could give evidence against our Lord Jesus Christ, Judas Iscariot was the man. A chosen apostle of Jesus, a constant companion in all His journeyings, a hearer of all His teaching, both in public and private – he must have known if our Lord had done any wrong, either in word or deed. A deserter from our Lord's company, a betrayer of Him into the hands of His enemies, it was his interest for his own character's sake to prove Jesus guilty. It would extenuate and excuse his own conduct if he could make out that His former master was an offender and an impostor.

Why then did not Judas Iscariot come forward? Why did he not stand forth before the Jewish council and specify his charges, if he had any to make? Why did he not venture to accompany the chief priests to Pilate and prove to the Romans that Jesus was a malefactor? There is but one answer to these questions. Judas did not come forward as a witness because his conscience would not let him. Bad as he was, he knew he could prove nothing against Christ. Wicked as he was, he knew well that his Master was holy, harmless, innocent, blameless, and true. Let this never be forgotten. The absence of Judas Iscariot at our Lord's trial is one among many proofs that the Lamb of God was without blemish – a sinless man.

We see, for another thing in the end of Judas, that *there is such a thing as repentance which is too late.* We are told plainly that Judas *felt remorse and returned the thirty pieces of silver to the chief priests and elders.* We are even told that he went to the priests and said, "*I have sinned.*" And yet it is clear that he did not repent unto salvation.

This is a point which deserves special attention. It is a common saying that "it is never too late to repent." The saying, no doubt, is true, if repentance be true; but *unfortunately, late repentance is often not genuine.* It is possible for a man to feel his sins and be sorry for them – to be under strong convictions of guilt and express deep remorse – to be pierced in conscience and exhibit much distress of mind – and yet, for all this, not repent with his heart. Present danger, or the fear of death, may account for all his feelings, and the Holy Spirit may have done no work whatsoever in his soul.

Let us beware of trusting to a late repentance. *Now is the acceptable time, behold, now is the day of salvation.* One penitent thief was saved in the hour of death, that no man might despair, but only one, that no man might presume. Let us put off nothing that concerns our souls, and above all not put off repentance under the vain idea that it is a thing in our own power. The words of Solomon on this subject are very fearful: *"Then they will call on me, but I will not answer; they will seek me diligently but they will not find me"* (Proverbs 1:28).

Let us see, for another thing in the end of Judas, *how little comfort ungodliness brings a man at the end.*

We are told that he cast down the thirty pieces of silver for which he had sold his Master, in the temple, and went away in bitterness of soul. That money was dearly earned. It brought him no pleasure, even when he had it. *Ill-gotten gains do not profit* (Proverbs 10:2).

Sin is, in truth, the hardest of all masters. In its service there are plenty of fair promises but an utter lack of performance. Its pleasures are but for a season. Its wages are sorrow, remorse, self-accusation, and too often death. Those who sow to the flesh do indeed reap corruption.

Are we tempted to commit sin? Let us remember the words of Scripture: *Your sin will find you out,* and resist the temptation. Let us be sure that sooner or later, in this life or in the life to come, in this world or in the judgment day, sin and the sinner will meet face to face and have a bitter reckoning. Let us be sure that of all trades, sin is the most unprofitable. Judas, Achan, Gehazi, Ananias, and Sapphira all found it so to their cost. Well might Paul say, *What benefit were you then deriving from the things of which you are now ashamed?* (Romans 6:21).

Finally, let us see in the case of Judas *to what a miserable end a man may come if he has great privileges and does not use them rightly.* We are told that this unhappy man *went away and hanged himself.* What a dreadful death to die! An apostle of Christ, a former preacher of the gospel, a companion of Peter and John commits suicide and rushes into God's presence unprepared and unforgiven.

Let us never forget that no sinners are so sinful as sinners against light and knowledge. None are so provoking to God. None, if we look at Scripture, have been so often removed from this world by sudden and fearful visitations. Let us remember Lot's wife, Pharaoh, Korah, Dathan, Abiram, and King Saul of Israel. They are all cases in point. It is a solemn saying of Bunyan "that none fall so deep into the pit, as those who fall backward." It is written in Proverbs, *A man who hardens his neck after much reproof will suddenly be broken beyond remedy* (Proverbs 29:1). May we all strive to live up to our light. There is such a thing as sin against the Holy Spirit. *Clear knowledge of truth in the head, combined with deliberate love of sin in the heart* go a long way towards it.

And now what is the state of our hearts? Are we ever tempted to rest on our knowledge and profession of religion? Let us remember Judas and beware. Are we disposed to cling to the world and give money a prominent place in our minds? Again, let us remember Judas and beware. Are we trifling with any one sin and flattering ourselves that we may repent by and by? Once more, let us remember Judas and beware. He is set up before us as a beacon. Let us look well at him and not make shipwreck.

Matthew 27:11-26

Now Jesus stood before the governor, and the governor questioned Him, saying, "Are You the King of the Jews?" And Jesus said to him, "It is as you say." And while He was being accused by the chief priests and elders, He did not answer. Then Pilate said to Him, "Do You not hear how many things they testify against You?" And He did not answer him with regard to even a single charge, so the governor was quite amazed. Now at the feast the governor was accustomed to release for the people any one prisoner whom they wanted. At that time they were holding a notorious prisoner, called Barabbas. So when the people gathered together, Pilate said to them, "Whom do you want me to release for you? Barabbas, or Jesus who is called Christ?" For he knew that because of envy they had handed Him over. While he was sitting on the judgment seat, his wife sent him a message, saying, "Have nothing to do with that righteous Man; for last night I suffered greatly in a dream because of Him." But the chief priests and the elders persuaded the crowds to ask for Barabbas and to put Jesus to death. But the governor said to them, "Which of the two do you want me to release for you?" And they said, "Barabbas." Pilate said to them, "Then what shall I do with Jesus who is called Christ?" They all said, "Crucify Him!" And he said, "Why, what evil has He done?" But they kept shouting all the more, saying, "Crucify Him!" When Pilate saw that he was accomplishing nothing, but rather that a riot was starting, he took water and washed his hands in front of the crowd, saying, "I am innocent of this Man's blood; see to that yourselves." And all the people said, "His blood shall be on us and on our children!" Then he released Barabbas for them; but after having Jesus scourged, he handed Him over to be crucified. (Matthew 27:11-26)

These verses describe our Lord's appearance before Pontius Pilate, the Roman governor. That sight must have been astonishing to the angels of God. He who will one day judge the world allowed Himself to be judged and condemned, though *He had done no violence, nor was there any deceit in His mouth* (Isaiah 53:9). He from whose lips Pilate and Caiaphas will one day receive their eternal sentence suffered silently an unjust sentence to be passed upon Him. Those silent sufferings fulfilled the words of Isaiah: *Like a sheep that is silent before its shearers, so He did not open His mouth* (Isaiah 53:7). To those *silent sufferings* believers owe all their peace and hope. Through them they will have boldness in the day of judgment, who in themselves would have nothing to say.

Let us learn from the conduct of Pilate *how pitiful is the condition of an unprincipled great man.*

Pilate appears to have been inwardly satisfied that our Lord had done nothing worthy of death. We are told distinctly that *he knew that because of envy they had handed Him over.* Left to the exercise of his own unbiased judgment, he would probably have dismissed the charges against our Lord and let Him go free.

But Pilate was governor of a jealous and turbulent people. His great desire was to procure favor with them and please them. He cared little how much he sinned against God and conscience so long as he had the praise of man. Though willing to save our Lord's life, he was afraid to do it if it offended the Jews. And so, after a feeble attempt to divert the fury of the people from Jesus to Barabbas – and a feebler attempt to satisfy his own conscience by washing his hands publicly before the people – he at last condemned one whom he himself called a *just person.* He rejected the strange and mysterious warning which his wife sent to him after her dream. He stifled the remonstrances of his own conscience. *He handed Him over to be crucified.*

Behold in this miserable man a lively emblem of many a ruler of this world! How many there are who know well that their public acts are wrong and yet have not the courage to act up to their knowledge. They fear the people! They dread being laughed at! They cannot bear being unpopular! Like dead fish, they float with the tide. The praise of man is the idol before which they bow down, and to that idol they sacrifice conscience, inward peace, and an immortal soul.

Whatever our position in life may be, let us seek to be guided by principle and not by expediency. The praise of man is a poor, feeble, and uncertain thing. It is here today and gone tomorrow. Let us strive to please God, and then we may care little who else is pleased. Let us fear God, and then there is no one else of whom we need be afraid.

Let us learn from the conduct of the Jews described in these verses *the desperate wickedness of human nature.*

The behavior of Pilate afforded the chief priests and elders an occasion of reconsidering what they were about. The difficulties he raised about condemning our Lord gave time for second thoughts. But there were no second thoughts in the minds of our Lord's enemies. They pressed on with their wicked deed. They rejected the compromise that Pilate offered. They actually preferred having a wretched felon named Barabbas set at liberty rather than Jesus. They clamored loudly for our Lord's crucifixion. And they wound up all by recklessly taking on themselves all the guilt of our Lord's death in words of portentous meaning: *"His blood shall be on us and on our children."*

And what had our Lord done that the Jews should hate Him so? He was no robber or murderer. He was no blasphemer of their God or reviler of their prophets. He was one whose life was love. He was one who *went about doing good and healing all who were oppressed by the devil* (Acts 10:38). He was innocent of any transgression against the law of God or man. And yet the Jews hated Him and never rested until He was slain! They hated Him because He told them the truth. They hated Him because He testified of their works that they were evil. They hated the light because it made their own darkness visible. In a word, they hated Christ because He was righteous and they were wicked, because He was holy and they were unholy – because He testified against sin, and they were determined to keep their sins and not let them go.

Let us observe this. There are few things so little believed and realized as the corruption of human nature. Men imagine that if they saw a perfect person they would love and admire him. They flatter themselves that it is the inconsistency of professing Christians which they dislike and not their religion. They forget that when a really perfect man was on earth, in the person of the Son of God, He was hated and put to death. That single fact goes far to prove the truth of Edwards' remark: "Unconverted men would kill God, if they could get at Him."

Let us never be surprised at the wickedness there is in the world. Let us mourn over it and labor to make it less, but let us never be surprised at its extent. There is nothing which the heart of man is not capable of conceiving, or the hand of man of doing. As long as we live, let us mistrust our own hearts. Even when renewed by the Spirit, they are still *more deceitful than all else and . . . desperately sick* (Jeremiah 17:9).

Matthew 27:27-44

Then the soldiers of the governor took Jesus into the Praetorium and gathered the whole Roman cohort around Him. They stripped Him and put a scarlet robe on Him. And after twisting together a crown of thorns, they put it on His head, and a reed in His right hand; and they knelt down before Him and mocked Him, saying, "Hail, King of the Jews!" They spat on Him, and took the reed and began to beat Him on the head. After they had mocked Him, they took the scarlet robe off Him and put His own garments back on Him, and led Him away to crucify Him. As they were coming out, they found a man of Cyrene named Simon, whom they pressed into service to bear His cross. And when they came to a place called Golgotha, which means Place of a Skull, they gave Him wine to drink mixed with gall; and after tasting it, He was unwilling to drink. And when they had crucified Him, they divided up His garments among themselves by casting lots. And sitting down, they began to keep watch over Him there. And above His head they put up the charge against Him which read, "THIS IS JESUS THE KING OF THE JEWS." At that time two robbers were crucified with Him, one on the right and one on the left. And those passing by were hurling abuse at Him, wagging their heads and saying, "You who are going to destroy the temple and rebuild it in three days, save Yourself! If You are the Son of God, come down from the cross." In the same way the chief priests also, along with the scribes and elders, were mocking Him and saying, "He saved others; He cannot save Himself. He is the King of Israel; let Him now come down from the cross, and we will believe in Him. He trusts in God; let Him rescue Him now, if He delights in Him; for He said, 'I am the Son of God.'" The robbers who had been crucified with Him were also insulting Him with the same words. (Matthew 27:27-44)

These verses describe the sufferings of our Lord Jesus Christ after His condemnation by Pilate – His sufferings in the hands of the brutal

Roman soldiers, and His final sufferings on the cross. They form a marvelous record.

They are marvelous when we remember who the sufferer is – the eternal Son of God! They are marvelous when we remember the people for whom these sufferings were endured. We and our sins were the cause of all this sorrow. He *died for our sins* (1 Corinthians 15:3).

Let us observe in the first place, *the extent and reality of our Lord's sufferings.*

The catalogue of all the pains endured by our Lord's body is indeed a fearful one. Seldom has such suffering been inflicted on one body in the last few hours of a life. The most savage tribes, in their refinement of cruelty, could not have heaped more agonizing tortures on an enemy than were accumulated on the flesh and bones of our beloved Master. Never let it be forgotten that He had a real human body, a body exactly like our own, just as sensitive, just as vulnerable, and just as capable of feeling intense pain. And then let us see what that body endured.

Our Lord, we must remember, had already passed a night without sleep and endured excessive fatigue. He had been taken from Gethsemane to the Jewish council, and from the council to Pilate's judgment hall. He had been twice placed on trial and twice unjustly condemned. He had been already scourged and beaten cruelly with rods. And now, after all this suffering, He was delivered up to the Roman soldiers, a body of men no doubt expert in cruelty, and of all people least likely to behave with delicacy or compassion. Then harsh men at once proceeded to work their will. They *gathered the whole Roman cohort.* They stripped our Lord of His clothing and put on Him, in mockery, a scarlet robe. They braided a crown of sharp thorns and in derision placed it on His head. They then bowed the knee before Him in mockery as nothing better than a pretended king. They spit upon Him. They smote Him on the head. And finally having put His own robe back on Him, they led Him out of the city to a place called Golgotha, and there they crucified Him between two thieves.

But what was a crucifixion? Let us try to realize it and understand its misery. The person crucified was laid on his back on a piece of timber with a cross-piece nailed to it near one end – or on the trunk of a tree with branching arms, which served the same purpose. His hands were spread out on the cross-piece and nails driven through each of them, fastening them to the wood. His feet in like manner were nailed to the upright part of the cross. And then the body having been securely fastened, the cross was raised up and fixed firmly in the ground. And there hung the unhappy sufferer until pain and exhaustion brought him to his end – not dying suddenly, for no vital part of him was injured – but enduring the most excruciating agony from his hands and feet and unable to move. Such was the death of the cross. Such was the death that Jesus died for us! For six long hours He hung there before a gazing crowd, naked and bleeding from head to foot – His head pierced with thorns – His back lacerated with scourging – His hands and feet torn with nails – and mocked and reviled by His cruel enemies to the very end.

Let us meditate frequently on these things. Let us often read over the story of Christ's cross and passion. Let us remember, not least, that all these horrible sufferings were borne without a murmur. No word of impatience crossed our Lord's lips. In His death, no less than in His life, He was perfect. To the very last, Satan found nothing in Him (John 14:30).

Let us observe, in the second place, that *all our Lord Jesus Christ's sufferings were vicarious.* He suffered not for His own sins but for ours. He was eminently our substitute in all His passion.

This is a truth of the deepest importance. Without it, the story of our Lord's sufferings, with all its minute details, must always seem mysterious and inexplicable. It is a truth, however, of which the Scriptures speak frequently, and that too with no uncertain sound. We are told that Christ *bore our sins in His body on the cross,* that He *died for sins once for all, the just for the unjust,* that God *made Him who knew no sin to be sin on our behalf, so that we might become the righteousness of God in Him,* that He *[became] a curse for us,* that He was offered *to bear the sins of many,* that *He was pierced through for our transgressions, He was crushed for our iniquities,* and that *the* LORD *has caused the iniquity of us all to fall on Him* (1 Peter 2:24; 3:18; 2 Corinthians 5:21; Galatians 3:13; Hebrews 9:28; Isaiah 53:5-6). May we all remember these texts well. They are among the foundation stones of the gospel.

But we must not be content with a vague general belief that Christ's sufferings on the cross were vicarious. We are meant to see this truth in every part of His passion. We may follow Him all the way through, from the bar of Pilate to the minute of His death, and see Him at every step as our mighty Substitute, our Representative, our Head, our Surety, our Proxy – the divine Friend who undertook to stand in our stead, and by the priceless merit of His sufferings, to purchase our redemption. Was He scourged? It was that *by His scourging we are healed.* Was He condemned though innocent? It was that we might be acquitted though guilty. Did He wear a crown of thorns? It was that we might wear the crown of glory. Was He stripped of His clothing? It was that we might be clothed in everlasting righteousness. Was He mocked and reviled? It was that we might be honored and blessed. Was He reckoned a malefactor and numbered among transgressors? It was that we might be reckoned innocent and justified from all sin. Was He declared unable to save Himself? It was that He might be able to save others to the uttermost. Did He die at last, and experience the most painful and disgraceful of deaths? It was that we might live forevermore and be exalted to the highest glory. Let us ponder these things well. They are worth remembering. The very key to peace is a right apprehension of the vicarious sufferings of Christ.

Let us leave the story of our Lord's passion with feelings of deep thankfulness. Our sins are many and great. But a great atonement has been made for them. There was an infinite merit in all Christ's sufferings. They were the sufferings of One who was God as well as man. Surely it is fit, right, and our bounden duty to praise God daily because Christ has died.

Last, but not least, *let us ever learn from the story of the passion to hate sin with a great hatred.* Sin was the cause of all our Savior's suffering. Our sins braided the crown of thorns. Our sins drove the nails into His hands and feet. On account of our sins His blood was shed. Surely the thought of Christ crucified should make us loathe all sin. Well says the Homily of the Passion, "Let this image of Christ crucified be always printed in our hearts. Let it stir us up to the hatred of sin, and provoke our minds to the earnest love of Almighty God."

Matthew 27:45-56

Now from the sixth hour darkness fell upon all the land until the ninth hour. About the ninth hour Jesus cried out with a loud voice, saying, "Eli, Eli, lama sabachthani?" that is, "My God, My God, why have You forsaken Me?" And some of those who were standing there, when they heard it, began saying, "This man is calling for Elijah." Immediately one of them ran, and taking a sponge, filled it with sour wine and put it on a reed, and gave Him a drink. But the rest of them said, "Let us see if Elijah will come to save Him." And Jesus cried out again with a loud voice, and yielded up His spirit. And behold, the veil of the temple was torn in two from top to bottom; and the earth shook and the rocks were split. The tombs were opened, and many bodies of the saints who had fallen asleep were raised; and coming out of the tombs after His resurrection they entered the holy city and appeared to many. Now the centurion, and those who were with him keeping guard over Jesus, when they saw the earthquake and the things that were happening, became very frightened and said, "Truly this was the Son of God!" Many women were there looking on from a distance, who had followed Jesus from Galilee while ministering to Him. Among them was Mary Magdalene, and Mary the mother of James and Joseph, and the mother of the sons of Zebedee. (Matthew 27:45-56)

In these verses we read the conclusion of our Lord Jesus Christ's passion. After six hours of agonizing suffering, He became obedient even unto death and *yielded up His spirit*. Three points in the narrative demand a special notice. To them let us confine our attention.

Let us observe, in the first place, *the remarkable words which Jesus uttered shortly before His death: "My God, My God, why have You forsaken Me?"*

There is a deep mystery in these words which no mortal man can fathom. No doubt they were not wrung from our Lord by mere bodily pain. Such an explanation is utterly unsatisfactory and dishonorable to our blessed Savior. They were meant to express the real pressure on His soul of the enormous burden of the world's sins. They were meant to show how truly and literally He was our substitute, was made sin and a curse for us, and endured God's righteous anger against the world's sin in His own person. At that dreadful moment, the iniquity of us all was laid upon Him to the uttermost. It pleased the Lord to crush Him and put Him to grief (Isaiah 53:10). He bore our sins. He carried our transgressions. Heavy must have been that burden, real and literal must have been our Lord's substitution for us when He, the eternal Son of God, could speak of Himself as for a time *forsaken*.

Let the expression sink down into our hearts and not be forgotten. We can have no stronger proof of the sinfulness of sin, or of the vicarious nature of Christ's sufferings, than His cry, *"My God, My God, why have You forsaken Me?"* It is a cry that should stir us up to hate sin and encourage us to trust in Christ.

Let us observe, in the second place, *how much is contained in the words which describe our Lord's end.* We are simply told, He *yielded up His spirit.*

There never was a last breath drawn of such deep importance as this. There never was an event on which so much depended. The Roman soldiers and the gaping crowd around the cross saw nothing remarkable. They only saw a person dying as others die, with all the usual agony and suffering which attend a crucifixion. But they knew nothing of the eternal interests which were involved in the whole transaction.

That death discharged in full the mighty debt which sinners owe to God, and threw open the door of life to every believer. That death satisfied the righteous claims of God's holy law, and enabled God to be just and yet the justifier of the ungodly. That death was no mere example of self-sacrifice, but a complete atonement and propitiation for man's sin, affecting the condition and prospects of all mankind. That death solved the hard problem of how God could be perfectly holy and yet perfectly merciful. It opened to the world a fountain for all sin and uncleanness. It was a complete victory over Satan, and it spoiled him openly. It finished the transgression, made reconciliation for iniquity, and brought in everlasting righteousness. It proved the sinfulness of sin when it needed such a sacrifice to atone for it. It proved the love of God for sinners when He sent His own Son to make the atonement. Never, in fact, was there, or could there be again, such a death. No wonder that the earth quaked when Jesus died, in our stead, on the accursed tree. The solid frame of the world might well tremble and be amazed when the soul of Christ was made an offering for sin (Isaiah 53:10).

Let us observe, in the last place, *what a remarkable miracle occurred at the hour of our Lord's death in the very midst of the Jewish temple.* We are told that *the veil of the temple was torn in two.* The curtain which separated the holy of holies from the rest of the temple, and through which the high priest alone might pass, was split from top to bottom.

Of all the wonderful signs which accompanied our Lord's death, none was more significant than this. The midday darkness for three hours must have been a startling event. The earthquake, which split the rocks, must have been a tremendous shock. But there was a meaning in the sudden tearing of the veil from top to bottom which must have pierced the heart of any intelligent Jew. The conscience of Caiaphas, the high priest, must have been hard indeed if the tidings of that torn veil did not fill him with dismay.

The tearing of the veil proclaimed *the termination and passing away of the ceremonial law.* It was a sign that the old dispensation of sacrifices and ordinances was no longer needed. Its work was done. Its occupation was gone from the moment that Christ died. There was no more need of an earthly high priest, a mercy seat, a sprinkling of blood, an offering up of incense, and a day of atonement. The true High Priest had finally appeared. The true Lamb of God had been slain. The true mercy seat was at last revealed. The figures and shadows were no longer needed. May we all remember this! To set up an altar, and a sacrifice, and a priesthood *now* is to light a candle at noonday.

That tearing of the veil proclaimed the opening of the way of salvation to all mankind. The way into the presence of God was largely unknown to the Gentile, and only seen dimly by the Jew, until Christ died. But Christ having now offered up a perfect sacrifice and obtained eternal redemption, the darkness and mystery were to pass away. All were to be invited now to draw near to God with boldness, and approach Him with confidence, by faith in Jesus. A door was thrown open and a way of life set before the whole world. May we all remember this! From the time that Jesus died, the way of peace was never meant to be shrouded in mystery. There was to be no reserve. The gospel was the revelation of a mystery which had been hidden from ages and generations. To clothe religion *now* with mystery is to mistake the grand characteristic of Christianity.

Let us turn from the story of the crucifixion every time we read it with hearts full of praise. Let us praise God for the confidence it gives us as to the ground of our hope of pardon. Our sins may be many and great, but the payment made by our Great Substitute far outweighs them all. Let us praise God for the view it gives us of the love of our Father in heaven. He that spared not His own Son, but delivered Him up for us all, will surely with Him give us all things. Not least, let us praise God for the view it gives us of the sympathy of Jesus with all His believing people. He can be touched with the feeling of our infirmities. He knows what suffering is. *Jesus is just the Savior that an infirm body, with a weak heart, in an evil world requires.*

Matthew 27:57-66

When it was evening, there came a rich man from Arimathea, named Joseph, who himself had also become a disciple of Jesus. This man went to Pilate and asked for the body of Jesus. Then Pilate ordered it to be given to him. And Joseph took the body and wrapped it in a clean linen cloth, and laid it in his own new tomb, which he had hewn out in the rock; and he rolled a large stone against the entrance of the tomb and went away. And Mary Magdalene was there, and the other Mary, sitting opposite the grave. Now on the next day, the day after the preparation, the chief priests and the Pharisees gathered together with Pilate, and said, "Sir, we remember that when He was still alive that deceiver said, 'After three days I am to rise again.' Therefore, give orders for the grave to be made secure until the third day, otherwise His disciples may come and steal Him away and say to the

people, 'He has risen from the dead,' and the last deception will
be worse than the first." Pilate said to them, "You have a guard;
go, make it as secure as you know how." And they went and made
the grave secure, and along with the guard they set a seal on the
stone. (Matthew 27:57-66)

These verses contain the history of our Lord Jesus Christ's burial. There
was yet one thing needful in order to make it certain that our Redeemer
accomplished that great work of redemption which He undertook. That
holy body, in which He bore our sins on the cross, must actually be
laid in the grave and rise again. His resurrection was to be the seal and
headstone of all the work.

The infinite wisdom of God foresaw the objections of unbelievers and
infidels and provided against them. Did the Son of God really die? Did
He really rise again? Might there not have been some delusion as to the
reality of His death? Might there not have been imposition or deception
as to the reality of His resurrection? All these and many more objections
would doubtless have been raised if opportunity had been given. But
He who knows the end from the beginning prevented the possibility of
such objections being made. By His overruling providence, He ordered
things so that the death and burial of Jesus were placed beyond a doubt.
Pilate gives consent to His burial. A loving disciple wraps the body in
linen and lays it in a new tomb hewn out of a rock *where no one had ever*
lain. The chief priests themselves set a guard over the place where His
body was deposited. Jews and Gentiles, friends and enemies, all alike
testify to the great fact that Christ did really and actually die and was
laid in a grave. It is a fact that can never be questioned. He was really
crushed. He really *suffered*. He really *died*. He was really *buried*. Let us
mark this well. It deserves recollection.

Let us learn, for one thing from these verses, that *our Lord Jesus*
Christ has friends of whom little is known.

We cannot have a more striking example of this truth than we see in
the passage now before us. A man named Joseph of Arimathea comes
forward when our Lord was dead and asks permission to bury Him. We
have never heard of this man at any former period of our Lord's earthly

ministry. We never hear of him again. We know nothing but that he was a disciple who loved Christ and did Him honor. At the time when the apostles had forsaken our Lord – at a time when it was a dangerous thing to confess regard for Him – at a time when there seemed to be no earthly advantage to be gained by confessing His discipleship – at such a time as this Joseph comes boldly forward, begs for the body of Jesus, and lays it in his own new tomb.

This fact is full of comfort and encouragement. It shows us that there are some quiet, retiring souls on earth who know the Lord and the Lord knows them, and yet they are little known by the church. It shows us that there are diversities of gifts among Christ's people. There are some who glorify Christ passively and some who glorify Him actively. There are some whose vocation it is to build the church and fill a public place, and there are some who only come forward, like Joseph, in times of special need. But each and all are led by one Spirit, and each and all glorify God in their several ways.

Let these things teach us to be more hopeful. Let us believe that many shall yet come from the east and west and sit down with Abraham and Isaac and Jacob in the kingdom of heaven. There may be in some dark corners of Christendom many who, like Simeon, Anna, and Joseph of Arimathea, are at present little known who shall shine brightly among the Lord's jewels in the day of His appearing.

Let us learn, for another thing from these verses, that *God can make the devices of wicked men work to His own glory.*

We are taught that lesson in a striking manner by the conduct of the priests and Pharisees after our Lord was buried. The restless enmity of these unhappy men could not sleep even when the body of Jesus was in the grave. They called to mind the words which they remembered He had said about "rising again." They resolved, as they thought, to make His rising again impossible. They went to Pilate. They obtained from him a guard of Roman soldiers. They set a watch over the tomb of our Lord. They placed a seal upon the stone. In short, they did all they could *for the grave to be made secure.*

They little realized what they were doing. They little thought that unwittingly they were providing the most complete evidence of the truth of Christ's coming resurrection. They were actually making it impossible to prove that there was any deception or imposition. Their seal, their guard, and their precautions were all to become witnesses, in a few hours, that Christ had risen. They might as well have tried to stop the tides of the sea, or to prevent the sun from rising, as to prevent Jesus from coming forth from the tomb. They were taken in their own craftiness (1 Corinthians 3:19). Their own devices became instruments to show forth God's glory.

The history of the church of Christ is full of examples of a similar kind. The very things that have seemed most unfavorable to God's people have often turned out to be for their good. What harm did the persecution which arose about Stephen do to the church of Christ? Those who were scattered went everywhere preaching the word (Acts 8:4). What harm did imprisonment do to Paul? It gave him time to write many of those Epistles which are now read all over the world. What real harm did the persecution of Bloody Mary do to the cause of the English Reformation? The blood of the martyrs became the seed of the church. What harm does persecution do to the people of God on this very day? It only drives them nearer to Christ. It only makes them cling more closely to the throne of grace, the Bible, and prayer.

Let all true Christians lay these things to heart and take courage. We live in a world where all things are ordered by a hand of perfect wisdom, and where all things are working together continually for the good of the body of Christ. The powers of this world are only tools in the hand of God. He is ever using them for His own purposes, however little they may be aware of it. They are the instruments by which He is ever squaring and polishing the living stones of His spiritual temple, and all their schemes and plans will only turn to His praise. Let us be patient in the days of trouble and darkness, and look forward. The very things which now seem against us are all working together for God's glory. We see but half now. Yet in a little while we shall see all. And we shall then discover that all the persecution we now endure was, like the seal and the guard, tending to God's glory. God can make the wrath of man praise Him (Psalm 76:10).

Matthew Chapter 28

Matthew 28:1-10

*Now after the Sabbath, as it began to dawn toward the first day
of the week, Mary Magdalene and the other Mary came to look
at the grave. And behold, a severe earthquake had occurred,
for an angel of the Lord descended from heaven and came and
rolled away the stone and sat upon it. And his appearance was
like lightning, and his clothing as white as snow. The guards
shook for fear of him and became like dead men. The angel said
to the women, "Do not be afraid; for I know that you are looking for Jesus who has been crucified. He is not here, for He has
risen, just as He said. Come, see the place where He was lying.
Go quickly and tell His disciples that He has risen from the dead;
and behold, He is going ahead of you into Galilee, there you will
see Him; behold, I have told you." And they left the tomb quickly
with fear and great joy and ran to report it to His disciples. And
behold, Jesus met them and greeted them. And they came up
and took hold of His feet and worshiped Him. Then Jesus said
to them, "Do not be afraid; go and take word to My brethren to
leave for Galilee, and there they will see Me." (Matthew 28:1-10)*

THE PRINCIPAL SUBJECT OF THESE VERSES IS THE RESUR-
RECTION OF OUR LORD JESUS CHRIST FROM THE DEAD. It
is one of those truths which lie at the very foundation of Christianity
and has therefore received special attention in the four Gospels. All
four evangelists describe minutely how our Lord was crucified. All four
relate with no less clearness that He rose again.

We need not wonder that so much importance is attached to our Lord's resurrection. It is the seal and headstone of the great work of redemption which He came to do. It is the crowning proof that He has paid the debt which He undertook to pay on our behalf, He won the battle which He fought to deliver us from hell, and He is accepted as our surety and our substitute by our Father in heaven. Had He never come forth from the prison of the grave, how could we ever have been sure that our ransom had been fully paid (1 Corinthians 15:17)? Had He never risen from His conflict with the last enemy, how could we have felt confident that He has overcome death and him that had the power of death, that is, the devil (Hebrews 2:14)? But thanks be unto God, we are not left in doubt. The Lord Jesus really *was raised because of our justification.* True Christians are *born again to a living hope through the resurrection of Jesus Christ from the dead.* They may boldly say with Paul, *Who is the one who condemns? Christ Jesus is He who died, yes, rather who is raised* (Romans 4:25; 1 Peter 1:3; Romans 8:34).

We have reason to be very thankful that this wonderful truth of our religion is so clearly and fully proved. It is a striking circumstance that of all the facts of our Lord's earthly ministry, none are so incontrovertibly established as the fact that He rose again. The wisdom of God, who knows the unbelief of human nature, has provided a great cloud of witnesses on the subject. Never was there a fact which the friends of God were so slow to believe as the resurrection of Christ. Never was there a fact which the enemies of God were so anxious to disprove. And yet, in spite of the unbelief of professed friends and the enmity of foes, the fact was thoroughly established. Its evidences will always appear to a fair and impartial mind unanswerable. It would be impossible to prove anything in the world if we refuse to believe that Jesus rose again.

Let us notice in these verses *the glory and majesty with which Christ rose from the dead.* We are told that *a severe earthquake had occurred.* We are told that *an angel of the Lord descended from heaven and came and rolled away the stone and sat upon it.* We need not suppose that our blessed Lord needed the help of any angel when He came forth from the grave. We need not for a moment doubt that He rose again by His own power. But it pleased God that His resurrection should be accompanied and followed by signs and wonders. It seemed good that the earth should shake and a glorious angel appear when the Son of God arose from the dead as a conqueror.

Let us not fail to see in the manner of our Lord's resurrection *a type and pledge of the resurrection of His believing people.* The grave could not hold Him beyond the appointed time, and it shall not be able to hold His people. A glorious angel was a witness of His rising, and glorious angels shall be the messengers who shall gather believers when they rise again. He rose with a renewed body, and yet a body real, true, and material, and so also shall His people have a glorious body and be like their Head. *We will be like Him, because we will see Him just as He is* (1 John 3:2).

Let us take comfort in this thought. Trial, sorrow, and persecution are often the portion of God's people. Sickness, weakness, and pain often hurt and wear their poor earthly body. But their good time is yet to come. Let them wait patiently, and they shall have a glorious resurrection. When we die, where we are buried, and what kind of a funeral we have matters little. The great question to be asked is this: "How shall we rise again?"

Let us notice, in the next place, *the terror which Christ's enemies felt at the time of His resurrection.* We are told that at the sight of the angel, *the guards shook for fear of him and became like dead men.* Those hardy Roman soldiers, though not unused to dreadful sights, saw a sight which made them recoil. Their courage melted at once at the appearance of one angel of God.

Let us again see in this fact a type and an emblem of things yet to come. What will the ungodly and the wicked do at the last day when the trumpet shall sound and Christ shall come in glory to judge the world? What will they do when they see *all* the dead, both small and great, coming forth from their graves, and *all* the angels of God assembled around the great white throne? What fears and terrors will possess their souls when they find they can no longer avoid God's presence and must finally meet Him face to face? Oh! that men were wise and would consider their latter end! Oh! that they would remember that there is a resurrection and a judgment and that there is such a thing as *the wrath of the Lamb!*

Let us notice, in the next place, *the words of comfort which the angel addressed to the friends of Christ.* We read that he said, *"Do not be afraid; for I know that you are looking for Jesus who has been crucified."*

These words were spoken with a deep meaning. They were meant to cheer the hearts of believers in every age in the prospect of the resurrection. They were intended to remind us that true Christians have no cause for alarm, whatever may come upon the world. The Lord shall appear in the clouds of heaven and the earth be burned up. The graves shall give up the dead that are in them, and the last day shall come. The judgment shall be set, and the books shall be opened. The angels shall sift the wheat from the chaff and divide between the good fish and the bad. But in all this there is nothing that need make believers afraid. Clothed in the righteousness of Christ, they shall be found without spot and blameless. Safe in the one true ark, they shall not be hurt when the flood of God's wrath breaks on the earth. Then shall the words of the Lord receive their complete fulfillment: *"When these things begin to take place, straighten up and lift up your heads, because your redemption is drawing near."* Then shall the wicked and unbelieving see how true was that word, *Blessed is the nation whose God is the* LORD (Psalm 33:12).

Let us notice, finally, *the gracious message which the Lord sent to the disciples after His resurrection.* He appeared in person to the women who had come to do honor to His body. Last at the cross and first at the tomb, they were the first privileged to see Him after He rose. And to them He gives commission to carry tidings to His disciples. His first thought is for His little scattered flock. *"Go and take word to My brethren."*

There is something deeply touching in those simple words, *My brethren.* They deserve a thousand thoughts. Weak, frail, and erring as the disciples were, Jesus still calls them His *brethren.* He comforts them, as Joseph did his brethren who had sold him, saying, *"I am your brother Joseph."* Much as they had come short of their profession – sadly as they had yielded to the fear of man, they are still His *brethren.* Glorious as He was in Himself – a conqueror over death and hell and the grave, the Son of God is still *gentle and humble in heart*. He calls His disciples *brethren*.

Let us turn from the passage with comfortable thoughts if we know anything of true religion. Let us see in these words of Christ an encouragement to trust and not be afraid. Our Savior is one who never forgets His people. He pities their infirmities. He does not despise them. He knows their weaknesses and yet does not cast them away. Our Great High Priest is also our elder Brother.

Matthew 28:11-20

Now while they were on their way, some of the guard came into the city and reported to the chief priests all that had happened. And when they had assembled with the elders and consulted together, they gave a large sum of money to the soldiers, and said, "You are to say, 'His disciples came by night and stole Him away while we were asleep.' And if this should come to the governor's ears, we will win him over and keep you out of trouble." And they took the money and did as they had been instructed; and this story was widely spread among the Jews, and is to this day. But the eleven disciples proceeded to Galilee, to the mountain which Jesus had designated. When they saw Him, they worshiped Him; but some were doubtful. And Jesus came up and spoke to them, saying, "All authority has been given to Me in heaven and on earth. Go therefore and make disciples of all the nations, baptizing them in the name of the Father and the Son and the Holy Spirit, teaching them to observe all that I commanded you; and lo, I am with you always, even to the end of the age." (Matthew 28:11-20)

These verses form the conclusion of the Gospel of Matthew. They begin by showing us *what absurdities blind prejudice will believe rather than believe the truth*. They go on to show us what weakness there is in the hearts of some disciples and how slow they are to believe. They finish by telling us some of the last words spoken by our Lord upon earth – words so remarkable that they demand and deserve all our attention.

Let us observe, in the first place, *the honor which God has put on our Lord Jesus Christ.* Our Lord says, *"All authority has been given to Me in heaven and on earth."*

This is a truth which is declared by Paul to the Philippians: *God highly exalted Him, and bestowed on Him the name which is above every name* (Philippians 2:9). It is a truth which in nowise takes away from the true notion of Christ's divinity, as some have ignorantly supposed. It is simply a declaration that in the counsels of the eternal Trinity, Jesus, as Son of Man, is appointed heir of all things, He is the Mediator between God and man – the salvation of all who are saved is laid upon Him – and He is the great fountain of mercy, grace, life, and peace. It was for this *joy set before Him [that He] endured the cross* (Hebrews 12:2).

Let us embrace this truth reverently and cling to it firmly. Christ is He who has the keys of death and hell. Christ is the anointed High Priest who alone can absolve sinners. Christ is the fountain of living waters in whom alone we can be cleansed. Christ is the Prince and Savior who alone can give repentance and remission of sins. In Him all fullness dwells. He is the Way, the Door, the Light, the life, the Shepherd, and the altar of refuge. He that has the Son has life, and he that has not the Son has not life. May we all strive to understand this. No doubt men may easily think too little of God the Father and God the Spirit, but no man ever thought too much of Christ.

Let us observe, in the second place, *the duty which Jesus lays on His disciples.* He bids them to *go therefore and make disciples of all the nations.* They were not to confine their knowledge to themselves but communicate it to others. They were not to suppose that salvation was revealed only to the Jews but to make it known to all the world. They were to strive to make disciples of all nations and to tell the whole earth that Christ had died for sinners.

Let us never forget that this solemn injunction is still in full force. It is still the bounden duty of every disciple of Christ to do all he can in person, and by prayer, to make others acquainted with Jesus. Where is our faith if we neglect this duty? Where is our charity? It may well be questioned whether a man knows the value of the gospel himself if he does not desire to make it known to all the world.

Let us observe, in the third place, *the public profession which Jesus requires of those who believe His gospel.* He tells His apostles to baptize those whom they receive as disciples.

It is very difficult to conceive when we read this last command of our Lord's how men can avoid the conclusion that baptism is necessary, when possible of course (there are rare instances when baptism is not possible, such as in cases of severe illness, etc.). It seems impossible to explain the word that we have here of anything but an *outward ordinance* to be administered to those who believe. That outward baptism is not absolutely necessary to salvation, the case of the penitent thief plainly shows. He went to paradise unbaptized. That outward baptism alone often confers no benefit, the case of Simon the magician plainly shows. Although baptized, he remained *in the gall of bitterness and in the bondage of iniquity* (Acts 8:23). But that baptism is a matter of entire indifference, and need not be used at all, is an assertion which seems at variance with our Lord's words in this place.

The plain, practical lesson of the words is the necessity of a *public confession of faith in Christ.* It is not enough to be a *secret* disciple. We must not be ashamed to let men see whose we are and whom we serve. We must not behave as if we did not like to be thought Christians, but we must take up our cross and confess our Master before the world. His words are very solemn: *"Whoever is ashamed of Me . . . the Son of Man will also be ashamed of him when He comes in the glory of His Father with the holy angels"* (Mark 8:38).

Let us observe, in the fourth place, *the obedience which Jesus requires of all who profess themselves His disciples.* He bids the apostles to *"[teach] them to observe all that I commanded you."*

This is a searching expression. It shows the uselessness of a mere name and form of Christianity. It shows that they only are to be counted true Christians who live in a practical obedience to His Word and strive to do the things that He has commanded. The water of baptism and the bread and wine of the Lord's Supper alone will save no man's soul. It profits nothing that we go to a place of worship and hear Christ's ministers and approve of the gospel, if our religion goes no further than this. What are our lives? What is our daily conduct at home and abroad? Is the Sermon on the Mount our rule and standard? Do we strive to copy Christ's example? Do we seek to do the things that He commanded? These are questions that must be answered in the affirmative if we would prove ourselves born again and children of God. Obedience is the only proof of reality. Faith without works is dead, being alone. *"You are My friends,"* says Jesus, *"if you do what I command you"* (John 15:14).

Let us observe, in the fifth place, *the solemn mention of the blessed Trinity which our Lord makes in these verses.* He bids the apostles to baptize *in the name of the Father and the Son and the Holy Spirit.*

This is one of those great plain texts which directly teach the mighty doctrine of the Trinity. It speaks of Father, Son, and Holy Spirit as three distinct persons, and speaks of all three as co-equal. Such as the Father is, such is the Son and such is the Holy Spirit. And yet these three are One.

This truth is a great mystery. Let it be enough to receive and believe it, and let us ever abstain from all attempts at explanation. It is childish folly to refuse assent to things that we do not understand. We are poor crawling worms of a day, and at our best we know little about God and eternity. Suffice it for us to receive the doctrine of the Trinity in unity, with humility and reverence, and to ask no vain questions. Let us believe that no sinful soul could be saved without the work of all three persons in the blessed Trinity, and let us rejoice that Father, Son, and Holy Spirit, who cooperated to make man, do always cooperate to save him. Here let us pause. We may receive practically what we cannot explain theoretically.

Finally, let us observe in these verses *the gracious promise with which Jesus closes His words.* He says to His disciples, *"I am with you always, even to the end of the age."*

It is impossible to conceive words more comforting, strengthening, cheering, and sanctifying than these. Though left alone like orphan children in a cold and unkind world, the disciples were not to think they were deserted. Their Master would be ever with them. Though commissioned to do a work as hard as that of Moses when sent to Pharaoh, they were not to be discouraged. Their Master would certainly be with them. No words could be more suited to the position of those to whom they were first spoken. No words could be imagined more consolatory to believers in every age of the world. Let all true Christians lay hold on these words and keep them in mind. Christ is with us always. Christ is with us wherever we go. He came to be *Immanuel, God with us*, when He first came into the world. He declares that He is ever Immanuel, *with us*, when He comes to the end of His earthly ministry and is about to leave the world. He is with us daily to pardon and forgive – with us daily to sanctify and strengthen – with us daily to defend and keep – with us daily to lead and to guide – with us in sorrow and with us in joy – with us in sickness and with us in health – with us in life and with us in death – with us in time and with us in eternity.

What stronger consolation could believers desire than this? Whatever happens, they at least are never completely friendless and alone. Christ is ever with them. They may look into the grave and say with David, *Even though I walk through the valley of the shadow of death, I fear no evil, for You are with me.* They may look forward beyond the grave and say with Paul, *We shall always be with the Lord* (Psalm 23:4; 1 Thessalonians 4:17). He has said it, and He will stand to it: *"I am with you always, even to the end of the age." "I will never desert you, nor will I ever forsake you."* We could ask nothing more. Let us go on believing and not be afraid. It is everything to be a real Christian. None have such a King, such a High Priest, such a constant companion, and such an unfailing Friend as the true servants of Christ.

J. C. Ryle – A Brief Biography

JOHN CHARLES RYLE was born into a wealthy, affluent, socially elite family on May 10, 1816 – the firstborn son of John Ryle, a banker, and his wife Susanna (Wirksworth) Ryle. As the firstborn, John lived a privileged life and was set to inherit all of his father's estate and pursue a career in Parliament. His future promised to be planned and comfortable with no material needs.

J. C. Ryle attended a private school and then earned academic scholarships to Eton (1828) and the University of Oxford (1834), but he excelled in sports. He particularly made his mark in rowing and cricket. Though his pursuit of sports was short lived, he claimed that they gave him leadership gifts. "It gave me a power of commanding, managing, organizing and directing, seeing through men's capabilities and using every man in the post to which he was best suited, bearing and forbearing, keeping men around me in good temper, which I have found of infinite use on lots of occasions in life, though in very different matters."

In 1837, before graduation, Ryle contracted a serious chest infection, which caused him to turn to the Bible and prayer for the first time in over fourteen years. One Sunday he entered church late as Ephesians 2:8 was being read – slowly, phrase by phrase. John felt the Lord was speaking to him personally, and he claims to have been converted at that moment through the Word without any commentary or sermon.

His biographer wrote, "He came under conviction, was converted, and from that moment to the last recorded syllable of this life, no doubt ever lingered in John's mind that the Word of God was living and powerful, sharper than any two-edged sword."

After graduation from Oxford, John went to London to study law for his career in politics, but in 1841, his father's bank crashed. That was the end of the career in politics, for he had no funding to continue.

In later years, John wrote, "We got up one summer's morning with all the world before us as usual, and went to bed that same night completely and entirely ruined. The immediate consequences were bitter and painful in the extreme, and humiliating to the utmost degree."

And at another time, he said, "The plain fact was there was no one of the family whom it touched more than it did me. My father and mother were no longer young and in the downhill of life; my brothers and sisters, of course, never expected to live at Henbury (the family home) and naturally never thought of it as their house after a certain time. I, on the contrary, as the eldest son, twenty-five, with all the world before me, lost everything, and saw the whole future of my life turned upside down and thrown into confusion."

After this financial ruin from abundance, Ryle was a commoner – all in a day. For the first time in his life, he needed a job. His education qualified him for the clergy, so with his Oxford degree, he was ordained and entered the ministry of the Church of England. He proceeded in a totally different direction with his first assignment in the ministry at Exbury in Hampshire, but it was a rural area riddled with disease. His recurring lung infection made a difficult couple of years until he was transferred to St. Thomas in Winchester. With his commanding presence, passionately held principles, and warm disposition, John's congregation grew so large and strong it needed different accommodations.

Ryle accepted a position at that time in Helmington, Suffolk, where he had much time to read theologians like Wesley, Bunyan, Knox, Calvin, and Luther. He was a contemporary of Charles Spurgeon, Dwight Moody, George Mueller, and Hudson Taylor. He lived in the age of Dickens, Darwin, and the American Civil War. All of these influenced Ryle's understanding and theology.

His writing career began from the tragedy of the Great Yarmouth suspension bridge. On May 9, 1845, a large crowd gathered for the official grand opening festivities, but the bridge collapsed and more than a hundred people plunged into the water and drowned. The incident shocked the whole country but it led Ryle to write his first tract. He spoke of life's uncertainties and God's sure provision of salvation through Jesus Christ. Thousands of copies were sold.

That same year, he married Matilda Plumptre, but she died after only two years, leaving him with an infant daughter. In 1850, he married Jessie Walker, but she had a lingering sickness, which caused Ryle to care for her and their growing family (three sons and another daughter) for ten years until she died. In 1861, he was transferred to Stradbroke, Suffolk, where he married Henrietta Clowes.

Stradbroke, Suffolk, was Ryle's last parish, and he gained a reputation for his straightforward preaching and evangelism. Besides his travelling and preaching, he spent time writing. He wrote more than 300 pamphlets, tracts, and books. His books include *Expository Thoughts on the Gospels* (7 Volumes, 1856-1869), *Principles for Churchmen* (1884), *Home Truths, Knots Untied, Old Paths,* and *Holiness.*

His *Christian Leaders of the Eighteenth Century* (1869) is described as having "short, pithy sentences, compelling logic and penetrating insight into spiritual power." This seems to be the case with most of his writing as he preached and wrote with five main guidelines: (1) Have a clear view of the subject, (2) Use simple words, (3) Use a simple style of composition, (4) Be direct, and (5) Use plenty of anecdotes and illustrations.

In all of his success with writing, he used the royalties to pay his father's debts. He may have felt indebted to that financial ruin, for he said, "I have not the least doubts, it was all for the best. If I had not been ruined, I should never have been a clergyman, never preached a sermon, or written a tract or book."

In spite of all of the trials that Ryle experienced – financial ruin, loss of three wives, his own poor health – he learned several life lessons. First, care and tend to your own family. Second, swim against the tide when you need to. He was evangelical before it was popular and he held to principles of Scripture: justification by faith alone, substitutionary atonement, the Trinity, and preaching. Third, model Christian attitudes toward your opponents. Fourth, learn and understand church history. Important benefits come from past generations. Fifth, serve in old age; "die in the harness." And, sixth, persevere through your trials.

These were life principles that Ryle learned as he lived his life, as he preached, as he wrote, and as he spread the gospel. He was forever a supporter of evangelism and a critic of ritualism.

J. C. Ryle was recommended by Prime Minister Benjamin Disraeli to be Bishop of Liverpool in 1880 where he then worked to build churches and mission halls to reach the whole city. He retired in 1900 at the age of 83 and died later that year. His successor described him as "a man of granite with a heart of a child."

G. C. B. Davies said "a commanding presence and fearless advocacy of his principles were combined with a kind and understanding attitude in his personal relationships."[2]

---

2   Sources:

William P. Farley, "J. C. Ryle: A 19th-century Evangelical," *Enrichment Journal, http://enrichmentjournal.ag.org/200604/200604_120_jcryle.cfm.*

"J. C. Ryle," *The Banner of Truth, https://banneroftruth.org/us/about/banner-authors/j-c-ryle/.*

"J. C. Ryle," *Theopedia, https://www.theopedia.com/john-charles-ryle.*

David Holloway, "J. C. Ryle – The Man, The Minister and The Missionary," *Bible Bulletin Board, http://www.biblebb.com/files/ryle/j_c_ryle.htm.*

Other Similar Titles

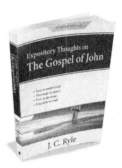

Expository Thoughts on the Gospel of John,
by J. C. Ryle

A Commentary

In the beginning was the Word, and the Word was with God, and the Word was God. – John 1:1

Wisdom, encouragement, and exhortation is contained in these pages. Not because of the author's brilliance, but because of the words of truth contained in the gospel of John. And just as the Apostle John didn't draw any attention to himself, so also J. C. Ryle clearly and wonderfully directs his words and our thoughts towards the inspired words of scripture. If we truly love God, we will love His word; and the more study His word, the more we will love God.

Available where books are sold.

Holiness
by J. C. Ryle

A thorough study of sin, salvation by faith, and the Christian's journey of sanctification.

He who wants a correct understanding of holiness must first begin by examining the vast and solemn subject of sin. He must dig down very deep if he wants to build high. Wrong views about holiness are generally traceable to wrong views about human corruption.

Practical holiness and entire self-consecration to God are not given adequate attention by modern Christians. The unsaved sometimes rightly complain that Christians are not as kind and unselfish and good-natured as those who make no profession of faith. Far too many Christians make a verbal proclamation of faith, yet remain unchanged in heart and lifestyle. But Scripture makes it clear that holiness, in its place and proportion, is quite as important as justification. Holiness, without which no one shall see the Lord (Hebrews 12:14). It is imperative that Christians are biblically and truly holy.

The aim of this book is to instruct you, equip you, and encourage you in the pursuit of holiness.

Available where books are sold.

The Ten Commandments,
by Dwight L. Moody

The ten commandments are not popular today. Atheists want them nowhere in sight. Many Christians say they are outdated. But Dwight L. Moody challenges us to take a closer look. Which of the ten commandments can we honestly say are not good? Which of the ten commandments can we break and not suffer the consequences, both here and in eternity?

This book will challenge you to examine God's rules for life. God doesn't ask anything of us that is difficult or unreasonable, and this is certainly true with Jesus Christ as our strength and the Holy Spirit to guide us. This book is a challenging yet refreshing look at some of the oldest, most well-known words of God.

Available where books are sold.

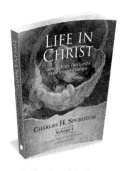

Life in Christ,
by Charles H. Spurgeon

Volume 1

Men who were led by the hand or groped their way along the wall to reach Jesus were touched by his finger and went home without a guide, rejoicing that Jesus Christ had opened their eyes. Jesus is still able to perform such miracles. And, with the power of the Holy Spirit, his Word will be expounded and we'll watch for the signs to follow, expecting to see them at once. Why shouldn't those who read this be blessed with the light of heaven? This is my heart's inmost desire.

I can't put fine words together. I've never studied speech. In fact, my heart loathes the very thought of intentionally speaking with fine words when souls are in danger of eternal separation from God. No, I work to speak straight to your hearts and consciences, and if there is anyone with faith to receive, God will bless them with fresh revelation.

– Charles H. Spurgeon

Available where books are sold.

According to Promise,
by Charles H. Spurgeon

The first part of this book is meant to be a sieve to separate the chaff from the wheat. Use it on your own soul. It may be the most profitable and beneficial work you have ever done. He who looked into his accounts and found that his business was losing money was saved from bankruptcy. This may happen also to you. If, however, you discover that your heavenly business is prospering, it will be a great comfort to you. You cannot lose by honestly searching your own heart.

The second part of this book examines God's promises to His children. The promises of God not only exceed all precedent, but they also exceed all imitation. No one has been able to compete with God in the language of liberality. The promises of God are as much above all other promises as the heavens are above the earth.

Available where books are sold.

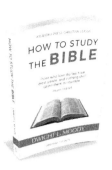

How to Study the Bible,
by Dwight L. Moody

There is no situation in life for which you cannot find some word of consolation in Scripture. If you are in affliction, if you are in adversity and trial, there is a promise for you. In joy and sorrow, in health and in sickness, in poverty and in riches, in every condition of life, God has a promise stored up in His Word for you.

This classic book by Dwight L. Moody brings to light the necessity of studying the Scriptures, presents methods which help stimulate excitement for the Scriptures, and offers tools to help you comprehend the difficult passages in the Scriptures. To live a victorious Christian life, you must read and understand what God is saying to you. Moody is a master of using stories to illustrate what he is saying, and you will be both inspired and convicted to pursue truth from the pages of God's Word.

Available where books are sold.

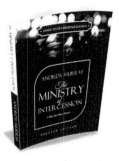

The Ministry of Intercession,
by Andrew Murray

If the answer to prayer is so positively promised in scripture, why are there so many unanswered prayers today (often misinterpreted as a "no")? Scripture teaches us that answer to prayer depends upon certain conditions. Christ spoke of faith, of perseverance, of praying in His name, of praying in the will of God. But all these conditions were summed up in the one central statement: If ye abide in me and my words abide in you, ye shall ask what ye will, and it shall be done unto you. It becomes clear that the power to pray the effectual prayer of faith depends upon the life.

Let Andrew Murray show you what it means to live in Christ, and let his challenge for genuine intercessory prayer change your life – and the lives of those you are praying for.

Available where books are sold.

Absolute Surrender,
by Andrew Murray

God waits to bless us in a way beyond what we expect. From the beginning, ear has not heard, neither has the eye seen, what God has prepared for those who wait for Him (Isaiah 64:4). God has prepared unheard of things, things you never can think of, blessings much more wonderful than you can imagine and mightier than you can conceive. They are divine blessings. Oh, come at once and say, "I give myself absolutely to God, to His will, to do only what God wants." God will enable you to carry out the surrender necessary, if you come to Him with a sincere heart.

Available where books are sold.

Printed in Great Britain
by Amazon

52946460R00210